"Property"
and the Making of
the International System

————— ◊ —————

Critical Perspectives
on World Politics
———— ◇ ————
R. B. J. Walker, *Series Editor*

"Property" and the Making of the International System

Kurt Burch

LYNNE
RIENNER
PUBLISHERS

BOULDER
LONDON

For Pamm

Published in the United States of America in 1998 by
Lynne Rienner Publishers, Inc.
1800 30th Street, Boulder, Colorado 80301

and in the United Kingdom by
Lynne Rienner Publishers, Inc.
3 Henrietta Street, Covent Garden, London WC2E 8LU

Library of Congress Cataloging-in-Publication Data
Burch, Kurt, 1958–
    "Property" and the making of the international system   /   by Kurt
  Burch.
        p.   cm.—(Critical perspectives on world politics)
    Includes bibliographical references and index.
    ISBN 1-55587-622-6 (hc   :   alk. paper)
    1. International relations.   2. Sovereignty.   3. Property.
  I. Title.   II. Series.
  JZ1305.B87   1997
  320.1'5—dc21   97-21297
                                                                      CIP

British Cataloguing in Publication Data
A Cataloguing in Publication record for this book
is available from the British Library.

Printed and bound in the United States of America

⊗   The paper used in this publication meets the requirements
     of the American National Standard for Permanence of
     Paper for Printed Library Materials Z39.48-1984.

    5 4 3 2 1

Contents

Preface

On the eve of the 1996 Republican National Convention, defeated party nominee Patrick Buchanan exhorted a partisan crowd that the United States "must reclaim its lost sovereignty." If America can send troops to protect the borders of Bosnia and Kuwait, he asked, why can't it also use troops to protect its own borders from illegal immigrants who threaten the common culture? He also asked, suspiciously, By what turn of events does U.S. trade law come under the review of the new World Trade Organization?

> Our servants are becoming our masters. You have my word: As long as there is life in me, I will spend the rest of my days fighting to restore the lost sovereignty of the United States, and to rescue the Republic I love from the grip of their godless New World Order. (*Washington Post*, August 12, 1996:A16)

Buchanan's oratory exemplifies internal and external understandings of sovereignty. He believes that as an internal matter sovereign states must exercise supreme jurisdiction and authority within well-defined and well-protected borders that encompass relatively homogenous cultures. Buchanan further believes that sovereign states must suffer no external superiors and no higher authority. Sovereignty is Janus-faced: "It simultaneously faces both outward at other states and inward at its own population" (Jackson, 1990:28).

Buchanan also distinguishes political life from economic concerns. While the political system is corrupted by venal leaders, the economic system comprises "hardworking individuals" who strive and endeavor. By more clearly distinguishing politics from economics, a society may restore the good faith and free function of government and preserve the freedoms of individuals. In Buchanan's judgment, government should protect individuals' rights, not rob them of resources and money. The split between the two systems must be strengthened, though governments must possess the authority to advance national economic interests.

Buchanan invokes the defining ontological elements of the modern international system: The concept *sovereignty* distinguishes domestic societies from the international system of competitive states; a conceptual split between politics and economics distinguishes public from private life. This conceptual framework constitutes the character and condition of both the global system and modern life. It has done so for several centuries. Yet the framework is neither fixed nor beyond contested meanings.

For example, two weeks after Buchanan's speech many U.S. politicians trumpeted outrage at Saddam Hussein's "invasion" of the city of Irbil, located within Iraq's well-defined borders but within the U.S.-sanctioned and UN-authorized no-fly zone. Yet French troops routinely parachute into the sovereign territory of small African countries to quell violence or intercede for French citizens, as they did in June 1997 in Brazzaville, the capital of the Congo Republic. Also, in May and June 1997, amid virtually no international protest, Turkish military forces entered northern Iraq to confront Kurdish guerrillas. Diplomats and journalists reported the Turkish "incursion" and "foray," but made no mention of "invasion" (*New York Times,* June 12, 1997:A25; June 13:A6). Amid such contradictory examples, what is sovereignty? What does it mean? Why do virtually all significant actors regard it as the constitutive feature of global life, but few can agree on its meaning or purpose?

This book hazards answers, but it does not offer a straight answer. Rather, I construct an argument. Initial chapters frame the problem. Middle chapters deliver the material for constructing an answer. The penultimate chapter arranges the elements into a coherent account of the constitution of the global system and the modern worldview. The final chapter concludes and briefly considers implications.

The book provides historical evidence concerning prominent understandings of the concept *property* and related social practices, often involving terms associated with property. This focus helps illustrate the social construction of sovereignty, the conceptual split between politics and economics, and the modern worldview, hence the constitution of the international system. To illustrate these contentions I adopt the perspective of a conceptual historian.

I focus on property and property rights in the seventeenth century because actors in that era constructed the foundations and conceptual frameworks of the modern world and the international system. The seventeenth century witnessed the formation of sovereign states and a state system, the elaboration of a body of positive international law to manage interstate relations, the development of novel bodies of domestic law to govern citizens, and the promotion of international capitalist production and exchange. Actors repeatedly framed their views on these subjects and marked their practices by invoking their understandings of property rights. Since the seventeenth century significant global and national actors have continually reinforced these constructions. Property and property rights are worthy subjects because they occur prominently in seventeenth-century thought and debate. Also, one can render property rights in the vocabulary of social construction because they are rules governing resources and social relations.

I conclude that the seventeenth-century bifurcation of the concept *property* into landed and mobile forms helped to create the conceptual foundation for a state system (real, territorial property) and capitalism (mobile, intangible property). At the same time, property rights necessarily develop into less contingent and more exclusive forms. Exclusive territorial rights establish the foundations for modern sovereignty. Relatively exclusive rights to mobile property reinforce the conceptual split between politics and economics. Thus, seventeenth-century actors in northwestern Europe constructed the ontological foundations of the modern global system, and with it the modern era and the liberal worldview.

Acknowledgments

As gladly would he learn, and gladly would he teach.

Geoffrey Chaucer, *Canterbury Tales*

I am fortunate to know many dear friends, loving family members, helpful colleagues, and provocative inspirations. This project bears my name, but many contributed. The virtues I share; the shortcomings I shoulder alone.

Nick Onuf deserves special mention. He epitomizes the Chaucer epigraph. He is the model of professional diligence and devotion to which I aspire and he is the most humane man I know. I am lucky to call him my colleague, luckier still to call him my friend.

Other friends—teachers all—contributed without reading a single page. For their patience and generosity, I thank Andy Brod, Connie Fawcett, Greg and Rose Holmes, Sandra Keowen, Chris Klyza, Eric Leeper, Ed Mihalkanin, Jim Roberts, Steve Rosow, Elaine Vaurio, and Vivian Wu. Several families warmly adopted me at various stages, conferring all of their blessings and bounty but few of their burdens. Thanks to the Holmes, Kotellos, Onuf, and Youseffi clans. My immediate family has also been supportive and proud. My mom glowed with the news that I had finished the manuscript. My dad beamed, too, especially when I told him that two books he'd given me more than twenty years ago found their way into my book.

Others have inspired me by their work. Few scholars are as challenging as Richard Ashley, as spirited as Richard Bernstein, as insightful as Robert Cox, as creative as Craig Murphy, or as probing as R. B. J. Walker. Similarly, the classrooms of Raymond Duvall and Terence Ball and correspondence with James Farr excited in me novel interests I would later develop. Although I traveled to the University of Minnesota to study what one faculty member called "Dust Bowl empiricism," I left with a fascination and affection for international political economy and political theory, especially the mysteries of language and the opportunities opened by critical theory and the linguistic turn in philosophy. Some consequences of this fascination appear in the following chapters.

Others exploring the same terrain also shaped my thinking and scouted important leads. Some of these talented people I know well, others I know little or have not met: John Agnew, David Blaney, Roxanne Doty, Naeem Inayatullah, Frank Klink, Friedrich Kratochwil, Tim Luke, Mark Neufeld, Spike Peterson, Ralph Pettman, Steve Rosow, Mark Rupert, Eric Selbin, Christine Sylvester, Cindy Weber, Jutta Weldes, and Alex Wendt.

Special thanks to Yale Ferguson and Candace Archer as well as Nick Onuf for reading the entire manuscript and sharing valuable comments. Spike Peterson and Robert Denemark critiqued Chapter 7. Carrie Mullen contributed sage advice and warm encouragement. Gia Hamilton and Alice Colwell, project and manuscript editors, were excellent allies. Lynne Rienner delightfully supported this project. With affection and patience, Pamm Smith made completing the book possible.

1

Introduction

My book [offers] . . . an attempt to deal with a large and complex subject simply by thinking it through.

Hedley Bull (1977:x)

This is a book of social theory that poses grand questions about the character of the international system. How did the modern international system of states arise? How are global capitalism and the state system related? How were these fundamental political and economic aspects of the international system generated and joined? My answers explore the processes of social construction, or co-constitution.

In brief: Actors in the seventeenth century constructed states and a state system by constructing the concept sovereignty and the conceptual split between politics and economics in order to demarcate and legitimize apparently distinct social realms (see Figure 1). Significant actors created the conceptual distinctiveness and thresholds of these realms. Property rights provided a means and medium for constructing this conceptual framework and modern worldview—other factors contributed, but property and property rights were key. Sovereignty was initially a property right of rulers; the bifurcation of property rights into real and mobile forms helped to create the conceptual foundation for a territorial state system and a fluid system of international capitalism. The result is a pair of conceptual crosshairs that constitute the basic ontological framework of modern social relations, thereby heralding the modern era. By disciplining space and time in this manner, the international system and the global political economy become central elements of the modern world and the modern worldview.

	POLITICAL	ECONOMIC
INTERNATIONAL		
NATIONAL		

Figure 1   The Conceptual Framework of the Modern World(view)

1

I build this explanation from a philosophical stance called construc-tivism, which claims that social relations and social actors continuously constitute each other: As the character of social relations constitutes social actors and their identities, so the behaviors of social actors constitute social relations. Giddens (1984) introduces social scientists to structuration, his attempt to explain "the duality of structure," or the simultaneous co-consti-tution of agents and structures. Onuf (1985) addresses the role of rules in co-constitution and social thought. Wendt (1987), drawing more from sci-entific realism than from Giddens, traces the agent-structure problem in international relations (IR) theory. His article sparked a structuration vogue in IR and international political economy (IPE) scholarship that has not yet subsided, though it is being widely co-opted and diluted. Onuf (1989) gives these issues their deepest attention and clearest articulation to date. In so doing he changes the label to "constructivism," outlines a specific orienta-tion to social construction, and warns that "a useful phrase has become a cliché, an overworked excuse to say nothing further" (Onuf, 1989:55). Wendt (e.g., 1992, 1995) has become the most prominent U.S. proponent of constructivism, which he claims is "a family of theories." These include postmodernism, neo-Marxism, feminism, and constructivism, each sharing a critical orientation and a concern for social construction. Onuf (e.g., 1989, 1994, 1997a,b,c) receives greater attention in Europe. He advances a specific theory of constructivism based on the performative character of language, rules, and consequent rule. He offers the most refined statement of his views in "A Constructivist Manifesto" (1997a).[1]

Rules, particularly those allocating resources, are the medium of social construction (e.g., Onuf, 1989:63–65). For example, parents and children reshape family life by creating and negotiating rules over bedtime, allowance, and curfew. Simultaneously, parents and children acquire roles and earn reputations in family life by the choices they make—to abide by, challenge, or evade rules. Actors similarly construct and reshape the inter-national system through rules (e.g., Onuf, 1997b:101–109; Roberts, 1997:155–157), while at the same time the global system constitutes specif-ic actors, notably states, that behave by making rule-based choices. Diplomacy within families and among governments (and all manner of counseling) often seeks to make apparent the nearly invisible web of rules and roles that entangle and motivate behavior, thereby exemplifying social construction. Counseling and diplomacy consider how structured social relations, whether in families or societies, constitute actors' identities, such as "good child," "terrorist scourge," or "renegade state." For example, modern society no longer constitutes chivalrous knights, alchemists, and crusaders as actors, except metaphorically. Nor did medieval Europe know spin doctors or fitness experts. Counseling and diplomacy also explore how agents' choices simultaneously constitute the character of those structures, such as "a loving home," "the almighty Church," "a repressive bloc," or "an imperial system" (Burch, 1996; Doty, 1996).

In contrast to constructivism's social theory foundations, the fields of international relations and international political economy offer little insight into the constitution of the international system. So I defy disciplinary practices and premises by beginning with neither states nor the state system. Indeed, I begin with neither agents nor structures. To focus on either violates the constructivist premises of co-constitution. Instead, I address the mechanism or medium of social construction by focusing on social rules. In particular, I focus on property rights, the specific social rules that identify and allocate resources (property). In this volume I offer a conceptual history of property rights, notably in seventeenth-century England, to demonstrate the social construction of the modern international system and to illustrate constructivism as a foundation for social science approaches. Property rights are among the most significant social rules because they allocate resources used in other interactions, especially those involving rule and governance.

States, a state system, capitalism, and the modern era historically emerge, converge, and cohere in northwestern Europe in the 1600s. Amid these profound social changes, individuals' worldviews also dramatically changed. Thus, I ask: How did actors in the early modern era conceive the international system, its components, their relationships, and their historical development? Property was a central element—a constitutive principle—around which actors organized their worldviews. I investigate how legal thinkers, policymakers, bankers, and financiers more than three hundred years ago used changing conceptions of property rights and consequent property rules to help construct a novel, modern world and worldview. Yet why bother to look?

Five reasons make the motivating questions important. Two reasons concern social construction, three address the character of the international system.

First, in exploring the making of the international system, I contribute a significant empirical case to the growing body of constructivist work. Several empirical studies have appeared in recent years (e.g., Burch, 1994, 1996; C. Weber, 1995; Wendt and Friedheim, 1995; Biersteker and Weber, 1996; Doty, 1996; Burch and Denemark, 1997).

Second, by responding to philosophical critiques in recent decades of (social) science and Enlightenment foundations, I contribute as well to critical theory and to the restructuring of social and political theory (Bernstein, 1976). Indeed, with this volume I hope to meet Bernstein's (1976:174, 235) challenge that adequate theory must be simultaneously empirical, interpretive, and critical. Many observers may be wary of such a project. A widespread conviction holds that to challenge philosophic foundations or some ultimate groundings of knowledge is to foreshadow a descent into relativism and nihilism (e.g., Bernstein, 1983:2–3; Ball et al., 1989:3). For others, it beckons a transition to postmodern understandings and/or a postmodern era. Concerning foundations, Toulmin (1990:4) asks, "What ideas or assumptions about nature or society have lain at the foundation of the 'modern' program for human improvement? And how has the Western imagination come to outgrow these ideas and assumptions?" One answer holds that widespread social change challenges prevailing wisdoms, erodes foundations, and sparks anxieties. In this spirit Walker (1993:x, 10) notes that "profound transformations are currently in progress . . . modernity is an evaporating condition."

As a third rationale, this book responds to pleas to investigate the emergence of the modern world, pleas that arise from a widespread sense of profound social change and the possible dawning of a postmodern era. Many commentators proclaim that the late twentieth century is an era of historical discontinuity and disorientation. Toulmin (1990:3) declares, "We are now stranded and uncertain of our location." Another observer similarly remarks, "If we are not to remain lost in the present we have little choice save to retrace our steps" (Ball et al., 1989:5). To address "our present quandary," Toulmin (1990:3) suggests reconstructing the philosophic, scientific, social, and historical assumptions upon which the culture of modernity was conceived and the international system constructed. For Walker (1993:ix), the quandary involves "the limits of the modern political imagination." Does "the modernist resolution of relations expressed by the principle of state sovereignty [offer] a plausible account of contemporary political practices" (Walker, 1993:14)? For Camilleri and Falk (1992:9), we confront "the way in which the very nature of boundaries, actors, and the political domain is defined and understood." In short, amid a widespread sense of social tumult, do members of modern societies know where they are, how to orient themselves, or how to think through their situations?

These authors direct us to "the problem of modernity" (Toulmin, 1990:5), "the paradox of modernity" (Walker, 1993:56), and "the ideology of modernity" and the "discourse of sovereignty" that gird conceptions of the social world (Camilleri and Falk, 1992:4, 2). Each directs scholars to consider the construction, character, and role of the international system in these transformations and quandaries. This volume addresses such concerns by exploring the social context and deep assumptions through which the ideology and conceptual frameworks of modernity emerged. Property is an apt instrument, and the international system is a quintessential manifestation of the modern world(view).

Fourth, questions about the character of the global system arise in literatures that critique conventional views in international relations and international political economy, the fields that claim proprietorship over international matters. For example, Ruggie (1983:273) wonders how one might account for "the most important contextual change in international politics in this *millennium:* the shift from the medieval to the modern international system." Ruggie squarely questions the character of the international system *and* social construction. In his terms, he asks about "generative structures" (p. 266): What structures generated the interstate system and the principles of sovereignty? What structures in turn do states and sovereignty generate? In this volume I specifically address generative structures, arguing that they must be understood in terms of property rights. Moreover, following Ruggie, I reduce generative structures to their (constitutive) principles, which govern the patterning of social interactions. Property rights are most significant in this regard because they allocate material resources (property) through the mechanism of rights (rules). Both resources and rules are necessary for agents to act and for structures to endure.

Fifth, in recent years IR and IPE have witnessed a revived interest in sovereignty (e.g., Bartelson, 1995:16). When sovereignty is understood as the "constitutive principle" or "foundation stone" of international society (James, 1986:278–279), explorations of sovereignty necessarily engage the character of the international system and the relationships between the domestic and international realms (Bartelson, 1995:52). Indeed,

> a history of sovereignty cannot begin by separating the sovereign state from its international outside, for it must be capable of accounting for the formation of the domestic and the international as imposed interpretations which organize modern political reality as well as our understanding of that reality as empirically given or analytically evident. Thus, a history of sovereignty must be a history of how and by what means this kind of differentiation . . . is carried out. (Bartelson, 1995:53–54)

In this book I explain important conceptual differentiations that inform sovereignty.

Before outlining my approach to Bartelson's challenge, I survey the analytic problems one encounters in the effort.

FRAMING THE ISSUES: ANALYTIC PROBLEMS

Problems raised by disciplinary boundaries, paradigms, and theory hinder investigations of the international system and the conceptual crosshairs that frame it. First, scholarly disciplines uniquely frame their subjects. For example, conventional IR and IPE premise an enduring self-help system that sets the context of state action (Waltz, 1979:66; Wendt, 1992:392). States, not the system, are generally at issue. Second, underlying paradigms inform disciplines and guide inquiry (Kuhn, 1970). For realism, the conventional paradigm in IR and IPE, both the state and the state system are generally unproblematic concerns since state *action* is the typical subject. Indeed, realism fails to provide an explicit theory of the state (Wendt, 1987:342). Rather than explain the state, theorists describe it as a power organization or "war machine" that produces national security (Jackson, 1990:39). The market, capitalism, and modernity are also typically unproblematic: "The state as the embodiment of politics and the market as the embodiment of economics are distinctive features of the modern world" (Gilpin, 1987:10). Moreover, the transition to the modern era may matter little: "the enduring anarchic character of international politics accounts for the striking sameness in the quality of international life through the millennia" (Waltz, 1979:66; also Gilpin, 1981:211).

Waltz's monolithically doctrinal depiction of the international system prompted several immediate retorts. Chase-Dunn (1981) criticizes strictly political characterizations of the global system and asks whether capitalism and the state system comprise for the modern world "one logic or two." He asserts that the state system is the political face of capitalism, so not autonomous (p. 21), because they share "a single, integrated logic" (p. 19). Cox (1981) distinguishes problem-solving theory from critical theory; Ruggie (1983) similarly contrasts descriptive accounts from generative ones, noting that Waltz (and problem-solving theorists more generally) cannot explain the development of the international system, its actors, or its relationships. As noted, Ruggie asks how one might explain the transition from the medieval world to the modern international system. For answers, he exhorts scholars to explore generative structures and to identify those underlying principles that pattern interstate interaction (Ruggie, 1983:266, note 16). Cox (1981) outlines critical theory in generative terms, noting that "it stands apart from the prevailing order of the world" to ask "how that order came about."

These framings shape this book's central features: critical perspective, millennial transition, consequent logic(s) of the international system, and a generative or constructivist explanation. These features inform the conceptual worldviews that constitute society and meaning, so also produce action, interaction, history, domination, and knowledge (e.g., Thompson, 1984:2).

Accounts about the character and development of the global order vary, often widely. Wallerstein (1984:29), for example, claims that "states . . . postdate, not antedate, capitalism; all are consequence, not cause." Similarly, Polanyi (1944:3) asserts that "the liberal state was itself a creation of the self regulating market." Mercantilists and other state-centered analysts (e.g., North and Thomas, 1973) tell the opposite tale. Hintze (1975:427), however, sees not causality but commonality: We must assume "a common spiritual ancestry for the modern state and for capitalism." It is intriguing that conventional scholars in IR and IPE express a remarkable disinterest:

> The historical relationship of state and market is a matter of intense scholarly controversy. Whether each developed autonomously, the market gave rise to the state, or the state to the market are important historical issues whose resolution is not really relevant [to understanding their interactions]. State and market, whatever their respective origins, have independent existences . . . and interact. (Gilpin, 1987:10, note 1)

These conflicting accounts lack any sense of social construction or critical theory. Each perspective depreciates history and social practices (Ashley, 1989:427).

Several issues become clear. The international system is not a significant analytic concern, even in IR and IPE. To the extent disciplines are attentive, their premises prejudge the conclusions. Those who study international politics presume that political dynamics dominate in the international system. For example, Morgenthau (1956:48, 10) writes bluntly that "historic evidence points to the primacy of politics over economics" and to "the autonomy of the political sphere." Many other IR scholars follow this lead (e.g., Waltz, 1979:79). Those studying international political economy presume an interplay of political and economic factors, but, again, the relative balance of factors depends on disciplinary training and background. Gilpin (1981:80), for example, approvingly quotes Albert Hirschman: "At any one historical stage, the economy functions *within* a given political and institutional framework" (emphasis added). However, "they do not operate independently of one another" (Gilpin, 1987:10). Disciplinary premises pose troubling analytic problems as one attempts to distinguish major from minor causes and to craft a textured account (Ashley, 1983). The problems loom large, as I show below, when the subject is the transition to the modern era.

Further, prominent scholarly fields, especially IR and IPE, do not address the social construction or history of the system. In turning to history, however, one similarly encounters problems in the boundaries and premises of other disciplines. Thus, to address the social construction of the international system, I harvest themes from diverse fields that contribute insight into the modern conception and construction of global relations. I then combine these themes to highlight the practices of construction and constitution. The elements are scattered throughout social science because the development of the international system is not a prominent puzzle. No scholarly fields are staked around it.

Scholarly views are firmly rooted in "fields," well staked and well demarcated by the boundaries of its paradigms and puzzles. Each "sees" its subject from its distinctive, allegedly superior "place" and terrain (Ashley, 1983). These fields are analogous to territorial property claims over particular subjects and puzzles: IR "claims" international matters; geography claims space; anthropology and sociology contest claims to culture. Pardon the extended simile, but property is like a seed germinating in each field. To pursue the questions I pose requires navigating through previously claimed proprietary fields to harvest elements from each, then combining them into a singular, distinctive account of the social construction of the international system. Since my interest is social construction, however, I collect indiscriminately from any fields staked out around themes akin to the emergence of the modern international system. History and political philosophy occupy proximate claims. To recast my project in historical terms, I explore the historical transition to the modern era and the creation of a modern worldview. To recast it as a philosophical inquiry, I explore the social construction of the defining concepts of the modern era and the modern international system.

The concept of property is to the scholarly fields what the concept of mobile property was to the fixed, territorial worldview of the seventeenth century: a fluid, intractable challenge to a fixed, static perspective. Many twentieth-century scholars and seventeenth-century citizens have trouble seeing and conceiving what is swirling within and among the various fields and realms that compose our worlds. Like early modern kingdoms, late modern scholarly fields have so "disciplined" their views that they see only with difficulty, if at all, the fluid circumstances that surround and constitute them (e.g., Onuf, 1997b). The irony, of course, is that modern scholarly disciplines possess a set of disciplinary property rights, if you will, that constitute each field as exclusive and autonomous, thus producing distinct academic departments, for example. Yet exclusivity and autonomy are precisely the social characteristics wrought by the transition to the modern era. For this reason, disciplinary fields are blindered, so "see" the transition only from their vantage. Disciplines cannot easily conceive the processes of social construction that constituted their agency, perspectives, and roles. As I illustrate below, inhabitants of the seventeenth century could easily recognize these characteristics as a self-property.

What kinds of views on the transition prevail? Some authors report on the transition in general terms. Others discriminate between transitions: from feudalism to capitalism, to liberalism, or to the modern era.[2] These literatures claim proprietorship over the transition but differently identify the key transformative elements. For his part, Toulmin (1990:7–9) defines the modern era as a set of conditions: the seventeenth-century emergence of the nation-state and sovereignty, a state system, industry and capitalism, science and positivist rationality, and a theory-centered style of philosophy. Others stake a scholarly claim to the transition in terms of clashing worldviews—whether feudal remnants, Christian universalism, apocalyptic chiliasm, renewed republicanism, or protoliberalism (e.g., Christianson, 1978; Ferguson, 1979).

Several authors focus on the specific crises of the seventeenth century as decisive events in the transition(s) (e.g., Aston, 1965; Trevor-Roper, 1965). Coates (1970) explores the major conflicts challenging English society. De Vries (1976) examines the economic consequences for European societies precipitated by the seventeenth-century "age of crisis." But world system theorists identify the key era as the long sixteenth century from 1450 to 1600 and share with Marxians a generally materialist position. Wallerstein (1974a:10) inaugurates world system theory by asking what the determining elements of the modern world system and their historical evolution are. What accounts for the historically specific character and development of the capitalist world economy (Wallerstein, 1974b:397)? Historical specificity leads in several directions, however.

Many scholars consider the development of joint-stock companies and capitalist-commercial entrepreneurship.[3] Others look to the formation of market society more generally (e.g., Polanyi, 1944; Macpherson, 1962). These concerns lead some to explore the domestic circumstances that prompted such changes. Many investigate the development of national law in Europe.[4] Several authors examine England as the model modern nation and France as its foremost rival, whereas others look more broadly to the development of the modern nation-state.[5] Still others examine sovereignty as the principle distinguishing states and their territorial authority.[6] Yet because England and France developed amid Europe's unique social, political, and economic competition, some scholars claim academic proprietorship over the development of the modern nation-state system (e.g., Tilly, 1975).

In the context of great power competition, a number of scholars and jurisprudents investigate the development of international law, the set of rules devised to manage sovereign behavior and coordinate the society of states.[7] However, discussions of sovereign behavior often quickly reduce to debates over sovereign rights. Many scholars lay academic claim to the study of rights generally and property rights particularly.[8] In disputes over property rights, the conceptual split between politics and economics develops (Burch, 1994). This split and the crafting of sovereign authority served socially valuable purposes in the seventeenth century. This new conceptual framing seemed desirable and "rational," in keeping with a philosophical "quest for certainty" (Toulmin, 1990:55–56, 69–80) that avoided the chronic violence of religious fratricide and the terror of regicide. Such certainty, following Descartes, animates rationality and positivism as philosophic foundations. Indeed, Bartelson (1995:238) declares that "the concept of sovereignty is so firmly linked with the epistemic and ontological foundations of political inquiry, that it hardly can be touched upon without simultaneously evoking questions about these foundations."

As a result, to investigate prevailing foundations and conceptual frameworks, one needs to establish alternative foundations. Alternative foundations also help to transcend the proprietary claims and standpoint perspectives of well-staked and well-garrisoned scholarly fields. Social construction offers one such alternative. The section below details the philosophical, theoretical, and methodological bases for the constructivist approach of this volume. Also, in Bartelson's (1995:54) terms, I outline how a constructivist approach illustrates the way in which the conceptual differentiations constituting the international system and the modern worldview were "carried out" and "imposed."

CONCEPTUAL HISTORIES, CONSTITUTIVE
PRINCIPLES, AND SOCIAL CONSTRUCTION

In the matter of philosophical foundations, I am a constructivist. I presume the co-constitution of social actors and their relations. In ontological terms, I regard concepts, not agents or structures, as basic units. In epistemological terms, I advocate a postpositivist critique sensitive to language and interpretation. As a matter of approach, I adopt the fully constructivist view that meaning and society are co-constituted, which places the agent-structure problem (Wendt, 1987) at the center of this analysis. Yet property rights and constitutive principles offer a solution. Property represents resources; rights are rules. This framing aligns neatly with Giddens's (1984) notions of structuration and Onuf's (1989, 1997a) insights into constructivism and social rules. These state-of-the-art treatments are finely complemented by Waldron's (1988) exemplary discussion of property rights. By labeling property rights as *constitutive principles,* I highlight their central role in the processes of co-constitution.

I use property rights to explain social construction, then use social construction to explain how actors, using understandings of property rights, crafted the conceptual crosshairs constituting the framework of modernity. In this framework the state system and global capitalism form an operative whole, though property rights distinguish its elements.

I take seriously the claim that the "limits of one's language mark the limits of one's world" (Ball et al., 1989:2) and that "behavior has no meaning at all outside of discourse" (Doty, 1996:25). To understand the construction of social relations, I attend to the concepts and conceptual frameworks that comprise worldviews. Three elements are key: conceptual histories, constitutive principles, and social construction. Property is relevant to each.

Conceptual Histories

In compiling conceptual histories, I attend to conceptual change. The changing meanings of concepts are both a means and marker of political innovation and of efforts to make and make sense of the world (e.g., Ball et al., 1989). Whether as catalyst or consequence, conceptual change often occurs during periods of dramatic social change: turmoil, revolution, dislocation, communicative breakdown, crisis, as when "those categories which were meant to define and control the world for us have boomeranged us into chaos; in which limbo we whirl, clutching the straws of our definitions" (Baldwin, 1955:14). During such crises, "the naturalness of the existing order [is] in danger of unraveling"; moments of crisis make more visible and dramatic "the representational practices that attempt to reaffirm or reconstruct identities," meanings, and even ideological foundations (Doty, 1996:13). In such circumstances, conceptual change remakes our understandings and outlines political possibilities. Since the meanings of concepts inevitably accrete and erode, conceptual change necessarily involves remaking the world. Thus, conceptual changes mark social changes. Conceptual histories chronicle the process and challenge the often narrow, barnacled, stultifying character of prevailing discourse, opening it to new questions and interpretations.

Insightful conceptual histories do not merely trace changing meanings but place those meanings in a broader social context that illuminates changing social beliefs, theories, perceptions, values, and attitudes (Skinner, 1989:20). The contexts are both social and conceptual. I explore the conceptual frameworks by which seventeenth-century individuals made sense of their world; I do so to investigate how their ways of thinking influenced their understandings and behavior. Historical sociology (e.g., Abrams, 1981), the "constitution of society" (Giddens, 1984), and "history in the ethnographic grain" (e.g., Darnton, 1984) are comparable. Undertaken in this spirit, conceptual histories illustrate that both epistemology and ontology affect worldviews and consequent behavior. Thus, this method underscores a substantive orientation: social construction and the linguistic constitution of social life.

Constitutive Principles

While rules are the medium of co-constitution, they do not directly lend themselves to the conceptual analysis I outline.[9] Constitutive principles do. By exploring constitutive principles, I link conceptual histories to rules. Rules both constitute and regulate social behavior; they "tell us how to carry on" (Onuf, 1989:51; cf. Wittgenstein, 1968:151, 179). In going on, human behaviors become patterned or institutionalized, as do all rule-related practices (Onuf, 1985:405). Principles are one type of social rules: those that inform us by asserting conditions, attributing value, and defining (Onuf, 1985:405; 1989:85–89). As patterned or institutionalized phenomena, rules fundamentally constitute forms of social rule that order and shape social relations, assign resources, and characterize interactions. (A typology of rules and rule appears on page 20.) Instructive principles declare that *x* counts as *y,* where *y* has value. In this sense, definitions of property create a patterned, fundamental, constitutive principle of social life. Indeed, I believe that property relations of some character exist in all social communities. Other rules confer rights and duties, including those to property. My treatment reflects a tension between constitutive *principles of* property and inextricable *rights to* property.[10]

In this sense, constitutive principles effectively generate distinctive, concentrated sets of recurring and pervasive social practices. They constitute patterned social behavior, hence social structures and society. Constitutive principles neither precede nor follow agents' activities; rather, they make up the co-constitutive setting. Concepts constitute practices (Farr, 1989:28–29), practices constitute social relations, social relations constitute agents, and agents simultaneously act by making choices in conceptually and linguistically constituted ways. These choices give meaning to concepts, patterns of social relations, and practices. By attending to the conceptual histories of constitutive principles, I locate the process of co-constitution in historical context and in actors' conceptual worldviews.

The concept property is a significant constitutive principle: "Property institutions are fundamental to social life, whatever form they take" (Reeve, 1986:7). Indeed, Reeve continues,

> property provides links between an economic system, a legal system, and a political system. To say this does not presuppose that neat boundaries can be put round the "systems" in question; property itself makes those boundaries ill-defined. (p. 7)

To a significant degree, property rights constitute the character of social life. Through the medium of property rights, individuals construct social relations, allocate and secure resources, and effect domination. For my analysis, property is significant in three related ways. First, as a constitutive principle, property plays a prominent ideological role. That is, as a central concept in many worldviews, property constitutes the character of social relations. Similarly, other concepts cohere around property, thereby forming a conceptual core of a worldview. Thus, property constitutes both society and meaning.

Second, as a specific principle embedded in language, property illustrates the performative, political, constitutive, rule-constituted character of language, first systematically introduced by Wittgenstein (1968; see also J. L. Austin, 1961; Searle, 1969; Kratochwil, 1989; Onuf, 1989:33–65, 78–95). That is, speaking, thinking, and understanding are intersubjectively political acts: "The political dimension of conceptual change and the conceptual dimension of political change, both being different sides of the same coin" (Ball et al., 1989:ix).

Third, understood as a social rule, property leads immediately to property rights, thus to social construction. As Onuf (1989:64) notes, "rules are the social component, resources the material component in all human endeavor. . . . Rules are needed to allocate resources and rules constitute a resource themselves." Waldron (1988:31) similarly defines property rights as a "system of rules governing the access to and control of . . . resources."

Social Construction

A focus on property and property rights—as simultaneously constitutive principles, linguistic principles, and social rules—offers tremendous analytical leverage for demonstrating the premises of social construction and for illustrating its processes and effects. It is at once interesting and helpful that no field claims academic proprietorship over property; by attending to property one avoids the prejudgments that disciplinary framings and paradigmatic premises necessarily introduce. And since property is neither actor nor structure, attention to it avoids the theoretical dilemma of the agent-structure problem.

To illustrate the social construction of the international system is another matter, however. A constructivist account must illustrate the co-constitution of agents and the international system. That is, an adequately constructivist approach must demonstrate both how individuals constituted states, a state system, and capitalism *and* how systemic-social relations constituted individuals' roles and choices. In turn, these conditions require explaining the construction of a conceptual framework for conceiving social relations. The concept sovereignty and the conceptual split between politics and economics form the component crosshairs of the framework, thereby constituting conceptually separate systems. Property rights also explain the constitution of the crosshairs.

In a broader view, concerns over property and property rights arise in each of the fields and puzzles noted above that are relevant to the transition from feudalism to the modern era. Property rights may be a specific subject of debate, as in the evolution of rights (Tuck, 1979), in debates over how to reconstitute authority in England after Cromwell (Pocock, 1957, 1975), and in the development of joint-stock companies (Scott, 1912/1968a,b,c). Or property issues may implicitly structure other concerns, as in the development of capitalism and liberalism, in the purposes served by novel national laws, in the debates over natural rights versus positive rights, and in the differences between clashing worldviews. Consider, for example, the hierarchically contingent property rights defining feudal relations versus the relatively autonomous and exclusive rights of the modern era.

With different vocabularies, these fields and themes illuminate strikingly similar insights that can be braided to the continuous thread marked by property. Indeed, attention to property and property rights highlights the similarities and overlapping meanings. Yet I do not intend to offer property and property rights as the sole explanation for the modern international system or for the crosshairs created by sovereignty and the conceptual split between politics and economics. Attention to property and property rights is only one of many conceivable discourses on sovereignty, modernity, and the international system; many other factors contribute as well, of course. Ideas about gender, class, religion, science, philosophy, security, legitimacy, and citizenship profoundly shape the European system and worldviews. Disputes over the nature of law, rights, justice, authority, and knowledge left deep imprints. Technological and social change—whether innovations in shipbuilding or mining or the emergence of an influential merchant class—also greatly influenced seventeenth-century developments.

I focus on property and property rights for four reasons. First, English citizens in the 1600s discussed most of the factors I note above in terms of property rights. Indeed, conceptions and categories of property rights effectively ordered English legal language, so structured the English worldview (see Chapter 4). Through this worldview, English citizens considered their pressing social concerns. Chapters 2 and 3 illustrate how conceptions of property (rights) pervasively shape diverse worldviews. Thus, attention to property rights offers a unique vantage on a wide range of seventeenth-century and contemporary concerns.

Next, as I mention above, constructivist accounts focus squarely on social rules. Among such rules, property rights are especially important because they directly link rules to resources and to the character of rule. A look at property rights, then, effectively illustrates constructivism in theory and social construction in practice.

Third, property rights neatly frame the relations between the state system and global capitalism. I am convinced that neither capitalism nor the state system arose spontaneously from the ashes of feudalism. Nor did they simply emerge in response to each other, though their subsequent development shows much reciprocal ratcheting. Instead, they have a common source in social practices. These practices one can conveniently label by reference to property rights. Specifically, what real and mobile property have in common as property is the single logic; their differences create conceptually separate systemic identities.

Fourth, though few have historicized property rights, I intend this volume as a step to that end. Rather than critique property as a foundational concept within the fields of IR and IPE, I address property and property rights to offer a disciplined critique of the foundations of the fields and the making of the international system.

To this end I add one important qualification. Although I focus on seventeenth-century Europe, especially England, I do not intend to draw universal conclusions from a Eurocentric explanation. I look to that era (the formal recognition of the Westphalian state system) and to England (because of its historical European and global influence) to discover the character of the worldview that would be exported to and imposed upon much of the planet. Global relations and conditions bear the unmistakable imprint of this worldview. Indeed, this worldview helped to *constitute* the international system and the modern era by establishing the foundations, frameworks, categories, and concepts by which much of the planet's population understands social life and international relations. I seek to understand the character of this dominant worldview, not to further impose it or to suggest it has a universal quality.

PURPOSES

Four purposes shape this book. The first is to demonstrate the social construction of the international system and the global political economy by demonstrating the social construction of the crosshairs. The second is to illustrate that the early modern character of the global political economy was unitary, lacking distinct political and economic aspects until the bifurcation of property rights constituted conceptually distinct systems. Third, I show that social change may be metered by changes in actors' conceptual frameworks and worldviews. Last, I seek to engage and draw from diverse fields and interests, including the development of the modern nation-state and state system, the modern world system, international law, capitalism, and the commercial revolution, as well as histories of the concepts property, rights, and sovereignty. I will score the effort a modest success if it speaks to audiences in historical sociology, history, international law, international political economy, critical international relations, the history of ideas, social theory, and political philosophy.

My argument unfolds in several chapters. Chapter 2 establishes property as a constitutive principle by illustrating its centrality in diverse historical contexts and ideological perspectives. Chapter 3 situates property as a constitutive principle in seventeenth-century England. Chapters 4–6 explore the role of property in the worldviews and practices of jurisprudents, policymakers, and capitalists. These three sets of actors correspond to what contemporary observers regard as distinct social spheres: law, politics, and economics. However, I illustrate that the spheres share similar understandings of property. Though meanings of property changed throughout the seventeenth century, each group of actors behaved in terms of its own understandings. Chapter 7 demonstrates that social turmoil and specific debates over royal authority led to conceptual innovations, including new understandings of property. Chapter 8 offers conclusions.

NOTES

1. In a forthcoming work, I distinguish between Wendt's structural-oriented constructivism, Onuf's rule-oriented constructivism, and weaker milieu-oriented constructivisms. Both Wendt and Onuf anticipate publication of new volumes in 1997, and each has been called a "master in the making" of international relations theory (Neumann and Waever, 1997). For other contributions to constructivism, see Burch and Denemark (1997).

2. Aston (1965) collects several notable reports on the transition. On the transition to capitalism, see Marx (1857–1858/1973, 1867/1977), Dobb (1946), Sweezy (1950), Kitch (1967), Postan (1972), Hilton (1976), Holton (1981), and Kriedte et al. (1981). These views privilege socioeconomic factors. On the transition to liberalism, see Seidman (1983), Arblaster (1984), and Rapaczynski (1987). This approach privileges sociopolitical explanations for the transition. On the transition to the modern era, see Max Weber (1958, 1978, 1981), who offers a broadly cultural account emphasizing diverse conditions.

3. The literature on joint-stock companies is vast (e.g., Epstein, 1908/1968; Scott, 1912/1968a,b,c; Hannay, 1926; Wood, 1935/1964; Davies, 1957; Cowles, 1960; Davis, 1962; Chaudhuri, 1965, 1978; Parry, 1966, 1981; Willan, 1968; Furber, 1976; Steensgaard, 1982, 1990; Kriedte, 1983; Andrews, 1984; Prakash, 1985; and Israel, 1989, 1990). Caton's *Politics of Progress* (1988), modeled on J.G.A. Pocock's landmark intellectual histories, offers a rich account of "the origins and development of the [modern, Western] commercial republic" from 1600 to 1835. Isaac Kramnick declares on the book jacket that Caton succeeds at "a monumental task, no less than clarifying and explicating the roots of modernity."

4. Tigar and Levy (1977) consider "law and the rise of capitalism." Hadden (1979) thoughtfully reviews their book. The literature on the development of English law is quite extensive. Pocock (1957) addresses the seventeenth-century English constitutional crisis and the legal innovations it sparked, such as the deeply rooted conception of an "ancient constitution." Little (1969/1984) examines the religious and political context of legal developments. Holdsworth (1936), Cam (1962), and Harding (1966) offer general, political, and social histories, respectively, of English law. Nenner (1977) takes an insightful look at legal culture and the legal worldview that permeated seventeenth-century English life. Renner (1949/1976) and Pawlisch (1985) consider the functions served by the law in England. Renner investigates "private law," while Pawlisch explores "legal imperialism" and the imposition of English law on Ireland.

5. Many treatments of England exist. Clay (1984a,b), for example, considers English "economic expansion and social change." Brustein (e.g., 1981, 1985) inves-

tigates forms of production and class rebellions in regions of France. Bonney (1978) addresses political change in seventeenth-century France; Beik (1985) similarly considers the development of French absolutism. Bonney (1981) explores the pressing problems posed by scant French finances. Investigations of the sorry state of British finances appear in Bryant (1934/1976), Howat (1974), Wilson (1977), Kenyon (1978), Jones (1987), Hutton (1989), and Miller (1991). On the development of the modern nation-state more generally, see Anderson (1974), Ardant (1975), Braun (1975), Poggi (1978), and Bonney (1995).

6. The historical touchstone is Bodin's *Six Books of the Commonwealth* (1576/1992) and his "majestic" definition: "Sovereignty is supreme and absolute power over citizens and subjects" (*Majestas est summa in cives ac subditos legibusque soluta potestas*) (p. 1; compare James, 1986:xi). See also Franklin (1978) on John Locke's views of sovereignty. Merriam (1900) offers a thickly informative, erudite treatise written in a distinctive turn-of-the-century style. In recent years sovereignty has become a central and controversial subject (e.g., Krasner, 1988; Hannum, 1990; Jackson, 1990; Walker and Mendlovitz, 1990; Onuf, 1991; Camilleri and Falk, 1992; Walker, 1993; Spruyt, 1994; Fowler and Bunck, 1995; Inayatullah and Blaney, 1995; Lyons and Mastanduno, 1995; Philpott, 1995; and Kuehls, 1996). Bartelson (1995) offers a demanding genealogy of sovereignty. Jackson (1990) insightfully distinguishes positive and negative sovereignty.

Hinsley (1986) and James (1986) have reputations as definitive works on sovereignty. However, I prefer de Jouvenal's (1957) unknown classic for its spirited prose and rich argument. Hinsley lacks a theoretical framework. James explores the use of the term *sovereignty* in contemporary political practice, so defines away many important questions when he records that "the concept of sovereignty is . . . the constitutive principle of inter-state relations and, theoretically speaking, the foundation stone of the international society" (pp. 278–279). Ruggie (1983) makes similar claims. In contrast, I argue that property and property rights are the constitutive principles; sovereignty and statehood are derivative.

7. For classics, see Hugo Grotius's *Law of War and Peace* (De jure belli ac pacis) (1625/1949) and his abbreviated *Prolegomena* (1625/1957). See also Samuel Pufendorf's *De jure naturae et gentium libri octo* (1672/1964) and *On the Duty of Man and Citizen According to Natural Law* (1673/1991). Onuma (1993) offers a masterful reconsideration of Grotius. Onuf (1997c:chs. 2–4) reinterprets the development of international law in light of republican themes in international thought.

8. The literature on rights is also vast, especially as it pertains to liberal thought (e.g., Shapiro, 1987). Tuck's (1979) notable treatment of natural rights and their role in the development of modern thought makes essential reading for both novice and initiated. The literature on property rights is equally extensive, in legal, economic, philosophic, and historical versions. Accessible introductions emphasizing conceptual and theoretical concerns appear in Lawson and Rudden (1982), Ryan (1984, 1987), Hunt (1986), Reeve (1986), Waldron (1988), Munzer (1990), and Paul et al. (1994). A benchmark publication is Manne (1975), which contains several early 1970s contributions on the relationship of property rights to economics and the law. Gaus (1980) prepared a helpful but now dated bibliography. Field (1989) modifies Demsetz's (1967) oft-cited argument to empirically demonstrate North and Thomas's (1973) effort. Field argues that land tenures will become more individual and less communal as the population grows and demand for land increases. Horne (1990) discusses the treatment of property rights in seventeenth-century English debates concerning the problems of poverty and the Poor Laws.

9. The study of rules typically falls to jurisprudents, philosophers, and theo-

retically inclined legal scholars (e.g., Hart, 1961; Gottlieb, 1974; Kennedy, 1986, 1987; Onuf, 1985, 1989; Kratochwil, 1989). The character of rules is much disputed.

10. My attention to constitutive principles draws from several related meanings of "principles," including constitutive elements, originating forces, fundamental premises, and characteristics of composition or organization. I build my understanding of constitutive principles from the literature on rules in order to focus attention on property rights as social rules and on principles as a basic form of rules. Rules enable individuals to become agents who make choices enabling them to act upon the world. These acts have material *and* social effects that make the world what it is. Agents use resources, made such through rules, to achieve their intentions (Onuf, 1997a:8). Thus, rules characterize agents, their behaviors, and their social relations.

Onuf (1985, 1989, 1994, 1997a; Onuf and Klink, 1989) develops a typology of rules and rule, which I use to inform this study. This understanding of rules begins by disavowing the oft-reported distinction between the constitutive and regulative function of rules; Onuf (e.g., 1989:51–52) argues that rules are simultaneously regulative *and* constitutive. In this view rules vary along at least three dimensions: content, formality, and form.

As a matter of content, rules vary from the general nature of principles to the specific composition of procedures. The formality of rules ranges from the highly formal character of legal laws to the informal quality of conventions and norms. The more formal the character of rules, the more likely the rules will become institutionalized. Indeed, all forms of rule yield some form of institutionalization as they become more formal.

Derived from a theory of performative language and speech acts, rules occur in three forms, each performing a unique function: instruction-rules, directive-rules, and commitment-rules (Searle, 1969; Onuf, 1989:78–95; cf. Leaper, 1991 and Goldstein, 1997:192). I draw the descriptions below from Onuf (1985:400–401; 1989:86–88; and 1997a:10–17).

Rules in the form of an assertive speech act inform agents about a state of affairs and about likely consequences for ignoring such information. Such rules are *instruction-rules*. The verbs that convey assertive speech acts include: affirm, attribute, characterize, declare, dissent, insist, report, and state. Assertive speech acts and instruction-rules state a belief and convey the speaker's intention that hearers accept this belief. Such rules take the form of "*x* counts as *y*." For example, consider Kenneth Waltz's (1979:96) claim: "To say that a state is sovereign means that it decides for itself how it will cope with its internal and external problems." This statement expresses a rule, conveyed as a fundamental principle with general content. The rule that "a white flag signals surrender" communicates more specific content.

Any rule in the form of a directive speech act, or imperative statement, is a *directive-rule*. Such rules tell agents what they must do, so specify what they should do. Directive verbs include: ask, caution, command, demand, forbid, and permit. Directive speech acts and directive-rules communicate a speaker's intention to have some act performed in some way. Directive-rules typically specify or imply the consequences for disregarding the rule. Such rules take the form of "*x* person or actor (must, may, should [not]) do *y*." Examples are many: "Don't drink and drive"; "Count your change before leaving the counter"; "No parking." Onuf noted in a personal exchange that the lack of a formal hierarchy in international relations precludes most authoritative directive-rules, save between great power and subordinant allies. However, not all imperative statements are directive-rules. For example, when Waltz (1979) thunders to his readers about sovereignty, power, or policymaking, he is not commanding specific behaviors. Rather, as a pundit, he encourages particular behaviors by communicating oft-repeated maxims in the form of rules of thumb.

Commissive speech acts convey promises to hearers. When other agents respond with promises of their own, the web of reciprocal promises yields *commitment-rules,* identifying specific rights and duties. Such rules indicate the speaker's intention to commit to a course of action by promising or accepting. These rules take the form of "I promise that I (can, will, should [not]) do *y.*" Wedding vows, contracts, and treaties supply examples.

Rules yield rule as a social condition. Indeed, each form of rules yields a different form of rule. In practice forms of rules and rule combine. Where instruction-rules prevail, ideas seem to dominate, thereby creating a condition of *hegemony.* Caste societies, professionalized standards, and cultural norms offer examples (Onuf, 1997b:94–101). Karl Marx and Antonio Gramsci are notable theorists of hegemony. Where directive-rules dominate, ranks are arranged in the pattern of a *hierarchy,* as in bureaucracies, corporations, and the military. Max Weber is a premier theorist in this vein.

Onuf (1997a:16) uses the post–World War II Pax Americana to illustrate aspects of both hegemony and hierarchy. As a "self-proclaimed defender of freedom and guarantor of prosperity," the United States claimed for itself a highly formal status and advanced a particular set of dominant ideas and values, indeed a distinctive ideology. Yet as a "self-appointed intervenor for the common good," U.S. policymakers appointed themselves to an informal office from which they could direct and command others, as well as enforce specific norms.

Where commitment-rules prevail, rights and duties dominate social life and agents perform multiple roles. The liberal-republican constitutional state illustrates this arrangement. The reciprocal exchange of promises, expressed in rights and duties, creates a form of rule called *heteronomy,* for which Immanuel Kant is the premier theorist. In this form of rule no one individual or group appears to rule. "International relations constitutes a condition of heteronomous rule because every state, as agent, claims a significant range of autonomy under the principle of sovereignty. . . . Heteronomy is a background condition forming international relations into a ruled institution, or society" (Onuf, 1997a:17).

Each form of rules and rule involves a specific character of property rights. The table on the next page summarizes these characteristics. This set of concepts frames and informs this volume. I return to the typology of rules and rule in Chapter 8.

A Typology of Rules and Rule

	Instruction-rules	Directive-rules	Commitment-rules
Speech acts	assertive	directive	commissive
Order social relations	by naming	by enabling	by conveying ownership or use; by coordinating
Expressions	to claim, assert	to order, command	to promise, oblige, commit
Formal form	principles	laws	rights and regulations
Form of rule	hegemony	hierarchy	heteronomy
Consequent institutions	networks	organizations	associations
Agents' institutional positions and roles	status-holders	office-holders	partners or members
Social exemplars	ruling class culture, ideology, values; professions; caste systems; the family	bureaucracies; corporations; the Roman Catholic Church; the military; the state as a legal order	liberal-republican constitutional state; the market; international relations
Social outcome	hegemonic actors monopolize meaning and the production and distribution of meaningful statements; hegemonic assertions constitute reality	orders create reality by enforcing conformity	exclusive property rights and the anonymity of the market mask social asymmetries as social equality
Consequent social interactions	ceremonial interaction among networks of positions	fears of sanction among ranked offices that distinguish relations between superiors and subordinates	competitive interactions involving bargaining and negotiation among associated individuals possessing ensembles of reciprocal rights and duties
Rules assigning access to resources	claims justified by reference to nature, justice, history, divinity, etc.	stipulated, assigned	exclusive, contracted, negotiated property rights

PART 1
PROPERTY AS A PRINCIPLE

2

Property as a Constitutive Principle

This chapter shows how property is a constitutive principle—a concept around which societies and actors constitute themselves, their worldviews, and their social relations.[1] I offer a conceptual history of property because language is the medium of social construction. Yet since rules are the medium and means by which actors construct their world, I also explore property rights. Although other principles shape behavior and society, after many centuries property remains a significant subject in public discourse, philosophy, and practice. However, divorcing the concept of property-as-ownership from rights-to-property remains difficult.

A brief sketch of the argument: By approximately 1450, the political traditions of moral and civic virtue had crumbled with the collapse of feudalism. Jurisprudential conceptions of property and property rights, drawn from Roman law, placed individuals and objects in counterpoint and helped erode the moral/civic conception of politics as individual-to-individual interaction. The Roman juristic tradition—which introduced the vocabulary of rights and "things"—helped to carve out a distinct "economic" realm in which individual-to-object relations prevailed. As a result, in the seventeenth century some individuals began to conceive two distinct systems of social relations. Some actors grounded their conceptions of these distinct social systems—polity and market—in changing meanings of property and property rights. By specifying rights to property, actors constituted as conceptually distinct the polity, the market, and their borders. The distinctions contributed to social and material asymmetries involving power, control, exploitation, and domination and introduced the transition to state-building and nascent capitalism.

Liberal thinkers later reified and justified the separation yet implicitly recognized the systems as conceptually separate but related in practice. The developing coherence of liberal ideology and the unfolding of the modern era are closely related episodes, both of them linked to conceptual innovations in property and property rights, notably a distinction between real and mobile property. This was a profound change, but perfectly in keeping with the productive spirit of the age. Real property became a conceptual foundation for the development of a territorial state system. In complementary fashion, mobile property set conceptual foundations for the growth of global capitalism. Property rights link the seemingly distinct systems into a single, coherent social reality no less whole than ancient and feudal understandings of politics and society.

From this constructivist view, one understands the modern era as the unity of global capitalism and the competitive state system. One also understands that actors construct the distinctions separating economics from politics and mobile property from real property to serve socially valuable purposes. To make the point, I locate property in distinct worldviews and eras.

THE ETYMOLOGY AND
CONCEPTUAL CONTEXT OF PROPERTY

The word *property* descends from adaptations through French and English of the Latin noun *proprietat-em* and the adjective *proprius,* meaning "one's own, proper."[2] It appears in French as the adjective *propre,* becoming a noun by adding the suffix *-té.* Remnants of Latin pronunciation produced the Old French *proprieté,* occurring in the twelfth century, from which, through apparent Anglo-French modifications, arose *propriety* and *proprete* in Middle English (c. 1150–c. 1475), as well as identical forms of *propreté* in both Middle English (ME) and French. With the transposing of the middle *r* and *e,* the word *property* evolved. Relatedly, a subsidiary ME form, *proprite,* corresponding to a French dialectical form of *propritei,* yielded (with corruptions) *properite,* thus *prosperite.* In like fashion, the ME *propre* and (corrupted) *propere* yielded *propfer, propferd,* and *propfit,* from which descended *prosper, proffer,* and *profit.* Thus, from Latin through French descend forms of the English words *proper, property, propriety, appropriate, prosperity, proffer,* and *profit.*

The Latin *proprietat,* representing "a distinctive quality or attribute of a person," normatively implies a "proper, suitable, or appropriate" quality. Such conditions represent "propriety" and "the quality of being proper." *Property* later came to apply to material characteristics of individual personality and thus to material possessions, which were viewed as extensions of individual personality. Thus developed our more modern sense of property as possessions. Here *property* conveys all of the senses of normative judgment (*propriety*) and personality characteristics (*properties*), extends them to material possessions (*personal property*), and approves the relationship (*proper, appropriate*). Property and property rights become inextricable. In the process a broad constellation of concepts, whether etymologically or conceptually related, encircles *property* and *property rights*. These include the cognates of *ownership, possession, use, title, domain, right,* and *rights*.

The word *propriety* developed similarly. In the seventeenth century *property* and *propriety* were synonyms: *propriety* meant the fact of being owned and referred to ownership or proprietorship and to the right of possession or use. More specifically, it meant possession or ownership of property, especially land or estate. These senses of possession, control, use, and so on were, of course, underscored by the normative judgments conveyed by the other senses of *propriety.*

In a similar manner developed the words *proprietary* and *proprietor.* By the seventeenth century, *proprietary* referred to the holding of property. Yet this word connotes restricted use and ownership, thus private property, as in trademarks and patents. In much this vein, *property* developed as a verb. In this now archaic sense it meant to make one's own, to take possession of, especially to make a tool of, use, or exploit.

The evolving senses of *property* and *propriety* illustrate three principles. First, *property* describes an individual's characteristics, thus raising normative judgments. Second, *property* represents material goods understood as extensions of an individual's personality. Third, *property* and *propriety* describe the relationship between an individual and a material object. In the latter sense, notions of *properness* arise, but actors introduced other terms to specify the relationship. This is especially true in the liberal world(view). However, Marx and others argue that these three features are socially deceptive because property represents not the relation of individual to object, but the broad social relations involved in the production of material objects.

Related words provide a conceptual context for *property.* In the possessive sense, *own* means that which belongs to someone. The terms *ownage* and *ownership* represent the state of being an owner, thereby establishing the legal right of possession, proprietorship, or dominion. An owner is one with rightful title. Thus to own is "to appropriate, to take possession of (as property)," or merely to hold or possess. In this sense, ownership or property is a right, which is limited but indefinite. To clarify this point, the *Oxford English Dictionary* quotes the legal scholar John Austin from an 1879 commentary. Reeve (1986: 42–43) similarly describes *ownership* and *property* as synonyms, but only in some contexts. Ownership, understood as "the greatest interest," was an important legal and social concern in ancient Rome. Yet most important in early modern England were rights to access, possession, and control of product, such as harvestable crops (Ryan, 1984:7; Reeve, 1986:43). By the modern era, actors understand one's "greatest interest" less as a matter of legal and social rules and more in terms of goals and aspirations. Indeed, a particular understanding of *inter-*

ests came to dominate the modern era and modern senses of rationality (Hirschman, 1977). By attending to interests, however, actors have no need to analyze the character or source of ownership and property because they are givens. Instead, actors may concentrate on how to protect an interest (Reeve, 1986:43).

Distinct from ownership, possession represents the fact of holding, occupying, or controlling property rather than legal, rightful ownership. Possession conveys exclusivity. Yet an owner may choose not to possess her possessions, as renting, loaning, and sharecropping illustrate. The term *possession* generally indicates a state of fact, carries legal significance, and relates to said property rights. One must then distinguish between *actual possession* and *legal possession,* such as the difference between a renting tenant and a freehold landlord. The latter may be the legal owner or any party whose use descends from the proper owner. The possibilities for confusion are many. Consequently, this is a significant issue in Anglo-Saxon law and a source of bewilderment for students of property (Reeve, 1986:21).

Notions of rights and title help distinguish among these concepts, their uses, and practical applications. *Title* conveys two related ideas. First, it represents "the union of all the elements constituting legal ownership." In this case a title conveys a legally just case for exclusive possession and offers the clearest legal identification of property and its relations to owners. More generally a title represents any claim or right, whether recognized or alleged. To declare "I am entitled to *x*" is to make a claim by asserting a right. Both the claim and right are property rights; *x* is either a property (this land, that cookie) or a property right (to harvest, to inherit, to occupy, to vote). In practice one recognizes property through property rights. When I hand my cash to the clerk, I pay not for the groceries but for rights over them (to take them away, to consume or distribute them) because I am now entitled to them.

Thus the concept of property implies rights to property as it stipulates an (appropriate) relation between an individual and an external object. Such relations necessarily color the social relations surrounding the individual and/or the object. Norms, ethics, and patterned social relations develop. Property is thus a constitutive principle that generates to considerable degree the organization and dynamics of a society. Similarly, individuals make choices about their behavior in terms of the existing assignments and distribution of property rights. That is, individuals reckon their possible choices in terms of the resources and rights available to them and to others. Property rights of varying formality and generality are inherent in all societies, but since property rights represent a relatively modern social *issue,* as opposed to social *feature,* I begin with a look at property.

VIEWS ON PROPERTY

Classical Views

Moral/Civic Tradition

For contrast with modern views on property, I briefly explore classical notions from ancient Greece. The terms *polis* (city, polity) and *oikos* (household, productive unit) serve as an introduction. The latter provided the material basis for political participation. The *oikos* represented control over property and freedom from toil. Individuals with such freedom enjoyed the leisure and independence to participate in political affairs. Military service provided another form of participation because without defense of the polity, neither citizenship nor liberty could endure. Of course only those with independent livelihoods and sufficient property possessed the time and means to serve militarily or politically. Thus the ownership of land and arms provided individuals the necessary autonomy to participate as citizens and to pursue virtue and liberty (Pocock, 1985:104).

To own property was to occupy a distinctive, virtuous political-moral sphere, the polity. In this view, "the function of property is to secure a morally worthwhile life for all members of society" (Ryan, 1987:71), though in practice this was a limited "society" comprising men almost exclusively. Political participation in the polity marked one as a citizen; citizens pursue virtue (e.g., Berlin, 1969; Ryan, 1984:ch. 3; Pocock, 1985:ch. 6). Thus property represented what a person *is*, the foundation and extension of political and psychological personality. Only in the *oikos* did property suggest production and exchange as well as identify subordinate gender, classes, and statuses. Otherwise property demarcated a moral/civic world: the relations among citizens in pursuit of the Aristotelian "good life."

Property rights, then, constitute the character of classical social relations and are in turn reinforced by the patterned social practices of Greek citizens. These practices constitute political participation, affirm moral/civic virtue, reproduce dominant social rule and inequalities, and underscore the significance of property.

Jurisprudential Tradition

Following Pocock (1985:ch. 6), one might say that a jurisprudential tradition, more Roman than Greek, was an equally relevant counterpoint and contributor to the modern world. In this tradition property marks social relations: "Property became a system of legally defined relations between persons and things, or between persons through things" (Pocock,

1985:104). While citizenship and liberty remained important, they became less central; participation eventually diminished almost entirely as the defining feature of political life. Participation remained central to republican thought and to advocates of democracy, but the jurisprudential elements in burgeoning liberal thought did not necessarily promote participation as a goal. Rather, the legal concepts of ownership and rights became paramount (Reeve, 1986:43; Ryan, 1987:8–22). In this context property rights became enmeshed with authority, order, and justice (e.g., Gaus, 1980:385). For example, *justice* came to mean "proper relations," which depend upon an orderly society administered by able authority. These relations could be derived from God (hence natural law and natural rights) or from positive social convention. Questions of authority, conferred rights, and consequent justice arise immediately; the answers inform several bodies of social thought.

The juristic tradition identifies property as the constitutive principle outlining social relations. Property also defines a set of practices necessary for participating in such relations. This tradition emphasizes rights but considers rights as individual "properties."

The Transition Toward Liberal Thought and the Modern Era

The jurisprudential tradition augurs several features of the modern world. In distinguishing individuals from objects and things, it asks, What might one do with one's "things"? Choices inevitably involve rights. The vocabulary and practices of ownership and rights were quickly converted into conceptions of "use." These bleed directly into production, exchange, and accumulation. Thus the jurisprudential tradition encouraged in two ways what would become a realm of seemingly distinct economic activity. First, the notion of rights or control over resources promoted trade, profit, and savings. Second, the legal tradition undermined political participation as the key (sole?) social activity. In short, it presages the crucial separation of political and economic realms: "Property was a juridical term before it was an economic one" (Pocock, 1985:56).

Reeve (1986:10) remarks that "putting boundaries round the political theory of property poses special difficulties, because property as a social institution is a legal, economic, and political phenomenon." The significance of property in these theoretical genres illustrates the division of the social world into discrete political and economic realms. For example, from Plato and Aristotle to von Hayek and Nozick, property occupies a central place in political theory. Its place is similarly significant in the "economic" analyses of Smith, Ricardo, and Engels and in the "political-economic" explorations of Locke, Rousseau, Marx, Friedman, and the like. It is only in the liberal era that political theory could be maintained as a distinct subject from moral theory, economic theory, legal theory, social theory, and philosophy. These arbitrary divisions are a historical product of academic chauvinism and the modern, liberal world: "Liberalism is a world of walls" (Walzer, 1984:315). Marx (1844/1964:103) more specifically remarks that "private property rests altogether on partitioning."

Walzer (1984:315) elaborates:

> The old preliberal . . . society was conceived as an organic and integrated whole. It might be viewed under the aspect of religion, or politics, or economy, or family, but all these interpenetrated one another and constituted a single reality. Confronting this world, liberal theorists preached and practiced the art of separation.

Perhaps the most distinctive separation divides politics from economics, power from wealth, or, more precisely, the state from the market. Other distinctions follow in the wake of this central dichotomy: The division of the liberal globe into the state system and capitalism, the divisions between liberalism and socialism/Marxism, and their relative emphases upon market exchange and modes of production, among others. To quote Walzer (1984:318–319) again:

> The contemporary social world is still an organic whole, less different from feudalism than we might think. . . . The art of separation is not an illusory or fantastic enterprise; it is a morally and politically necessary adaptation to the complexities of modern life. Liberal theory reflects and reinforces a long-term process of social differentiation.

Property was the wedge that split the state system and global capitalism; it was also the tie that bound them. As a result, the political world changed, and economics—a realm quite distinct from *oikos*—burst forth from the shadows of restricted household or manorial production to become society's prime mover. Economics became a system of relations between individuals and objects in the service of marketable production.[3] Politics as civic virtue and citizen participation, practiced among relatively equal though privileged actors, disappeared beneath the shadow of politics understood as a system of hierarchical relations among authorities and subjects.

The prevailing doctrine of the early modern era held that political authorities created and enforced rights; subjects held rights and avowed deference. Individual subjects held such rights over material objects. Rights to land were most important because they most clearly defined social relations. Disputes over interests in land largely defined political life. Once land became an object or thing tied to individuals by property rights, land became an economic resource. The notion of property as an economic resource—again, this overwhelmingly meant land—delimits the new economic realm that the juristic tradition carved from the moral/civic notion of politics. Thus economics comprises those relationships among individuals and things. Pocock (1985:105) writes that

> the increasingly complex and dynamic relationships and processes which we call "economics" began to surpass in importance the political relations among people, swallowing up the ancient *polis* as they swallowed up the *oikos*.

These new notions of economics were rivaling, if not eclipsing, the seemingly permanent centrality of the polity or community. Economic relations were vanquishing classical participatory politics with alienated politics (Marx, 1844/1964). Wolin (1960) offers strikingly similar comments about the political consequences of liberalism. In complementing the relations of individuals to objects, the new economics crafted a political world in its own liberalized image.

Even so, the republican and moral/civic view that politics involved individuals at all was disappearing. Nor was liberal individualism yet coherently developed as a worldview. Over time, authority came to be vested less in an individual than in the Crown and ultimately in the state as sites of sovereign authority. Such authority became an institutional condition called sovereignty. By the seventeenth century, the Crown and the state were no longer individuals; they were things, although Louis XIV's exclamation "l'état, c'est moi" blurs the distinction and pundits promoted and decried absolute royal authority (e.g., respectively, Robert Filmer in *Patriarcha* and John Locke in *Two Treatises*). Individual subjects, too, became faceless and uniform, since they had lost political personality. They became a group, the masses, the rabble. For example, Hobbes (1642/1983:19) and Filmer (e.g., 1680/1949:82) refer to the population as a whole as "the multitude," thus fueling an already extensive debate on the character and rights of the people and sovereigns (see Daly, 1979:84–96). However, even seventeenth-century Whig critics of Filmer's royalist sympathies—notably Edward Gee, James Tyrell, and Locke—discuss "the people" and "the rabble": "'The people' were not a mass of theoretically equal political units, but an organic and articulated whole composed of parts which were related to each other through different types of subordination sanctioned by natural laws of association. In this society, the basic unit was the family, not the individual" (Daly, 1979:92; see also Horne, 1990:48; on subordination and association through levels and parts-wholes relations, see Lovejoy, 1936, and Onuf, 1997c:ch. 8). A recurring strand of political theory fears the participation of the majority and regards democracy as a corrupt form of rule. For elites, the distressing specter of mass armies and social revolutions in the eighteenth century revived these dreads. "Not only Constant, but Mill and de Tocqueville held that negative liberty was threatened by mass society. . . . They were all the more fearful because the threat to liberty that they feared came from the whole mass of the citizens" (Ryan, 1987:39).

It is not surprising that liberalism fostered both political and economic theories of property, each with a moral/civic and jurisprudential justification. However, an instrumental utilitarian justification, thoroughly modern and capitalist, also emerged. This became the logic, practice, and justification for sharply separating individuals from objects by conceiving material "things" as tools or means in the service of a goal. Instrumental utilitarianism represents the victory of reason over passions, of interests and goals over desires (Hirschman, 1977).

Modern Views

In the modern era, property became far less significant in political discourse than did the rights attached to it. The evolution of liberalism, the political theory of modernity, and the consequences of the seventeenth century made that certain (Gray, 1986:ix, 82).

Liberal Political Theories

Moral/Civic Tradition.   Theorists in the moral/civic tradition argue that a nurturing community best promotes moral worth (e.g., Ryan, 1987:ch. 6). Yet morality remains rooted in individual personality. Property serves individuals and community; land was the most privileged and significant form of property. The implicit issue was stability. Since land bears the imprint of our love and labor, it represents a manifestation of our personality. A complete, virtuous individual must be a member of a moral community, which recognizes the sanctity of the individual, sustains the good life, and provides meaning to an individual's existence (Ryan, 1987:70). In liberal-modern versions, the individual remains distinct from society and through rights acquires a degree of autonomy. Yet only as a community member does an individual possess rights. Framed by this logic, liberal-modern variants of the moral/civic tradition emphasize property rights rather than property.

Natural rights theorists hail individual rights, but the divine foundations raise serious qualms for many commentators. Utilitarian theory offers an attractive concern for community welfare, but individual rights became too greatly subordinated. Thus the modern moral/civic tradition attempts to mix the best features of the alternatives by justifying the delicate balance of individual and community interests supporting the tradition (e.g., Ryan, 1987:73–74). The revival of republican thought (Pocock, 1975; Shapiro, 1990; Rahe, 1992; Zuckert, 1994) and the backlash against liberal entitlements like welfare and affirmative action reflect contemporary adjustments in this balance.

The moral/civic tradition often virtually disappears into the conservative juristic discourse on rights or into the socialist critiques of liberalism. Nevertheless, theorists in this tradition clearly indicate how property structures social institutions, particularly its significance for shaping political relations. Just as clearly they declare how property relations constitute and reinforce patterned social practices.

Jurisprudential Tradition.   Issues of rights dominate matters of property in the jurisprudential tradition. Locke (1690/1965:340–341, sec. 44; 344, sec. 51) illustrates this point in the chapter "Of Property" from the *Second Treatise:*

> Man (by being Master of himself, and *Proprietor of his own Person,* and the actions or *Labour* of it) had still in himself *the great Foundation of Property.* . . . A Man had a Right to all he could imploy his Labour upon. (emphasis in original)

Locke holds that property grounds political society but rights to property characterize society (Locke, 1690/1965:366–367, sec. 87). Indeed, property rights generate humankind's basic social institutions. The purpose of civil society is to preserve members' property (pp. 367–368, secs. 87–88) so that they may attain "a secure Enjoyment of their Properties" (p. 375, sec. 95). Locke misleadingly suggests, however, that individuals have merely a right to all that they can work upon. Many rights are at issue, including myriad property rights.[4]

Instrumental Utilitarianism.   Jeremy Bentham and James Mill assert with others that property is essential for individual survival and the good life. Individuals must be able to appropriate and dispose of objects, thus utility dictates the necessity of property rights over such items. This necessity demands a legal defense of ownership to promote general welfare. North and Thomas (1973) adopt this view in their treatment of state-building in early modern Europe. As do the jurisprudential theorists, instrumental utilitarians transform treatments of property into considerations of the property rights that constitute basic social institutions and practices.

Liberal Economic Theories

The economic theories are largely derivatives of the political theories.

Moral/Civic Tradition.   The moral/civic tradition generally discounts economic activity as anathema to its premises. Nevertheless, these theorists recognize the moral merit of working diligently at our everyday tasks because it serves God's will and improves both our individuality and community. The economic realm consists of work and labor; property represents the essential tools and materials necessary to perform one's duties. Weber's (1958) *Protestant Ethic and the Spirit of Capitalism* reflects aspects of this view.

Jurisprudential and Utilitarian Traditions.   In the jurisprudential and utilitarian traditions, the political realm protects basic (property) rights in civil society. Such rights allow individuals to dispose of property, especially through contracted agreements to produce, distribute, exchange, and ultimately consume objects, whether natural or produced. Such activity constitutes the economic realm. Utilitarians assert that economic activity should promote community welfare, but they do not necessarily argue the central place of property in shaping social life.

In both jurisprudential and utilitarian writers, property plays a key role in establishing the form and arrangement of significant social institutions, as well as the pattern of social relations that consequently arise. More specifically, property generates social institutions and social practices while also providing the means to conduct such practices.

These formulations do not consider how property rights are socially constructed. Marx (1844/1964:106) makes a similar point when he observes that British "political economy starts with the fact of private property, but it does not explain it to us." I explore rights below only after discussing property in ideological perspectives critical of liberalism.

Critiques of Liberalism: Socialism, Marxism, and Feminism

Early Socialists.   Blunt criticism of nascent liberalism and capitalism emerged as early as the 1600s. In 1649 the Leveller Gerrard Winstanley condemned the inequalities arising from private property and market exchange, "the cheating art of buying and selling" (quoted in Hunt, 1986:60). Many prominent socialists—notably Gracchus Babeuf (1760–1797), Louis Blanc (1811–1882), Auguste Blanchqui (1805–1881), Charles Fourier (1772–1837), William Godwin (1756–1836), Pierre Joseph Proudhon (1890–1865), Henri de Saint-Simon (1760–1825), and Wilhelm Weitling (1808–1871)—similarly attacked private property, capitalism, and liberalism. They argued that private property relations cause significant social problems (Struik, 1964:25–31; Hunt, 1986:60–66).

Some, like Thomas Hodgskin (1787–1869), writing in 1825, critically approached the issue of property from within the liberal framework (Hunt, 1986:54–55). He argued that interdependent labor, not capital, was the actual productive force. Only by abolishing private ownership of the means of production could society ensure a competitive market, he declared. His advocacy of free market socialism did not satisfy others, who assaulted liberal foundations generally. For example, William Thompson and Robert Owen were conspicuous British critics of liberalism and capitalism. In 1824 Thompson lambasted the social evils that arose from the competitive principles engendered by private property and market forces. Owen criticized the social inequalities that liberal and capitalist activities, especially those involving private property, produced. Both Thompson and Owen advocated socialism, involving the dissolution of private property and a new distribution of property rights, as a protest against the inequalities and social ills wrought by capitalism.

Babeuf and Blanchqui advocated the abolition of private property by violently toppling the existing, hence supportive, governments. Godwin expressed the hallmarks of nineteenth-century socialism: The belief that private property is the source of social ills and that the existing liberal-capitalist governments would never redress these evils because of their intimate links to the capitalist class. He saw education, reason, and justice as the means by which society would abolish private property and introduce new property relations. Saint-Simon did not condemn private property but did attack the social inequalities and injustices it creates. He introduced the recently commonplace argument that government should oversee production and distribution. Fourier condemned the "irrational" social organization; monumental waste of time, effort, and resources; and extreme inequalities and injustices engendered by liberal-capitalist society and private property.

Proudhon bluntly declared that "property is theft" and "the mother of tyranny." In the same era, Balzac remarked that "behind every great fortune there is a crime." Proudhon thought that because the state coercively enforced unequal property rights, injustice and social inequalities were unavoidable unless private property and the state were abolished. Adam Smith (1776/1937:670, 674) makes intriguingly similar condemnations in *The Wealth of Nations:*

> Wherever there is great property, there is great inequality. For one very rich man, there must be at least five hundred poor, and the affluence of the few supposes the indigence of the many. . . . Civil government supposes a certain subordination. But as the necessity of civil government gradually

grows up with the acquisition of valuable property, so the principle causes which naturally introduce subordination gradually grow up with the growth of that valuable property. . . . Civil government, so far as it is instituted for the security of property, is in reality instituted for the defense of the rich against the poor, or of those who have some property against those who have none at all.

Marx. Property anchors Marx's critical view of liberalism, capitalism, and the liberal-bourgeois state. To introduce these critiques, he addresses British political economists from Adam Smith's time, particularly the abstractions, delusions, hypocrisy, and cynicism he sees in their treatments of private property. Marx (1844/1964:128–129) declares that their work "carries to its logical conclusion the denial of man."

In contrast to mercantilists and physiocrats (who viewed precious metals and land, respectively, as the chief sources of wealth), Marx claims British political economists made great strides in recognizing labor as the source of wealth. However, the British dehumanized humankind by making people prisoners of the concept of private property, since the relation of person to property is no longer a relation of individual to object. Instead, humans themselves are this "essence of private property" (Marx, 1844/1964:129). Said differently, the juristic relation of individuals to objects (property rights) becomes corrupted as it eclipses its corollary, propriety. By this conceptual shift-and-fade of liberal-modernity, property becomes more significant than humankind. Indeed, property engulfs humanity. Yet many British political economists portray the social injustices and inequalities that thereby arise as reasonable and necessary. Indeed, British political economy reifies private property and inequality as natural.

Marx argues instead that alienated and estranged labor produces private property, which becomes the receptacle and source of all wealth. We (re)produce ourselves as a species, as humanity, by laboring in and upon the natural world (Arthur, 1970:21). Yet capitalist relations tear this bond, making the relationships alien. An individual's labor is estranged in three ways: (1) the individual from the object she produces, (2) the individual from self in the act of production, and (3) the individual from humanity and humanness.

Alienated labor directly produces private property because it produces a good that belongs to the capitalist, not to the laborer. This is the first estrangement. In a definitional sense, estranged labor produces private property at the moment a human sells her labor—her personal, private property—to a buyer (Marx, 1867/1977:292). This is the second estrangement. The paying of wages and the creation of private property are then identical, a unity, as mediated through labor. Alienation is the result (the third estrangement). Private property is a summary expression of these estrangements (Marx, 1844/1964:119).

Yet Marx introduces a chicken-and-egg dilemma: Alienated labor produces private property, but private property appears necessary to produce alienated labor. Marx attempts a resolution by considering private property in specifically capitalist social contexts. Earlier societies knew possessions and personal property, but none understood private property and the relevant property relations as legal terms describing the relations of production (Marx, 1859/1970:21). For Marx, relations of production constitute the economic structure of society (Marx, 1859/1970:20). In contrast, ownership is "the simplest legal relation" in society (Marx, 1859/1970:207). Although liberal legal doctrine describes possession as the simplest social relation, it is not the most fundamental legal relation.

Marx illustrates that property is a constitutive principle: A product and catalyst of social practices. Human activity changes the meaning of private property over time: "to attribute powers to private property, to make it the subject which originates activity and to make man merely its object, is pure superstition" (Arthur, 1970:18). Thus in *German Ideology* (1845–1846/1970) and in *Origin of the Family, Private Property and the State* (1884/1972), Marx and Engels offer a historical chronicle of labor and property. In the *Economic and Philosophical Manuscripts of 1844,* Marx provides the conceptual foundation for his later investigations, anchored by the concepts of private property and alienation:

> Just as we have derived the concept of private property from the concept of estranged [and] alienated labor by analysis, so we can develop every category of political economy with the help of these two factors. (Marx, 1844/1964:118; emphasis removed)

Thus the French and British socialists, the British political economists, and the German philosophers consistently reckoned property as possessions owned by individuals. They thereby reduce the essential feature of property to good title. Indeed, the English legal system deflected a fundamental question that Roman law directly addressed: What does it mean to be an owner—how does something become mine? (Ryan, 1984:7, from Nicholas, 1962:15ff.). Thus classical liberal theorists aptly hail the significance of individual-to-object relationships created by property but minimize the defining social structures that property relations constitute (Suvorova and Romanov, 1986:38–39).

> Hence the general juridical notion from Locke to Ricardo is always that of *petty-bourgeois ownership,* while the relations of production they describe belong to the *capitalist mode* of production. (Marx, 1867/1977:1083; emphasis in original)

In the Marxian view, property represents the social or economic relations among individuals in the social production and appropriation of material values (Suvorova and Romanov, 1986:35). To understand property is to
understand capitalist relations. For example, the "relations of private property contain latent within them the relations of private property as *labor,* the
relations of private property as *capital,* and the *mutual* relation of these two
to one another" (Marx, 1844/1964:122; emphasis in original; see also p.
126).

> Originally the rights of property seemed to us to be grounded in a man's
> own labour [e.g., Locke]. Some such assumption was at least necessary,
> since only commodity-owners with equal rights confronted each other,
> and the sole means of appropriating the commodities of others was the
> alienation of a man's own commodities, commodities which, however,
> could only be produced by labor. Now, however, property turns out to be
> the *right,* on the part of the capitalist, to appropriate the unpaid labour of
> others or its product, and the impossibility, on the part of the worker, of
> appropriating his own product. (Marx, 1867/1977:730; emphasis added)

Marx's discussion of property shares features with the moral/civic and
jurisprudential traditions of liberalism, but he tries to dissolve the politics/
economics dichotomy. Moreover, Marx understands property as a constitutive principle that generates the most basic social institutions. Property generates consistent, coherent, extensive social practices that (re)produce
social structures and institutions. "The inner construction of modern society, or, capital in the totality of its relations, is therefore posited in the economic relations of modern landed property" (Marx, 1857–1858/1973:276;
see also Marx, 1844/1964:100–105).

Feminists.   Marxist feminists declare that private property and the relations
of production subjugate women (R. Hamilton, 1978:12). Other feminists,
says Grimshaw (1986:11), assert women's rights by drawing from the
moral/civic and jurisprudential traditions of liberal thought. The argument
is direct: There is no logically coherent reason to exclude women from the
(political) privileges enjoyed by men since women, too, have natural rights.
The only defense against extending such rights must be that society (or
males) values the subjugation of women (see Clark, 1979). Grimshaw
(1986:51) argues that resort to the "naturalness" of female subordination is
a deceptive attempt to hide the dominance exerted over women by (male)
political philosophy and (male-dominated) social practice. For example,
Clark (1979) believes that Locke's political theory of rights and property
presumes that women are a unique form of property. Indeed, Clark argues
that women occupy a social role as possessions, more similar to cattle and
land than to free, independent agents. In that case the issue of property is
central, whether explicit or implicit, in all feminist thought. Hartsock

(1983) and Connell (1987) indirectly address property and power in their analyses of the role of women in the market and the sexual division of labor.

Thus while only Marxist feminists appear to discuss property directly, the concept is unavoidably related to the issue of female subordination. Many feminists acknowledge the constitutive feature of property in generating significant social institutions but devote more attention to the consequent social practices. In this regard the issue of property for feminist theory is hard to distance from the centrality of rights.

CONSTITUTIVE PRINCIPLES

Property is a constitutive principle. It represents resources important to how social life is organized and how social practices are patterned. I introduce the notion of constitutive principles to explain (rather than describe or stipulate) how social structures and actors' identities are generated. Focusing on constitution brings agents' activities and social structuring to the fore. Thus the term *constitutive principles* captures the organized character of structures as well as the constitutive quality of agents' behaviors yet sees them in continuous interplay. These practices are rule-bound.

Just as the structuralist vocabulary of "organizing principles" describes and defines social structures (Lukes, 1977:8; Poulantzas, 1978:67–68; Giddens, 1979:45–48), constitutive principles bring into being specific roles, rules, and relations that constitute and fundamentally organize society. Constitutive principles differ from organizing principles as atomic particles differ from the periodic table of the elements and as genetic code differs from the taxonomy of the animal kingdom.

Consider, for example, George Kennan's famous Mr. X article. He declares that the intractable global relations confronting the United States after World War II constitute for it a unique identity as a nation with a historic mission to accept "the responsibilities of moral and political leadership that history plainly intended for [it] to bear" (Kennan, 1951:106). Indeed, in Kennan's judgment, "Providence" offered the United States the opportunity to exercise such leadership. Kennan's comments introduce global leadership as a constitutive principle, reinforced by notions of divine intervention, crusades, truth, and justice. Wedded to U.S. foreign policy, these principles constituted the Cold War as a state of affairs built upon an "innate antagonism between capitalism and socialism" (Kennan, 1951:95), cast the United States as a vigilant sentinel, crafted the USSR as an implacable foe and brooding outsider, and generated U.S. hegemony and leadership as a form of rule. To the degree other global actors then behaved in ways that reinforced this form of rule and its component rules, an international society with particular characteristics was constituted.

Similarly, when in the novel *Lord of the Flies* the older boy Jack declares, "We'll hunt [and] I'm going to be chief" (Golding, 1959:123), he declares the authority of chieftains as a constitutive principle. He thereby significantly helps to constitute warrior tribal life as the character of the boys' island society, creates identities as hunter-warriors for the other boys, introduces hunting and play as the dominant social practices, and generates absolute monarchy as a condition of (his) rule. To the extent other boys acted in their new roles, adopted their new identities, and reinforced the new rules, they crafted their island society. Further, as other boys, notably Piggy and Ralph, resisted these constitutive rules and structuring social relations, they helped craft the specific character of the developing society, and in turn their identities were constituted.

These examples illustrate how constitutive principles generate social relations by constituting social structures and actors. Constitutive principles represent enduring human practices identifiable by the rules constituting and regulating that behavior. Property and property rights serve constitutive functions. Indeed, Jack declares his role as chief as a personal property: "His [Jack's] tone conveyed a warning, given out of the pride of ownership. . . . Authority sat on his shoulder" (Golding, 1959:138). He secures his authority by appropriating the conch shell and Piggy's eyeglasses, the two most socially significant items of property on the island. In a similar way, Kennan reckons U.S. leadership as a matter of properties, because the United States possesses the most effective attributes or properties for dealing with the Soviet threat and because the opportunity for global leadership is a divine gift (Kennan, 1951:103–105; Burch, 1996).

Speaking generally, constitutive principles are those fundamental concepts embedded in rules by which actors organize their societies, from which societies generate actors' identities and interests, and through which forms of rule emerge.

CONCLUSION

This chapter illustrates that property is a constitutive principle. At the same time, property is difficult to separate conceptually from property rights. While property is a resource at issue in social practice, property rights are the rules that conduct, restrict, and (re)produce such practices. Property rights also identify what is properly called property and what one may do with it. In identifying *what* counts as property and *how* one may dispose of it, property rights serve as fundamental social rules. Such rules are constitutive principles.

Having informed property and illustrated constitutive principles in a general sense, I address these subjects in the next chapter in the specific context of seventeenth-century England.

NOTES

1. The subject of property and property rights is immense. See the select bibliographies in Gaus (1980), Reeve (1986), Ryan (1987), and Waldron (1988). To the degree possible, I distinguish between conceptual and historical discussions.

2. I draw the etymologies and definitions in this book from the *Oxford English Dictionary* (1989) and/or *Black's Law Dictionary* (1990).

The etymology of *property* also draws from the *Middle English Dictionary* (1954). See the *Thesaurus of Old English* (1995:636–647, sec. 15) for a contrasting treatment of the Anglo-Saxon vocabulary concerning property and property relations. These Anglo-Saxon words and phrases differ strikingly from the Latin and French, especially Norman, influences on Middle English generally and on English vocabulary concerning property specifically. The Middle English adoption of Norman French occurred most markedly in the social fields that the Normans dominated: law and government, the Church, and military matters. Each bore on property relations.

Scholars divide the development of the English language into three eras: Old English (c. 450–c. 1150), Middle English (c. 1150–c. 1475), and Modern English (c. 1475–present).

3. It is ironic that one of the motives for "economic" activity in this period was to acquire (sufficient, necessary) property to entertain the possibility of participating in the "good life." And it is telling that such motives helped disintegrate the classical notion of the virtuous good life. The transformation is well illustrated by contemporary understandings: The "good life" now means material consumption.

4. Sreenivasan (1995:4) interprets and evaluates Locke's arguments about property in terms of twentieth-century philosophical disputes. Dunn (1969:ch. 6) explores Robert Filmer's works as catalysts for Locke's thinking. Daly (1979) provides a detailed analysis of Filmer's thought.

3

Specifying Property as a Constitutive Principle in Seventeenth-Century England

A great watershed lying across the history of Western civiliza-tion, the 17th century marks the beginning of the distinctively modern world.

Richard S. Westfall (1973:1)

Myriad social trends converged and clashed in the seventeenth century. As Chapter 1 notes, equally myriad scholarly fields, literatures, and approach-es survey the swirling welter of the century. This was an era "burning with the questions of the rights of rulers and the duties of subjects, forerunners of an approaching war" (Hobbes, 1642/1983:19). It was a "period of con-siderable and often violent political change" (Greenleaf, 1964:10), "unher-alded collapse" (Pocock, 1975:348), and "general crisis" (Toulmin, 1990:17). I ease the task of relating the diverse strands of these events and debates by juxtaposing a pair of contemporary interpretations.

C. B. Macpherson (1962) discusses "possessive individualism" as a feature of developing market exchange relations. J.G.A. Pocock (1975, 1985) responds to Macpherson by considering how actors reconstructed medieval authority to forge modern political authority and form states. By my reading, Macpherson and Pocock each illustrate only one element of the conceptual bifurcation of property, so see only a portion of the larger social picture. Political theorists typically read these as conflicting accounts. I read them as complements, as masterful comments on different aspects of the same coherent social reality. Indeed, Macpherson's attention to "eco-nomic" concerns and Pocock's focus on "political" matters reflect the con-ceptual bifurcation I explore.

This turn to conceptual history warrants comment, for IR and IPE theo-rists may wonder at the reason, and political theorists may balk at an extended commentary on a well-known debate. The seeming debate between Macpherson and Pocock appears familiar because its frame of reference seems self-evident at first glance: Are seventeenth-century changes in the meaning and character of property and property rights a reflection of changing economic conditions or of changing political circumstances? To pose the question in this way illustrates two important features I want to explore. First, this question—cast in terms of a debate—presumes that distinct economic and political causes (and social realms) exist. This distinction is one of my subjects. Second, the question assumes that property rights have only a singular character, yet I intend to demonstrate that understandings of property rights split into two separate classes of meaning. This bifurcated meaning creates a conceptual framework for reckoning seemingly distinct realms of politics and economics. This novel reading will intrigue theorists and inform IR scholars. For the latter, the turn to conceptual histories allows us to explore the worldview or ideology of the early modern era. From this view one sees that the conceptual framework by which twentieth-century IR scholars arrange and classify the world does not exist in the seventeenth century. That is, the international system is neither "natural" nor "self-evident." Indeed, one sees and makes sense of the international system from particular (historical, conceptual) vantage points. As actors constructed a modern worldview, they constituted a conceptual framework that identifies and characterizes an international system. In this regard, the turn to conceptual history may intrigue IR theorists because it challenges many of the field's foundations and illustrates how those foundations were laid. I conclude that mainstream IR theory, as one of the foremost embodiments of the modern worldview, is as much an ideology and a central feature of modernity and the international system as it is an explanation of them (Walker, 1993).

However, I offer two cautions at the outset. One considers related efforts; the other outlines what this chapter does not attempt. First, although several authors similarly explore the era, I pursue novel goals, though we share approaches. For example, Dunn (1969), Tully (1980), and Ashcraft (1986) investigate the context and character of Locke's views on property. Their approaches illuminate my effort. Dunn offers "an extended archaeological excavation of Locke's mind" (p. ix) in order to place Locke's arguments into the historical context of the seventeenth century. Tully (1980:e.g., p. x) attempts to recover from the *Two Treatises of Government* the original context and meanings Locke intended to convey in his theory of property. Tully and Ashcraft have a common purpose, though Ashcraft expands the context to the revolutionary politics of the seventeenth century and explores the broad range of Locke's political thought (e.g., p. ix).

As matters of method, each of these authors emphasizes historical context and interpretation. They argue that one can recover meanings only by placing oneself as nearly as possible in the historical, social, practical contexts being explored. Dunn, Tully, and Ashcraft probe deeply with their sharp focus on Locke. My subject requires a broader but more shallow excavation of the conceptual frameworks of the era. I search for the load-bearing walls and foundations, so to speak, by concentrating on the narrower theme of property. In this regard Dunn (p. 66) notes the "centrality and paradigmatic quality of the analysis of property for the whole theory of politics." Dunn's point conveys the essence of my argument so far.

Tully offers a linguisitic caution, however, that is generally applicable. He warns readers that misunderstandings of Locke arise "from wrenching his argument out of its linguistic context and reading it in the light of our quite different vocabulary" (p. xiv). For example, Tully informs us that the modern dichotomy of private versus common "has no place" in the seventeenth century. Thus in a broader sense we must try "to understand a way of thinking about rights in which our opposed concepts do not exist." I agree wholeheartedly, since I similarly argue that the politics/economics dichotomy did not exist in the seventeenth century either. Indeed, the questions that motivate this work arise from "our quite different vocabulary."

Also, Ashcraft (1986:xii) expresses a critical motivation that I share: "This work is, in its entirety, an argument against methodological divisions and disciplinary boundaries." He and I also criticize conceptual and paradigmatic divisions. In sum, much of my work follows the leads these authors first scouted.

Yet my effort differs. They explore Locke and property. I explore the seventeenth century and property to understand the international system in the modern era. Similarly, Pennington (1993) looks to the political theory and legal discourse of the Middle Ages (1200–1600) to address the relationships between princely authority and the law. These relationships make up one of many contested elements that inform the modern worldview and the practices that constitute the international system. In a similar spirit, Bartelson (1995:2) investigates "the relationship between sovereignty and truth" by conducting a genealogical history. His concerns, though more abstract, still speak to the subjects I present. He notes that

> genealogy is a history of the present in terms of the past. . . . [It is] a history of logical spaces and their succession in time. . . . [A] genealogy must start from an analysis of the present, and explain the formation of this present in terms of its past; a genealogy has not as its task to tell what actually happened in the past, but to describe how the present became logically possible. (Bartelson, 1995:7–8).

I seek to explain the conceptual crosshairs that currently frame the international system and define contemporary social "space" by explaining how they were constituted. In a like vein, for perspective on twentieth-century philosophical disputes, Tuck (1979:2) investigates rights. Last, Ryan (1987:3) explores the concept property through a "philosophical analysis of ideas . . . of their coherence and their implications." Of course "some reference to historical context is inescapable. The problem, then, is one of how *much* and *what* context is inescapable" (Ryan, 1987:3). I take the premises of Ryan, Tuck, and Bartelson to heart, and I wed them to the conceptual and historically sociological approaches I share with Dunn, Tully, Ashcraft, and many others. Yet we differ markedly in the scope and depth of our subjects.

My second caution is preemptive. This chapter does not attempt a historical account or evaluation of seventeenth-century events. Nor does it offer a philosophical analysis of the contested themes. Rather, I use the masterful excursions into seventeenth-century political theory by Macpherson (1962) and Pocock (1975) to frame, inform, and signify important elements of the social and political changes in the era. I do so in the spirit of Tuck's (1979:2) claim that "understanding a political language involves understanding the literature of political theory, and that applies to the speakers of the language as much as to its historians."

In this chapter I argue simply that to understand the dizzying events of the era, we would find it valuable to attend to the concepts property and property rights. Yet to understand the turmoil at all, we need guidance. Other factors were important, but property rights were fundamental. The well-established theoretical template of the Macpherson-Pocock debate illuminates and frames three important aspects: seventeenth-century social relations and political theory, the place of property in those relations and theories, and twentieth-century perspectives. I look to the seventeenth century to illustrate the constitution of a uniquely liberal-modern worldview and the related practices that constitute the international system. To explain that "modes of consciousness" (Pocock, 1975:334) changed and an era-auguring worldview emerged, I explore conceptual frameworks, the catalysts that prompted change, and the conceptual changes that occurred.

Macpherson and Pocock address these themes. Their work shaped others' scholarship on the early modern period, though respondents offer critical comments (e.g., Dunn, 1969; Tuck, 1979:3, 83, 133, 149; Tully, 1980; Ashcraft, 1986:150–151, 189–190; Simmons, 1992; Sreenivasan, 1995:30). By any standards Macpherson and Pocock are renowned scholars. For thirty-five years, Macpherson's volume has been benchmark scholarship; for twenty years Pocock's work has been the same. Moreover, Macpherson and Pocock exemplify competing views on liberalism, rights, state formation, statecraft, market society, property, and related themes. They also treat these concepts and issues as proper subjects for conceptual histories. Last, Macpherson and Pocock represent traditional, perhaps paradigmatic (world)views. Macpherson employs the juristic vocabulary of rights in the context of a Marxian concern for property, propriety, and exchange in the early liberal-modern era. Pocock works within the moral/civic tradition, relying on the vocabulary of moral virtue and civic authority.

Macpherson analyzes the rise of the commercial, bourgeois order from its feudal ancestry, focusing specifically upon changes in property rights and the development of "possessive individualism." Pocock questions Macpherson's analysis, reading possessive individualism as a consequence of the friction between governmental authority and individual liberty. He argues that the transformation Macpherson addresses is a political and philosophic reaction to the social upheavals surrounding the Cromwellian interregnum and the Glorious Revolution, not the flowering of the bourgeois world. In the tremendous wake of these disruptive social and political developments, new relations arose concerning the possession and disposition of property.

Macpherson and Pocock exemplify competing conceptions of seventeenth-century society and politics. In that era the contrasts between the communitarian politics of ancient republics and the fragmented, individualized politics of an emerging modern order became pointed and politically charged. This is the "Machiavellian moment" (Pocock, 1975) in Anglo politics. Yet Macpherson's and Pocock's views apply not only to this moment but to a long era of social and political transformation in southern and western Europe.

Macpherson represents modernity. He sees the past from the perspective of the present, reading the seventeenth century in terms of nascent-to-burgeoning liberalism and capitalism. He excavates seventeenth-century political thought in search of clues identifying the origins of capitalist markets, liberal politics, and "market society," much as the Leakeys excavate Olduvai Gorge. Macpherson knows the present and seeks its source.

Pocock knows the past and traces its trajectory. He represents the politics of the ancient polis or Italian city-states (Pocock, 1975:ch. 3; 1977:41). Republican elements of the Greco-Roman past configured the seventeenth century and beyond. With the irrevocable dissolution of feudalism, European actors confronted a perplexing problem of society: how to reconcile the republican tradition of individual fulfillment through political participation with the Christian doctrine of fulfillment after death? When seventeenth-century English political authority collapsed, the "problem of society" became more a matter of its forging than of its form. English citizens could shape their futures only by borrowing from the past. To (re)craft political authority was to confront questions about the foundations and purposes of authority, especially its effects upon individual liberties. Pocock (1975, 1980) reads the era of Machiavelli to Andrew Jackson in western

Europe and North America as a contest between traditional republican and emerging liberal values.

For Macpherson, Pocock, and seventeenth-century actors, property was a central concern.

PROPERTY AS A CONSTITUTIVE PRINCIPLE

> *Every one as he is himselfe, so he hath a selfe propriety, else he could not be himselfe.*

> Richard Overton, Leveller spokesman, 1646

The epigraph above is symbolic. Macpherson reads it as a statement about proprietary interests, property rights, and thus also about property. It is a statement of possessive individualism. Alternatively, Pocock interprets it as a claim about individual liberty and the property requirements for good government. For him, the quotation states a condition for civic virtue. Each theorist recognizes property as a principle constituting the character of social relations and political governance. That is, property as a concept is a shorthand reference to human practices that generate social relations. Both authors also illustrate the constitutive role of property in seventeenth-century worldviews and in the political debates of the era.

Macpherson and "Possessive Individualism"

Macpherson (1962) reads Hobbes, Locke, Harrington, and Puritan thinkers as advocates of political individualism. For Macpherson, such individualism is the root of modern liberal-democratic theory, market society, and the liberal state. Although Tuck (1979:3), for example, sees *moral* individualism in the fourteenth century, Macpherson concentrates on *political* individualism in the liberal, market context of the seventeenth century. Liberal individualism has a possessive quality "found in its conception of the individual as essentially the proprietor of his own person or capacities . . . as an owner of himself" (Macpherson, 1962:3). Berlin (1969:122) calls the situation negative liberty: "Over himself, over his own body and mind, the individual is sovereign." To own one's self is to possess the capacity to exercise self-direction, self-determination, and self-control. Individuals make choices. They make choices in market contexts. "This was the liberal society and state. . . . This was the market economy. . . . [This was] a society based on . . . individual choices" (Macpherson, 1966:6–7). In this view, liberal society and market society are indistinguishable.

> Society becomes a lot of free, equal individuals related to each other as proprietors of their own capacities. . . . Society consists of relations of exchange between proprietors. (Macpherson, 1962:3)

These are Macpherson's "possessive individuals." Seven features define them. First, human freedom occurs when individuals escape dependence upon the will of another. Such freedom suggests, second, that freedom manifests itself in voluntary relationships. Third, the occasion to make exclusive personal choices implies that all individuals must hold property rights in their persons and abilities; they are self-proprietors. Fourth, any individual may alienate all but the whole of her or his personal self-property, including the property or capacity of personal labor. Consequently, fifth, human society necessarily entails marketlike social relations among sole proprietors of personal capacities and characteristics. Sixth, since personal freedom is reducible to freedom from dependence, limitations on personal liberties can arise only in the course of securing similar freedoms for others. Last, political society is an institutionalized means for protecting self-propriety, personal property, and the orderly exchange relations among individual sole proprietors.

What one possesses in these circumstances, as a possessive individual—that is, what one is proprietor over—is rights and obligations (see Hohfeld, 1964; Tuck, 1979:1–7). Macpherson uses the terms *proprietor* and *owner* to convey just this fundamental sense. Indeed, "political society becomes a calculated device for the protection of this property and for the maintenance of an orderly relation of exchange" (Macpherson, 1962:3; recall Smith, 1776/1937:670, 674). By my reading, the phrase "this property" carries several meanings: property as the exclusive property right in one's self, as rights and obligations affecting choice-making, as physical objects, and as the rightness or propriety of relations among individuals and between individuals and objects. (I discuss these latter three features of property in Chapter 2.) While Macpherson does not invoke the word *propriety,* he does emphasize the virtues of social "cohesion." Such cohesion is the necessary foundation for political obligation (Macpherson, 1962:83, 87–90, 271–276). As this is Macpherson's ultimate point, one can read a sense of propriety into his discussion of cohesive social relations. In the context of seventeenth-century England, he describes these relations as cohesive because individuals saw themselves as essentially equal—that is, they saw themselves as having more in common than not. What they shared, what bound them into a cohesive society, was "the equal subservience of all men to the determination of the market" (Macpherson, 1962:87).

In short, because Macpherson sees property as a constitutive principle generating the organization and dynamics of social relations, he discusses the property *rights* exercised by possessive individuals. As such, he invokes juristic conceptions of property and society.

Pocock, the (Re)Construction of Authority, and Political Personality

For Pocock, property arose as a political and philosophical issue following the English civil war during the mid-seventeenth-century crises over the "radical need to reconstruct authority" (Pocock, 1985:57). The place of property in reconstructing society was central because it was a prerequisite for political authority and civic virtue, both necessary elements. Pocock (1985:109) further argues that each of the two dominant ways of reconceiving social life centered on forms of property:

> We must think . . . of an enduring conflict between two explicitly post-feudal ideals, one agrarian and the other commercial, one ancient and the other modern.

The agrarian ideal, drawing from the moral/civic tradition, emphasizes the political independence, personality, and worth conferred by landed property. The commercial ideal, Macpherson's subject, hails mobile property and exchange among possessive individuals in market society. For Pocock, property constitutes both relations of authority and political personality, hence individual virtue and civic worth. Together these features contribute significantly to the form and function of civil (and commercial) society.

Thus, in both the moral/civic and jurisprudential traditions property serves to constitute social relations generally and social actors in particular. In the section below, I explore this theme in detail as I elaborate Macpherson's and Pocock's broad arguments.

THE PROMINENCE OF PROPERTY IN THE (RE)CONSTITUTION OF ENGLISH SOCIETY

Macpherson and Market Society

Macpherson traces the simultaneous emergence of the market economy and liberal society in the seventeenth century. Market relations so fundamentally transformed social life that there no longer existed a "fundamental equality" among individuals (Macpherson, 1962:274). As social cohesion eroded, the liberal state became a purveyor of law, order, and civil liberties and an enforcer of property rights. Macpherson argues that Hobbes, Locke, the

Levellers, and Harrington constructed models of market society based on particular but evolving notions of property. I treat them in this order below, devoting most attention to Hobbes. Since Harrington is central for Pocock, the arrangement also offers an attractive segue to Pocock's views.

On Hobbes

For Macpherson, Hobbes envisions the social and political consequences of individuals making competitive choices in a market context administered by a central state.[1] In this worldview possessive individuals competitively confront one another as proprietors of their own capacities, understood as property rights in their persons. The state is necessary because individuals violently and endlessly compete for power. This unyielding threat of violence is "the natural condition of mankind," or the so-called state of nature.

While Hobbes depicts original individuals as asocial creatures, his intention to deduce the need for an unrestrained sovereign requires that he incorporate assumptions about socialized, civilized humans. The society he depicts is his own: His state of nature is an abstraction away from his experiences in seventeenth-century England (Macpherson, 1962:26–27). Thus, the state of nature is an "inference made from the passions" (Hobbes, 1651/1958:107). Passions are key because Hobbes believed that when authority disintegrates, individuals will violently pursue their competitive self-interests (Hobbes, 1651/1958:108). Undiluted warfare ensues:

> During the time men live without a common power to keep them in awe, they are in that condition which is called war, and such a war as is of every man against every man. (Hobbes, 1651/1958:107)

Stripped of order, society becomes a virtual fiction, a tornado of dislocated, suspicious individuals engaged in competition. This is an unrelenting, "restless desire of power after power that ceases only in death" for the limited stock of existing power (Hobbes, 1651/1958:86). Yet a ceaseless, competitive, zero-sum struggle for power over others describes social relations rather than universal personal motivations; it is a defensible assumption only in the context of an already universally competitive society (Macpherson, 1962:40, 45). Here we discover the essential characteristics of the competitive market (Macpherson, 1962:36–46).

Macpherson (1962:48ff.) reasons that only a possessive market society remains consistent with the elements of Hobbes's arguments:

> If a single criterion of the possessive market society is wanted it is that man's labour is a commodity, i.e., that a man's energy and skill are his own, yet are regarded *not as integral parts of his personality, but as possessions,* the use and disposal of which he is free to hand over to others

for a price. It is to emphasize this characteristic of the fully market society that I have called it the *possessive* market society. Possessive market *society* also implies that where labour has become a market commodity, market relations so shape or permeate all social relations that it may properly be called a market society, not merely a market economy. (Macpherson, 1962:48; emphasis in the two latter instances in original)

Macpherson's view of Hobbes rests squarely upon a conception of individual possessors: "All individuals are essentially related to each other as possessors of marketable commodities. . . . Everyone is a possessor of something, if only his capacity for labor" (Macpherson, 1962:55, 57). Hobbes (1651/1958:78) describes personal attributes in terms of "natural power" and "instrumental power." Macpherson understands these attributes as personal capacities or self-possessions over which individuals possess rights. By Macpherson's judgment Hobbes's individuals do not hold powers; it is not that they *are,* for example, strong, wise, or rich. Instead, Macpherson argues, they *possess* strength, wisdom, or wealth. Hobbes's competitive individuals do not over*power* each other. Rather, they arrange advantageous *exchanges*. They simply outcompete or outwit each other, so reap advantages.

Individuals are drawn into market relations as the only available means of parlaying their self-capacities into satisfaction and success. Market competition determines the benefits each derives from what she offers. Also, marketlike relations impute value to honor, virtue, and other forms of personal power. "Every man is in the market for power, either as supplier or demander, for everyone either has some power to offer to others or wants to acquire the power of some others" (Macpherson, 1962:39). These relations became increasingly familiar as nascent market operations and the development of unconditional rights to property eroded anachronistic feudal relations, especially militarily contingent land tenures. Exclusive private property rights sharply contrast with the highly contingent, overlapping property claims that comprised feudal life (Strayer, 1970; Anderson, 1974:32–38; Kratochwil, 1995:25–28). Possession of rights becomes central: What rights do individuals hold over property? What can one do with property? What objects and relations count as proprietary? Such questions signal jurisprudential configurations of political life. Similarly, questions about disposing of property raise matters of exchange and transfer, hence economic relations.

On Locke

Reason, natural rights, and property bond acquisitive, possessive individuals into a civil society. Locke, more clearly than Hobbes, argues that humans create political society to regulate the interactions of proprietors.[2]

Locke's state of nature contrasts with Hobbes's conception. In one of few references to Hobbes, Locke (1690/1965:321, para. 19) remarks that "some men have confounded" the difference between the state of nature and the state of war. For Locke, the state of nature is a harmonious social community based on reason. In this society individuals bear responsibility for enforcing the law of nature (Laslett, 1965:111). Locke stakes familiar ground when he declares that property is a right derived from natural law, or the "law of reason." This law represents God's will and is the source of individual freedom and equality (Locke, 1690/1965:348, para. 57).

The faculties of reason also establish the foundations of fellowship, community, and society (Locke, 1690/1965:429–430, para. 172). Individuals are first and foremost possessive beings because they possess reason. By reason they are free. Thus, despotic government and absolute monarchies are intolerable (Locke, 1690/1965:369, para. 90). Legitimate government offers the means for collectively enforcing the law of nature (Locke, 1690/1965:ch. 15). Locke emphasizes community and property when he declares:

> *Political Power* then I take to be a Right of making Laws with Penalties of Death . . . for the Regulating and Preserving of Property, and of employing the force of the Community in the Execution of such Laws. (Locke, 1690/1965:308, para. 3; emphasis in original)

Individuals transform community property into material personal possessions by mixing their labor with the raw resources in the state of nature. By their effort they create individual "Lives, Liberties, and Estates" (Locke, 1690/1965:395, para. 123). By mixing labor with resources, individuals also become citizens, so acquire political rights. Locke equates property with rights and conceives individual rights as marketable goods (Laslett, 1965:118). Thus, property becomes a tangible manifestation of rights (Laslett, 1965:116). Property and property rights symbolize the development of political society from a hypothetical state of nature. Thus, Locke created his views of society in the image of market man (Macpherson, 1962:169). Macpherson (1962:270) concludes that Locke's work rests on Hobbes's "sure foundations."

On the Levellers

Primarily former Parliament members, the Levellers formed a political movement during the English civil war. They advocated nearly universal suffrage, a written constitution, and religious tolerance. Macpherson believes the Levellers and Harrington were receptive to organizing England as a market society, but they did not articulate those premises or explore their consequences.

As did Hobbes and Locke, Levellers rooted their conceptions of society in visions of humans in nature. Property rights symbolize the innate, naturally derived freedoms that buttress individual human rights and privileges. Property, and therefore property rights, existed before the establishment of government. Consequently, people agree to establish governments in order to preserve property. One Leveller spokesman proclaimed during a political debate that "properties are the foundation of constitutions" (quoted in Macpherson, 1962:139). Advocates grounded this view in a broad conception of natural property rights that was itself founded on the principle of personal proprietorship (see Lilburne, 1646, in Macpherson, 1962:137). On this score Macpherson (1962:150) interprets the Leveller program as advancing all human rights—whether social, political, or economic—as matters of property rights. One realizes these rights by applying one's labor to the world. The rewards for such labor are individual rights of possession. These rights thereby create a society of possessive individuals.

From this grounding the Levellers deduced specific economic rights of ownership and acquisition. The most important right, however, was a right to unhindered trade. The Levellers, well in advance of any other individual theorist or group of thinkers in mid-seventeenth-century England, articulated a coherent vision of individuals behaving as proprietors over their personal attributes, abilities, and possessions. On this basis Macpherson (1962:56) judges Leveller thought to be possessive but Locke more so. Levellers adopted the premise of proprietary possession to ground individual freedoms. Thus, they grounded their identity as proprietors in a political system and their personalities as laboring individuals in an economic realm:

> If you insist that a man is human only as sole proprietor of himself, only in so far as he is free from all but market relations, you must convert the moral values into market values. (Macpherson, 1962:266)

Thus, modern society is coherent and whole but necessarily divided. Property sets the divisions.

On Harrington

Harrington offers an alternative. He analyzes the political consequences of the gradual transformation of property claims to land. The English feudal order endured until the reign of Henry VII (1485–1509). For example, Shakespeare clearly illustrates the feudal character of English life and nobility in the three plays centering on King Henry VI (1422–1461), as when Henry returns Richard Plantagenet to his princely status as a duke and substantial landholder in exchange for an oath of allegiance (*Henry VI Part 1*, act 3, scene 1). A generation later, Henry VII enacted statutes that undermined the power of the feudal nobility. These dictates eroded the military attachments and aristocratic advantages of land tenure, thereby forcing the nobility to enter market society (Macpherson, 1962:164–165, 172–173). By the time of Elizabeth I (1558–1603), the predominant control of (landed) property had shifted away from the nobility toward the people. This shift corresponds directly with constitutional changes during that era.

These transitions are unmistakable. Beginning in about 1500, English constitutional foundations started to shift, and by midcentury they were aligned in distinctly new ways. In the roughly fifty years between the reigns of Henry VII and Elizabeth I—the beginning of a longer, slower erosion of aristocratic domination—English political authority was transforming from monarchical to parliamentary rule. Over the next 100 years, these changes became widely apparent, relatively popular, and incontrovertibly entrenched.

> The shift he [Harrington] found was not from king and nobility to gentry but from king and nobility to the people. . . . He held, indeed, that property had shifted from nobility to gentry and people, and that power should shift accordingly. (Macpherson, 1962:171)[3]

Harrington argues that domestic order was not unsettled by these changes, however. Changes in political power followed shifts in the distribution of property. Thus, property constitutes forms of governance and social order. Indeed, Harrington conceives three forms of government, each distinguishable by the distribution of power and property. Drawing from Aristotle and Roman political theory, the three forms are government by the one ("absolute monarchy"), by the few ("mix'd monarchy"), and by the many ("a commonwealth").

For government to be stable, the distribution of power within society must conform to the distribution of property. In Harrington's view property is virtually a sole determinant of myriad social conditions: political authority, domestic order, social stability, class affiliation, interclass relations, and even international war and colonization. Property also constitutes competitive individuals—they seek to dominate others and their environment—but they are only modestly acquisitive. Still, individuals will not risk revolutionary social upheaval and dramatic shifts in government lest it upset the possibility of upward mobility and increased wealth. Government and society will remain stable in Harrington's view because the people "would not risk weakening the sanctity of property by any confiscatory measures" (Macpherson, 1962:188).

Harrington begins with Hobbesian assumptions yet derives a constitutional commonwealth rather than an absolute monarchy. Harrington asserts that a gentry class holding nonfeudal landed property can also found a commonwealth. Overstating the matter, Macpherson (1962:193) concludes that Harrington depends "on a concept of the economy which takes for granted the necessity or at least the superiority of capitalist relations of production, and a concept of equality which is essentially bourgeois." These conceptions depend fundamentally on property.

While Harrington's views do not conveniently fit Macpherson's model of possessive individualism and a burgeoning bourgeois market society, they do illustrate the central role of property and property rights in constituting society as a whole. Moreover, they also illustrate the split in the conceptual makeup of property.

Summary

Macpherson anchors his discussion of possessive individualism in the jurisprudential tradition's concern for rights. His argument is essentially constitutive. Property and property rights constitute social relations by generating specific, recurrent social practices and consequent social structures. The foremost structure is the competitive market and attendant class inequalities. Associated practices involve possessive relations. These include production and exchange.

Self-possession or self-proprietorship are the foremost property conceptions, though landed property remains significant throughout the era. Self-proprietorship becomes a means to personal freedom. Individuals are free insofar as they can avoid social relations except those they voluntarily join in their self-interest. Thus, individuals are choice-makers and personal proprietors who can alienate all but the whole of their (self-)properties, including personal labor. This is possessive individualism. What of consequent market society?

Since all individuals achieve their humanity and freedom by acting as self-proprietors, then human society is reducible to the relations among sole proprietors, thereby becoming a market society (Macpherson, 1962:264). Political society protects property and maintains order so that proprietors may trade. Said briefly, Macpherson marks the emergence of the bourgeois, capitalist order from highly conditional feudal relations. He identifies developing unconditional property rights and the competitive exchange relations they generate. However, Macpherson does not explain how or why they emerge, noting only that they develop. "He clearly presupposes here as proved what the argument is supposed to prove" (Tully, 1980:142–143).

While Macpherson's argument illustrates property as a constitutive principle, I also read it as consistent with the broader theme that capitalist relations and the state developed simultaneously and inextricably. For

Macpherson, this is the debut of liberalism. It is also the emergence of the modern world.

> To put this another way, . . . there came the society and the politics of choice, the society and politics of competition, the society and politics of the market. This was the liberal society and state. (Macpherson, 1966:6)

These changes swept individuals into the free market and transformed social life into market relations (Macpherson, 1966:7).

The market economy and liberal society represent slightly different views of the same broadly social phenomenon: The emergence of market society. Since market society requires stability and order, the demands became more pronounced not only for government efficiency but also for responsiveness. Individuals came to see governance as a consumable commodity. Governments were suppliers who expanded civil liberties and provided law and order. The liberal state became a modified, relaxed version of the original capital-accumulating state.

A picture becomes clear. The world is composed of possessive individuals, acting as sole self-proprietors, trading in capitalist markets as mediated, reinforced, and administered by a centralized state. However, Macpherson merely outlines this picture for us. It lacks focus and context. We do not know the source of possessive market principles or of the responsive state. To address these issues, we turn to J.G.A. Pocock, a contrasting voice in this contemporary debate.

Pocock and Legal Authority

Pocock introduces the paradox of liberalism and authority to interpret the social and political turmoil of seventeenth-century England. For him, any discussion of individualism, whether possessive or not, must address the rudiments of liberalism. Yet "it is impossible to assert even the most radical liberty without some conception of authority at the same time," hence the paradox (Pocock, 1985:54). The issue of political authority was central, even cosmic, since revolutionary tumult in England had destroyed sovereign control. Efforts to reestablish political authority invoked the concept of property.

The "Machiavellian Moment"

Authority collapsed in England in the wake of years of civil war and the beheading of King Charles in 1649. The collapse precipitated profound controversies over the foundations of society and the principles around which to refashion authority. Commentators invoked republican themes to make sense of the constitutional and social crisis (Nenner, 1977:197; Pocock, 1977:23; on republicanism more generally, see Onuf, 1997c). This is the "Machiavellian moment" writ large: a titanic clash of worldviews (Pocock, 1975). Republican thought presented *virtu,* moral/civic fulfillment, *vita civilis,* and political participation as the means to self-realization. The anxieties of *fortuna,* chance, *tyche,* and uncertain luck had abolished social and natural order (Pocock, 1975:36–39, 64–67; Toulmin, 1990:13–22). This symbolic conflict became the foundation for English public discourse when in 1642 the monarchy argued, in the *Answer to the Nineteen Propositions,* that "mindless and random" *fortuna* would prevail should republican virtues collapse (Pocock, 1977:21). Maintaining royal privilege was, of course, necessary to maintain the social balance fundamental to republican doctrine. Thus, both the monarchy and the opposition acknowledged Machiavelli's conception of the conflict between virtue and fortune as relevant to the English experience. However, other parties maintained quite different notions. Bodin (1576/1992), Hobbes (1651/1958), and Filmer (1680/1949) each dismissed as nonsense the idea of mixed, balanced government in the republican tradition.

Royalist counterarguments to the republican attack held that individuals were naturally subject to the authority of kings. Were citizens subject to sovereign authority wherever it was vested? What is the foundation of sovereignty or authority? How should citizens address de facto authority? Whom or what should citizens obey?

> Unless men inherited or acquired property, it was hard to see how they acquired an obligation to obey the laws of society as it positively existed. . . . Freedom must have a material base: that a man must own himself if he were not to be owned by another. (Pocock, 1977:27)

Thus authority, liberty, and property sit at the center of seventeenth-century efforts to reconstitute society. Republican vocabulary became an effective weapon against entrenched authority. Whether property and freedom were grounded in inheritable rights and positive law (thus, government → laws → property) or were grounded in nature and innate reason (thereby reason → property → government → laws) was not yet decided. Sword-bearing conquerors complicated the formulae. Nevertheless, the key concepts of authority, liberty, and property remained prominent.

Debates over political authority introduced property as the source of political personality. As property owners, individuals may claim, assert, and exercise liberties. So by what titles or property can authority be firmly grounded in society? Consequently, what rights should those who possess authority be entitled to hold? Harrington and Filmer, for example, argue that property is the means by which authority maintains itself. As noted, Harrington specifically argues that changes in the distribution of property explain the shifting locations of authority over time (Pocock, 1977:27).

Debates about the relationship of authority to property focused on governmental corruption and patronage, ultimately viewed as a novel and socially destabilizing form of property. Patronages eroded the constitutional foundations by which only those with landed property possessed sufficient personal independence to participate politically. In short, patronages altered prevailing notions and practices of politics. Broadening political participation undermined the moral, virtuous attributes that only (landed) property could bestow upon (privileged) individuals. The rising prominence and sociopolitical significance of mobile, nonlanded, especially commercial property undermined the moral foundations of government and individual virtue that landed property represented.

I address below three crucial points: the nature of authority, the place of property in considering the sources of social authority, and the specific concerns about patronage and political corruption.

On Authority

The Cromwellian interregnum mirrored the social and political uncertainty that followed the collapse of the Roman Empire. Filmer, Hobbes, Harrington, and Locke, among others, responded to their fractured circumstances much as Aquinas had to his. English citizens, like their Roman counterparts, confronted the disquieting prospect that authority had disintegrated and God had chosen not to reveal alternatives. The consequence in each case was a focus upon political authority and the subsequent ruler-ruled relationship, for which property always played a key role.

> Seventeenth century men were still premodern creatures for whom authority and magistracy were part of a natural and cosmic order. . . . The starting point of much of their most radical thinking was the unimaginable fact that, between 1642 and 1649, authority in England had simply collapsed. (Pocock, 1985:55)

Each individual had to "rediscover in the depths of his own being the means of reconstituting and obeying" social authority (Pocock, 1985:55; also 1975:348; 1977:15; 1980:10–11). A retreat to theology promised sectarian conflict and the prospect of renewed religious war. This was plainly too frightening in the waning years of the Thirty Years' War on the Continent and religious fratricide at home. Alternatively, anticlerical sentiments motivated Hobbes and Harrington to craft chillingly secular conceptions of natural politics (Pocock, 1977:77–99).

On Property as a Source of Authority

Property as a source of political authority became a subject of prominent public discussion: By what rights or principles can authority be secured in society? Pocock addresses the issue Macpherson raises but does not answer: Why were the concepts of possession and property changing? Pocock's (1985:58–61) jab at Macpherson is gentlemanly but substantial. He acknowledges that Macpherson addresses a significant issue but that he addresses it weakly. Macpherson's observation that relationships involving property were changing slowly but distinctly and that some theorists recorded the changes is a tantalizing entree, rendered unpalatable because he offers no reasons for the changes. Thus Macpherson's model of liberalism and possessive individualism becomes suspect. Does it leave out too much? Does it interpret the theorists in stilted ways? Pocock is especially suspicious of Macpherson's rendering of Harrington (Pocock, 1985:59).

The widespread sense of social collapse and cosmic chaos in the seventeenth century precipitated a quest for certainty and stability (Toulmin, 1990). Wren and Harrington addressed these issues. Matthew Wren, "one full-blooded possessive individualist" (Pocock, 1985:61), argues in a pair of works from 1657 and 1659 that society comprises competitive, bargaining individuals. The most powerful always stipulate the terms of exchange to the weaker parties, Wren argues. He claims that the model of bargaining man is especially applicable to an individualist society in which movable goods and wealth are significant (Pocock, 1985:61). With these Hobbesian assumptions, Wren reaches a similarly Hobbesian conclusion: Society requires an absolute sovereign to regulate the dynamic bargaining process. However, Harrington argues in *Oceana* (1656/1977) that commercial property alienates individuals, as it makes them coldly calculating and narrowly self-interested. Instead, he asserts that landownership confers stability and affords freedom of action to owners. These owners then enjoy the opportunity to pursue rational political interests. By this freedom of action, landowners can form a deliberative, just commonwealth.

Harrington's views are mildly liberal but are clearly anchored in traditional conceptions of society and politics drawn from the moral/civic tradition, or what Pocock calls civic humanism. Alternatively, Wren appears as a modern man (Pocock, 1977:140; 1985:62), condemning Hobbes and Harrington for their traditional, secular, anticlerical views. Wren's view of politics based on commercial exchanges argues that power is property and property is the measure of power. Thus, a possessive, power-seeking individual

> enters into exchange relationships less because he lacks what others have than because he has the power to force others to give him what he lacks,

in exchange for his excess of what they lack. Political power is set up to enforce the contracts which the strong impose upon the weak, and must be sovereign because strong and weak alike are constantly asserting the natural freedom to escape one's share of the bargain. Property and government are alike based on the excess of one's power over another's, which also gives rise to exchange; and the more effective the mechanisms of exchange the more effective the mechanisms of sovereignty. (Pocock, 1977:88–89)

Wren is then the consummate possessive individualist. His views and family ties to the clergy established a means for Puritan bishops to become point men for expanding liberalism. Indeed, these bishops became the foremost supporters of the so-called bourgeois ideology against the stolid conservatism of traditional elites (Pocock, 1985:63).

In this regard Wren and Harrington appear more significant than Hobbes or Locke. Both Wren and Harrington suggest that movable, commercial property alters personal psychology, political personality, and social relations. Commercial property compels individuals to behave competitively, violently, and acquisitively to the detriment of social order. The maintenance of social order requires a sovereign, whether absolute or not.

One cannot demean the political and philosophical significance of these views. While Macpherson recognizes the rise of a commercial, financial, bourgeois order in the political thought of the era, Wren and Harrington are speaking to a slightly different concern: The simultaneous revival of traditional elites and their renewed exercise of political power and social control. The consequence was the interplay of commercial and landed interests involving bourgeois and traditional values that marked modern and ancient conceptions of politics. This is the paradox of liberty and authority (Pocock, 1985:67–68).

Wren's support of commercial property over landed property illustrates how support for bourgeois relations came not only from an emerging commercial class but primarily from the restorationist class. This included socially displaced yet recovering aristocrats, bureaucrats, clergy, and other elites.

The ruling classes of England became significantly more commercial in their membership and behavior [because] . . . some of them discovered the utility from their point of view of a commercially based ideology. (Pocock, 1985:64)

After the return to power of traditional elites in 1660, the commercial ideology received substantial support. Political success led to consistency, theoretical and practical refinements, and a bandwagon effect. Recognition of the power and significance of mobile property was one of the features of the restoration program. Thus, the transition from individual-as-magistrate to individual-as-proprietor was well under way. By the last quarter of the seventeenth century, the tension between elites promoting traditional, land-ed values and the commercial advocates of mobile property had come to dominate deep politics. In microcosm, Harrington and Wren anticipated such disputes over the fundamental character of the polity.[4]

On Patronage

Debates over the merits of different forms of property escalated in the 1690s when government patronage began to involve mobile property rather than land. When mobile property became prominent during the Financial Revolution of the 1690s, it frightened traditional elements not because of its marketable characteristics but because it appeared to be yet another form of governmental bribery or payoff. Markets did not represent a telling threat because trading markets had already been absorbed into the social makeup. People recognized trade as a means to personal independence and virtue, although it was more crass than landed property. Instead, patronage in the form of "public credit," public office, and government stock was both scandalous and catastrophic for traditional classes. Depending upon your values and views, public credit, or "corruption," was

> a mode of property which rendered government dependent on its creditors and creditors dependent on government, in a relation incompatible with classical or agrarian virtue. It was a property not in the means of production, but in the relationships between government and the otherwise property-owning individual. (Pocock, 1985:69; also 1977:136–138)

By 1700, citizens could not deny the significance of commercial markets in society and the prominence of credit operations in public and private practice.[5] Perceptions of credit preceded and shaped perceptions of the market (Pocock, 1985:69). Markets and credit, as mobile forms of property, stand in contrast to landed property. Political thinkers began to offer ideological responses to the existing capitalist relations. They worried over the seeming dissolution of the moral/civic tradition and the disintegration of individual virtue, self-knowledge, and political action.

Rather than acknowledge the emergence of *Homo oeconomicus* from the breast of political man, Pocock prefers different analogies. He reads the events of the late seventeenth century in terms of an unfinished debate or an indistinguishable conflation:

> The dialogue between polity and economy remained a dialogue, . . . because both political man and commercial man were equipped with theories of property as the foundation of political personality which could not be separated from each other. (Pocock, 1985:70)

Summary

Pocock argues that possessive individualism arose in the social tumult surrounding efforts to reestablish authority in English society. Discussions of authority centered upon conceptions of property and concomitant property rights. Two forms of property emerged: real, landed property and mobile, commercial property. Pocock argues both were conceived in terms of the ancient, moral/civic tradition. By this view property was the foundation of political personality, individual virtue, and freedom. Debaters sought to justify or denigrate nonlanded property and its sociopolitical consequences. In this regard many prominent figures framed ideological conceptions of market man and market society to attack rather than promote them.

It is clear that Pocock regards property as a constitutive principle and argues that important seventeenth-century thinkers also believe so. The definitive feature of the moral/civic tradition is the premise that property constitutes political personality and social relations. Pocock interprets the sociopolitical controversies of the mid- to late-seventeenth century as thoughtful debates arising squarely within the confines of the moral/civic tradition yet colored by burgeoning market relations. In short, these controversies consider the constitutive effects of property upon politics and society. Property, perhaps more than any other social feature or institution, helped constitute social structures and individual agents in this era. Merchants and traditionalists advocated different conceptions of society by illustrating the virtues of different forms of property rights.

The emergence of market man and market society better signals the formation of the modern English state than a coming bourgeois order. The social foundation of authority looms large in Pocock's moral/civic reading of seventeenth-century English history. By the term *authority,* he suggests the exercise of control and the maintenance of order by government. In the postfeudal context of the seventeenth century, this means, in contemporary vocabulary, the exercise of authority by the state. However, Pocock assiduously avoids the expression *the state,* perhaps because it is largely an eighteenth-century use. Instead, Pocock prefers *government* to indicate authority and administration and *commonwealth* to represent the polity.

Yet two exceptions are revealing. In discussing debates around 1675 concerning patronage, Pocock (1985:66) contrasts the traditionalist parties in the country with the royal "court." The latter represents the personalized, monarchical rule of dynastic families. Elsewhere, Pocock (1980:11) defines the court as the sociopolitical apparatus "surrounding *the person* of the King" (emphasis added). Thus, the ruling head governs; government is but the means. Similarly, Pocock (1980:6) defines the Crown as governance by royal individuals or families. Pocock later changes this personalized conception of court and Crown. When discussing trends from "the later seventeenth and early eighteenth centuries," Pocock (1985:71) refers to "political sovereignty." Thus, by approximately 1700 the court and Crown had been transformed into a sovereign crown state, if not an impersonal, institution-alized state. Royal rule had become state administration, and the term *court* came to represent the "class of aristocratic managers of parliamentary poli-tics" (Pocock, 1980:12). That is, the court comprised managers or protobu-reaucrats of state institutions. Limited attempts by the Crown to respond to demands from the rising gentry class may have presaged such a transition (e.g., Trevor-Roper, 1953, 1965). Indeed, in responding to demands from the gentry class, the royal government (the court) grew in size, scope, and cost (Pocock, 1980:9).

> Property was the foundation of personality; but the acid test of personality was whether it required most to be affirmed in liberty or governed by authority. When modes of property arose that did not favor political virtue, they suggested private freedom and political sovereignty. (Pocock, 1985:70–71)

MACPHERSON, POCOCK, AND THE SIMULTANEOUS CONSTITUTION OF COMMERCIAL RELATIONS AND AUTHORITY

With the deterioration of traditional politics and the disintegration of the moral/civic worldview, the sources of political virtue also eroded. Market man and market society were both cause and effect of this transformation. Market relations emerge as actors displace traditional values and craft the institutions of the sovereign state. As bourgeois market relations devel-oped—arising from the developing systems of public credit and stocks—so, inextricably, did the modern, depersonalized state form. Each had antecedents, but fully recognizable states and capitalist relations arose and prospered only as an integrated set of practices and institutions marking the modern world order. Property rights are the markers. They are constitutive principles. Macpherson (1962:3) concisely announces one of the important themes of this book:

> It cannot be said that the seventeenth-century concepts of freedom, rights, obligation, and justice are all entirely derived from this concept of posses-sion, but it can be shown that they were powerfully shaped by it.

That is, property rights are constitutive principles that decisively shaped the modern worldview and the international system by shaping the conceptual, structural, and practical frameworks of the seventeenth century.

Once we recognize property as a constitutive principle, the vocabulary

of social construction effectively expresses the social and political developments of the seventeenth century. As a constitutive principle, property contributes to the constitution of capitalism and the state system as a coherent
social reality. The differences between real and mobile property contribute
to the differences between the two structures.

> Society becomes a lot of free equal individuals related to each other as
> proprietors of their own capacities and of what they have acquired by their
> exercise. (Macpherson, 1962:3)

Macpherson outlines the constitution and appearance of capitalist relations. He holds that human society consists of market relations. This view
"may appear in a theory not as a deduced proposition but as *the primary or
even the sole social assumption*" (Macpherson, 1962:264; emphasis added).
Market society works as a social vortex. Those with the least capital or
resources are most subject to its forces; they subject themselves to the privileged elements who exploit but sustain them. Class divisions, based originally upon landownership and the fiction of equal rights, arise
(Macpherson, 1962:53–58, 269), and modern capitalism arrives. Changes
in property rights herald its arrival.

The modern state emerges along with capitalism: "The possessive market model requires a compulsive framework of law" (Macpherson,
1962:57; also North and Thomas, 1973; Levi, 1987). Beyond enforcing
contracts and maintaining social stability to promote orderly exchange, the
state determines the contours of the social landscape. While establishing
"level playing fields" is a current policy vogue, states a few centuries ago
similarly sought "to move the hurdles to the advantage of some kinds of
competitors, or change the handicaps" (Macpherson, 1962:58). Indeed, the
state helped forge market society.

Pocock (1985:70) argues that "Macpherson's market model explained
only one group of phenomena and did not account for their opposites."
Macpherson's sharp distinctions unwittingly serve to decontextualize and
dehistoricize market man. In privileging market concerns over traditional
ones, in emphasizing self-proprietorship and commercial wealth over landed property, Macpherson was unable to recognize the paradox of liberty
and authority. What Macpherson missed was the dynamics of state formation. The state was not a secondary contributor to capitalist market relations. As Pocock sees it, the focal issue was the recrafting or reconstitution
of political authority. In seventeenth-century debates over the future form
of authority, capitalist concerns weighed heavily, but the nature, form, and
social consequences of property acquired precedence. These conceptions of
property arose in the context of state formation.

In this sense, Pocock (e.g., 1977:88–89) clearly subordinates the market or economy to political concerns. Though Pocock offers a richer account, he nonetheless manifests the very dichotomy separating politics and economics. Indeed, he reads the era in terms of a "dialogue between polity and economy" (Pocock, 1985:70). Pocock attempts to extend Macpherson's analyses by arguing that conceptions of market society and possessive individualism arose in the wake of debates over authority and property. By focusing attention on authority, Pocock is less able to see how commercial relations helped constitute a conceptual framework that partitioned social life into seemingly discrete spaces or fields. By this framework, authority acquires a distinctive status and becomes recognizable in its modern form as authority in and over a set of institutions. Moreover, while Pocock's attention to authority enriches the accounts, he does not extensively consider whether the vocabulary and conceptual histories of property and rights themselves helped inform the era's debates and establish a conceptual framework for making sense of the world. To answer the question "authority over what?" requires attending to the market as a seemingly distinct social sphere that appears to lack such authority. It also requires addressing the conceptual worldview that partitions social life into these realms. We return to Macpherson's themes, and we encounter property as a principle constituting a worldview and social relations.

In short, we enrich Macpherson and Pocock by reading them together. We better see their accounts as complementary when we attend to constitutive principles generally, property specifically, conceptual histories, and worldviews.

Regardless of relative emphases—market versus state, juristic versus moral/civic—one sees in Macpherson's and Pocock's works a clear support for the thesis that capitalist relations and an institutional-legal order emerged simultaneously and inextricably. Together, these authors offer a more complete picture of the tumultuous social conditions in which nascent capitalist features and vestigial feudal hierarchies uneasily coexisted. In the controversies over authority, diverse elements formed complementary unions. Rather than reconstituting authority, English elites augured the modern world order. Nascent capitalist features matured only in the nurturing circumstance of a powerful but minimally responsive state apparatus. Alternatively, the modern state achieved its depersonalized form and managerial function in the context of competitive rights-possessors who exchanged objects and obligations in an alienated, mechanical society.

In the following chapters I shift the focus from property as a principle to social behaviors related to property. By exploring the property-related practices of jurisprudents, government leaders, and financiers, I demonstrate in part the agent-structure interplay that frames social construction, while also focusing on property rights as constitutive principles and social rules, the medium of social construction.

NOTES

1. Tuck (1989:vii) bemoans biographers' inattention to Hobbes, calling him "the most neglected by posterity." Two recent biographies are by Rogow (1986) and Tuck (1989).

2. In this discussion I draw also from Laslett (1965). Other informative treatments of Locke include Dunn (1969), Franklin (1978), G. Parry (1978), Pocock and Ashcraft (1980), Tully (1980), Vaughn (1980), Ashcraft (1986), Wood (1986), and Buckle (1991).

3. Wallerstein (e.g., 1980) and Harrington similarly date significant social and cultural transitions in Europe.

4. Pocock consistently stresses the contributions of Harrington and Wren over Locke. Pocock (1985:65–67) strenuously argues that Locke should not be read as the foremost philosophical voice of this era. He was not the philosophical justifier of the Glorious Revolution of 1688 since he wrote his *Two Treatises* between 1679 and 1681, nor did he contribute to the political groundwork of any of the significant parties. Moreover, the most vitriolic debate of the era was "conducted with very little reference to anything he had said" (Pocock, 1985:67).

5. Brewer (1980:334–337) strongly defends this claim for the 1770s. One infers from his antecedents and examples that his chronological account corresponds well with the events closer to 1700 that I highlight.

PART 2
PROPERTY AND PRACTICES

4

Jurisprudents

Courts, judges, and judicial proceedings antedate national states and appear in so many unstately guises, it is easy to forget how large a part certain kinds of courts played in the day-to-day construction of Western states.

Charles Tilly (1975:6)

While religious and scientific worldviews were also significant in seventeenth-century England (Westfall, 1973), this chapter illustrates the legal worldview of the time by considering the practices of jurisprudents: those lawyers, judges, and theorists who thought about the law and acted by reference to legal principles. In considering legal practices, I consider discourse a form of practice. That is, to participate in legal discourse—indeed, in any discourse or language—is to engage in a particular practice or behavior. Discourse is both a mirror and maker of culture.[1]

Legal language was the political vernacular. Even republican, chiliastic, and commercial concerns were often expressed in legal terms. By exploring the distinctive character of legal discourse, one discovers the prominent role property plays in it.

Throughout the chapter I investigate the practices of jurisprudents that bear upon property. These practices arise primarily in efforts to constitute civil authority and promote market society. In this chapter I also substantiate the specific claim that changes in agents' practices marked a conceptual split in the notion of property around the year 1700. The similarities between real and mobile property establish the single, unified coherence of these diverse practices; similarities among conceptions of property cohere the practices of statecraft and capitalist commerce. The single social reality of these cohered practices—amid conceptual distinctions—marks the modern world order.

WIDELY SHARED LEGAL WORLDVIEW

[The law] conditioned men's thought and language and ulti-
mately their actions.

Howard Nenner (1977:x)

Statecraft and capitalist commerce are inextricable, unified activities mediated through practices involving property rights. For many agents, property
rights become manifest in legal relations. Legal discourse became the
means for debating social, political, and economic problems in seventeenth-century England. Actors used legal concepts as tools to craft solutions to pressing problems.

For two reasons, however, I do not focus on what Cam (1962) calls the
"law-finding and law-making" activities of legal professionals. I am not a
legal historian so lack the skills to untangle the many courts and overlapping jurisdictions of courts of equity, ecclesiastical law, martial law, civil
law, corporate law, communal law, and more than a dozen others cross-ref-
erenced through the English *Statutes of the Realm* (also see Tigar and Levy,
1977; Berman, 1983; Pocock, 1987:290). Further, as I illustrate below, it
becomes futile to investigate or inventory specific legal arguments, hold-
ings, or statutes as definite evidence of actors' practices concerning property. In the 1600s barristers and judges invoked the precedents of existing,
immemorial, uncodified custom when pleading, holding, or enacting. Since
these precedents were infrequently committed to written record, prevailing
notions, uses, and practices are difficult to identify in the *codified* law.
They are, in any event, "hardly to be altered by legislation" and so are also
missing from the lawmaking records (Pocock, 1987:260; see also Ferguson,
1979). Since social practices typically changed gradually, they slowly made
their marks on legal practices and the scant legal record. Indeed, legal practices registered such changes only after the fact. This tradition—that is, this
reliance upon community memory, oral recollection, and interpretation—
was greatly eroded by the dizzying pace and scope of seventeenth-century
events.

I focus instead on the practice of legal discourse and the ways jurisprudents articulate the legal worldview. I consider law a form of ideology and
regard legal discourse as a form of social practice.

Legal values condition perceptions, establish role expectations, provide
standards of legitimacy, and account for the institutional patterns of politics. To understand the political importance of law, it is not enough to consider the concrete manifestations of legal institutions or to take into
account the immediate reactions to or compliance with legal rulings.

These are important matters, to be sure, but they must be understood in the context in which politics is conducted. (Scheingold, 1974:xi)

Jurisprudents do not merely moderate the prevailing meanings and uses of property. Rather, they self-consciously employ a prevalent, definitive discourse. The law provides fundamental social symbols and concepts that "reflect values which are the building blocks of a political ideology" (Scheingold, 1974:13). At the core of the prevailing ideology of liberalism lies "a social perspective which perceives and explains human interaction largely in terms of rules and of the rights and obligations inherent in rules" (Scheingold, 1974:13). This view rests on a public *faith* in the political efficiency and ethical sufficiency of law as the principle of government.

The concept of rights and now the long-standing rights tradition are central to such understandings (Scheingold, 1974:7–8). This orientation sees rights as social rules and all official rules—laws included—as implying rights. To this end Scheingold, Giddens (1984), Onuf (1989), and I hold similar views. However, Onuf believes that rights are not social rules as such but are visible manifestations of less visible commitment-rules: "Only commitment-rules, in my opinion, imply or produce rights" (personal correspondence, November 1996). More generally, however, views from rights theorists and constructivists depart from conventional legal, jurisprudential, and philosophical uses (e.g., Hart, 1961; Rawls, 1971).[2]

Legal discourse represents and conveys a worldview that makes sense of the (political) world largely through the lenses of property and property rights. For example, Tuck (1979:2) distinguishes two dominant worldviews: Those of rights theorists and utilitarians. In the seventeenth century, legal discourse and its prevalent property concepts became the medium for debating the constitutional crises confronting English society (Pocock, 1957, 1987; Nenner, 1977). Though distinctions between political, religious, and legal matters were necessarily arbitrary, in each case property rights controversies were central (e.g., Berman, 1983; Little, 1969/1984:vii). For example, disputes between subjects and authority and between the Crown and houses of Parliament involved controversies over property rights. Thus, the parties recognized, disputed, and resolved the English constitutional crises in *legal* terms involving property rights.

As Macpherson (1962, 1975, 1978) and Pocock (1975, 1977, 1980, 1985) argue, the prominent political debates in mid- to late-seventeenth-century England illustrate that property constitutes not only social structures (the state, the capitalist market) and practices (statecraft, capitalist commerce) but also structures of thought. Through legal discourse individuals conceived, conditioned, and carried out their behaviors. In this sense, jurisprudents constructed the *conceptual* foundations for the state and capitalist markets. Property was central to the framing. Through the rules of property rights, actors conducted statecraft, conducted capitalist exchange, and constituted their social relations.

In seventeenth-century England, legal thought rivaled religious and scientific discourse in prominence and significance (Little, 1969/1984:27–32; Nenner, 1977:9–11; cf. Westfall, 1973). By relying upon precedent, legal reasoning incorporated revealed wisdom and met empirical science as an equal throughout the century. "Most gentlemen had a legal education of some sort, and thought of politics in legal terms" (Nenner, 1977:3, citing Hill, 1965:256). As a result, legal discourse, available to most men of substance and stature—but generally not to women because of the conventions of the time—provided a coherent worldview (Nenner, 1977:33). English citizens lived "in a legal universe in which the present and future were wedded to the past by a smooth continuity of omnicompetent law and custom" (Little, 1969/1984:31).

The ideology and practices of common law culture rested resolutely upon rights and duties, including preeminently a right to hold property exclusively against, for example, unauthorized claims or seizures (Tully, 1980:142–143).[3] Although the rights tradition defines the common law worldview, the law of real property was the irreducible foundation of the common law. Jurists and laymen alike argued that the law of real property was as old as time itself and certainly as old as the kingdom (Pocock, 1957).

Common law rules, principles, and training created a common law culture that embodied a coherent ideology or worldview. Indeed, common law culture represented the cohesion and group identity that shared understandings engender.

> To have been bred in that culture meant much more than having a knowledge of principles and rules. It meant having, as well, *a ready-made vocabulary of political discourse* and a particularized *view of the political world.* (Nenner, 1977:xi; emphasis added)

In this sense, the "common law provided a constant conceptual framework for political action" Nenner (1977:ix). Actors made sense of their world, identified its problems, devised resolutions, and guided their actions by common law precepts: "Throughout the century virtually every important controversy was formulated, and every position justified, in legal language and common-law paradigms" (Nenner, 1977:ix).

In the confusingly heady circumstances of revolutionary England, individuals turned to the law as a "cultural instinct" (Nenner, 1977:32). To buttress their claims, jurists frequently used three concepts drawn from private law concerns: inheritance, property, and contract. These legal concepts became especially significant metaphors for interpreting social relations as jurists employed them to impose order upon chaotic and uncertain conditions (Little, 1969/1984).

Inheritance

The concept of inheritance became a politically potent simile. In the seventeenth century, one conceived acquiring political rights by birthright. One further conceived that those rights could be protected by law and that such rights and the law itself were subject to inheritance (Nenner, 1977:33). For example, James I received in 1607 a petition from Parliament entitled "The Apology of the House of Commons to the King" that places inheritance at the center of its protest.

> With all humble and due respect to your Majesty, . . . we must truly avouch, first, that our privileges and liberties are our right and due inheritance, no less than our very lands and goods. Secondly, that they cannot be withheld from us, denied, or impaired, but with apparent wrong to the whole state of the realm (quoted in Sowards, 1969:699).

To ask "who owns or possesses the law?" was to raise a politically significant question with tremendous social consequences riding on the answer (Pocock, 1977:28–31; 1987:320–326). Following the English civil war and the corruption of the Puritan Revolution, marked dramatically by the beheading of King Charles I in January 1649, Oliver Cromwell's rule raised this question to cosmic heights. Such concern became especially pronounced after the failure of the Commonwealth and the institution of Cromwell's one-man rule during the Protectorate (1653–1658). Did Cromwell "own" the law or merely possess and control it? Did the "social contract" hold although the royal party had been banished and replaced? Is de facto control of the law sufficient to compel obligation? Does one acquire authority through the law, or can one acquire the law through coercive authority?

At least two possible interpretations arise of the relationship between law and authority. Each implies unique understandings of inheritance and rights. First, one may acquire legitimate title to exercise authority. Examples include inaugurations of duly-elected officials, coronations of rightful heirs apparent, and other traditional or legally sanctioned activities. Here the law *confers* authority. That is, through the legal *process* one acquires authority. Second, one may acquire authority through means other than the legal process. Invasions, coups, revolutions, and martyrdom provide such examples. Through such exercises of power or persona, one may *claim* the law as a prize or one may come to *control* or conquer it. In either case one may (re)claim as law some set of rules previously ignored or perverted. The U.S. invasion of Panama in 1989 was conducted on just this principle. Indeed, it was defended on the premise that the United States could "give back" to Panamanians the law and order corrupted by Noriega (C. Weber, 1995:ch. 6).

Acquiring the law by authority bleeds into this interpretation. Yet since in this case determining how to identify authority becomes key, one must carefully distinguish power, charisma, and other attributes from authority. Traditional English law held that authority acquires the law when it *creates* and promulgates such law. Yet English legal traditions ignored the sticky problem of justifying or legitimizing the "authority" of the agent(s).

Thus, two alternatives presented themselves as possible sources of authority: *jus conquestas* (law of conquest) versus *jus civitatis* (law of the commonwealth). The choice sharpened attention to the character of the civil law itself.

Property

Possession represents a property right. Indeed, all rights may be understood as property rights. It is difficult to imagine them in any other terms, although Tully (1980:142–143) prefers a narrower understanding. Rights theorists plumb the deep implications of the relationship between rights (*jus* or *ius*) and property (*dominium*). Telling issues include identifying what counts as property and what rights are attached. In relating these themes, Tuck's (1979) volume is a slender marvel.

> By the fourteenth century it was possible to argue that to have a right was to be the lord or *dominus* of one's relevant moral world, to possess *dominium*, that is to say, *property.* (Tuck, 1979:3; emphasis in original)

This view prevailed throughout the medieval era, and lawyers recognized *dominium* as a kind of *jus*, "and hence w[ere] prepared to talk about *property* rights" (Tuck, 1979:13). The logic of the argument led one to conclude that isolated individuals—that is, for example, alienated individuals in the state of nature—controlled their lives in a manner that could be described as *dominium*, or property. Many late medieval and early modern thinkers regarded this as a basic fact about humans, the premise upon which actors established their social and political relationships (Tuck, 1979:24). With alterations, these assumptions contribute to the individualist, liberal, classical rights theories of the seventeenth century: through Grotius to the English radicals of the 1640s, then to Locke and others. Yet upon the same premises,

> medieval rights theorists, Molina, Grotius [again], Selden, Selden's followers, and Hobbes all openly endorsed such institutions as slavery and the absolutist state. . . . When Rousseau repudiated the entire tradition as conservative, and chose Grotius as his main target, his instincts were absolutely right. (Tuck, 1979:3)

Renaissance understandings make the lineage of ideas more confusing (Tuck, 1979:ch 2). Renaissance thinkers focused upon positive law—*jus civile* and *jus gentium*—hence humans in social settings. The rights and duties attendant upon morality and law arose with civilization, not with the state of nature. *Dominium* was a phenomenon of the postnatural world. By this view, if there were no natural rights, there could be no natural dominion. Renaissance actors recognized property as a contingently multifaceted concept, not as a monolithic notion. Property exists in several forms, not all of which are cases of dominion: Consider, for example, *proprietas* (proper ownership), *possessio* (possession), *usufructus* (use and enjoyment without ownership), *jus utendi* (possession on behalf of the owner), and *simplex usus facti* (simple use) (Tuck, 1979:20). Only use or possession-for-use, not complete *dominium,* existed in the natural order.

Dominion, a feature of social, civilized humankind, must be stipulated and enforced. Thus, it can also be infringed, so, paradoxically, it can never be complete or unrestricted.

> *Dominium* could not be *ius.* . . . "It is said that *dominium* is one thing, and *ius* another: for those who have legitimate possession, use or usufruct have a *ius* of a kind, but they are not *domini*." (Tuck, 1979:47)

It follows, then, that liberty could not be a right (cf. Dworkin, 1977:ch. 12; see Berlin, 1969, on "negative liberty"). Indeed, liberty is the ability to act as one wants, unless prevented by force or by *jus*. Liberty must be a property or attribute of self-possession.

Only later, when the sources of authority—hence the sources of legitimate rights-granting—became an issue were these oppositions resolved. Yet as jurisprudents and philosophers elaborated these concepts, it became clear that the apparently definitive relationship between rights and property prevailed. One could imagine differences between natural and nonnatural dominion. Natural dominion comprised rights over or relations with basic, natural items. Nonnatural *dominium* was the product of social convention. Such conventions might be based in custom, law, or rules. These conventions might therefore entail rights. Indeed, Scheingold (1974:7, note 4) argues that they *must* involve rights.

Since the early Renaissance, concerns about dominion—especially nonnatural dominion, if one accepts the conceptual distinction—addressed trade relationships. Specifically, thinkers asked, what rights to use existed, or, obversely, what rights did use precipitate? In the early modern era, such issues became significant and directly relevant to a burgeoning commercial order.

> If one had property in anything which one used, in any way, if only for personal consumption and with no possibility of trade, then any intervention by an agent in the outside world was the exercise of a property right. Even one's own liberty, which was undoubtedly used to do things in the material world, counted as property—with the implication that it could, if the legal circumstances were right, be traded like any other property. *Dominium* did not appear when the laws allowed appropriation and exchange; it had been present from the beginning of time, even when appropriation and exchange were unnecessary, and there was no conceptual break at the point at which men decided to trade their property rather than merely consume it. (Tuck, 1979:29)

In brief, the *relation* of rights to property (and vice versa) is perhaps less significant than how the *character* of the concepts circumscribes and informs the relation. This points to the advantages of conceptual histories and reinforces the focus upon property. To repeat, it is difficult for the modern mind to understand rights as other than property rights. Although ancient and modern minds share this view, medieval skepticism leavens modern conceptions, introduces an antinomy between rights and property, raises finer distinctions among forms of property, and focuses the conceptions upon commercial applications.

Thus, Nenner (1977:36) calls property "the most confusing of the common law concepts." It confuses in multiple senses. As a legal concept, property denotes specific but divergent meanings depending upon its location in the varied contexts of common law, community law, ecclesiastical law, feudal law, or positive law. To pursue specific meanings, one enters the legal thicket inhabited by *dominium, domain, freehold, usufruct,* and myriad other terms of legal relations. As a term of rights, property overlaps the legal context but directs us to the Roman *jus, res,* rarely *lex,* and *dominium* again. The term *property rights* also attunes us to the normative connotations of "right" conveyed in *jus, recht, droit,* and *diritto* (Tuck, 1979:5–13). As a matter of objects and relations, *property* conjurs *proprietas.* Though, as Tuck (1979:8) quotes a renowned French theorist, "the Romans did not regard *dominium,* property, as a *ius*" or an objective virtue. Rather, a *jus* better represents "what is always fair or good" (*jus naturale*) or "what is best for all or most in a particular society" (*jus civile*).

Tully (1980:142) believes that amid such conceptual confusion, Locke and others employed a relatively narrow definition of *property:* "That something is one's own such that it cannot be taken without the owner's consent." However, Ryan (1984:7) draws an exactly opposite conclusion: "The English legal system discouraged a question which Roman law encouraged, namely, 'What is it to be the owner of something?' or 'How does a thing become Mine?'" (see also Nicholas, 1962:15). To different effect both Nenner and Macpherson quote Gilbert Burnet, the noted Scot historian-philosopher and clergyman, from 1687: "The first branch of property is the right that a man has to his life" (quoted in Nenner, 1977:38). Similarly, Locke (1690/1965:328–329) declares in the *Second Treatise* that "every man has a *Property* in his own *Person*. This no Body has any Right to but himself" (emphasis in original). In the latter quotations, Locke and Burnet make moral claims. As philosophic foundations, moral claims contrast with political claims about exclusive control and ownership of property in the face of royal threats to confiscate it.

One quickly infers rights to one's life from rights to one's person. And rights to life rapidly spill into rights to fundamental aspects of life that are not alienable, though held exclusively: religion, liberty, and happiness. Individuals viewed these values as rights that should be defended by the law. Thus, a little-noted seventeenth-century pamphleteer echoed and refined widespread sentiments we take to be specifically Lockean:

> The use of the Law consisteth principally in theis 2 thinges, the one to secure mans persons from death and violence, and th' other to dispose the propertie of Lands and goods. (quoted in Nenner, 1977:38)

Thus, in this era property represents a right secured in law. Speeches, writings, and legal thinking of the time unmistakably illustrate that property rights were becoming more private and exclusive (Reeve, 1986:45). These changes mark the construction of modern, exclusive, political relations from the feudal context of layered, contingent rights and moral frameworks.[4] Property rights are not merely the result of good title or advantageous, proper inheritance. Rather, property rights represent the fullest, most fundamental right that an individual can possess (e.g., Tigar and Levy, 1977:197).

Property rights are therefore constitutive and definitive. Property rights define individuals' characteristics and motivate their practices. Property rights also constitute the social structures that comprise social reality.

> The institution of property . . . posits a person (*persona*) and a thing (*res*) joined by a legal norm called property or ownership. Human society is dissolved into isolated individuals, and the world of goods split up into discrete items. One can no longer speak of a duty to use property or behave toward others in a certain way: all such duties as may be imposed by law are *prima facie* derogations from the fundamental "right of property." (Tigar and Levy, 1977:197; cf. Walzer, 1984:315–319)

Property-as-*dominium* is both a simile and a synecdoche. As a simile, seventeenth-century English use conveyed the concept property as or like a personal dominion, as an unrivaled right or possession ensconced in the natural, communal, and positive law. Thus, confronting society as a whole, individuals were the possessors of (property) rights that could not be rightfully or lawfully trammeled. In turn, understood as a synecdoche, such rights-bearing individuals represented society as a whole.[5] Indeed, all such individuals comprise society, meaning that the collective social whole possesses the same complete, unrivaled rights vis-à-vis the ruler. Thus, individuals possessing property rights constitute society; society, maintained through legal rules, secures individual rights and constitutes agents; the law (the social rules, the property rights) determines how agents organize and reproduce society. This is the process of social construction.

Contract

As individuals inherit property rights by birthright, all that remained was to conceive society as the relations among such individuals. Jurisprudents and juristic thinkers employed the concept of contract to express these relations. A contract conveys reciprocal rights and duties maintained through mutually binding obligations. Even natural rights involve relations we may conceive as contractual: We may be obliged to God as the natural source of the laws, but we are certainly obliged to respect each other's rights, or else the rights of all are (potentially) infringed. Reciprocity reigns. Heteronomy rules. Mutual obligation underscores social relations. Without this implied contract to oblige ourselves reciprocally, no society may exist at all (e.g., Little 1969/1984:2). In the vocabulary of social rules that Onuf (1989) introduces, a claim of reciprocal obligation asserts a right, directs others to recognize and obey the assertion, and implicitly promises to obey the reciprocal assertions of others. Efforts to impose obligations upon others nullify contracts because there exists no *mutual* obligation, no consideration from *each* party. Indeed, one might agree with the Sophists and Roman legislators that law itself is a contract: "All laws are but Contracts where the people agree one with another that such things shal [*sic*] be done" (quoted in Nenner, 1977:22).

The prominence of the social contract in political philosophy reflects the significance of this legal analogy. Yet the analogy is unworkable without identifying the relevant parties to the contract. Hobbes and Locke, for example, argue that the contract is among the people alone, not between the people and the ruler. For this reason, Hobbes and Locke may have enjoyed less influence upon seventeenth-century political debate than more practical pamphleteers who argued that the Crown and subjects were the parties to any social compact.

Actors employed legal analogies to apprehend troubling political circumstances and to make sense of the social turmoil and political upheaval marking the English constitutional crises. Pocock (1985:56) refers to this crisis-riddled era by discussing "the radical need to reconstruct authority."

Little (1969/1984:29) tells us that "the old unity of political and legal life was falling apart, and the question of authority was inevitable." Hill (1975) refers to "the world turned upside down," Christianson (1978) to "apocalyptic visions," Mendle (1985) to "dangerous positions." In these circumstances actors looked to the law to provide respite, relief, and resolutions (Tigar and Levy, 1977:ch. 19). To resort to a trite expression that nonetheless echoes the sentiments of the time, the law brought order to chaos.

> The law was the one constant in an era otherwise marked by constitutional uncertainty and political disarray. It afforded the one structure, both institutional and intellectual, which rendered the issues intelligible and which provided a forum for political debate. (Nenner, 1977:ix)

In this context the previous chapter acquires a new significance. While the foremost purpose of Chapter 3 is to illustrate property as a constitutive principle in the thought of this era, one can also read the theoretical work reviewed there as examples of legal discourse applied to pressing social issues. To call these issues constitutional crises in any narrowly political sense demeans their broadly social implications, including the simultaneous construction of the state and the development of capitalism.

Debating political concerns was perhaps the most significant practice that jurists engaged in during this era. The issues commanding jurists' attention were profound, whether we refer to revolution and restoration, constitutional crises, or a struggle for sovereignty. What remains compelling is the degree to which jurists, theorists, and policy advocates employed legal concepts or analogies to express themselves, and how deeply rooted these concepts were in notions of property.

APPLYING THE LEGAL WORLDVIEW THROUGH LEGAL DISCOURSE

Making Sense of Authority, Legitimacy, and Sovereignty: The Early Constitutional Crises

The seventeenth-century constitutional crises involved struggles among the Crown, Parliament, private property owners, and society at large over the law itself. The law was both the weapon and the prize in the controversies (Harding, 1966:228; Nenner, 1977:ch. 3). Although several scholars trace precursors of the revolutionary movement as far back as the eleventh and twelfth centuries (e.g., North and Thomas, 1973; Tigar and Levy, 1977; Kriedte et al., 1981; Berman, 1983), many others look to the attempts by Tudor rulers to establish personal monarchy or to institutionalize the

Crown. Later, James I (1603), the first Stuart ruler, openly claimed an autocracy and provoked debates over divine right. James's son, Charles I, extended such demands and was met in 1628 with the *Petition of Right,* penned by the renowned jurist Sir Edward Coke. Charles's efforts to wage war raised issues of "kingscraft" versus statecraft (Sowards, 1969:699) and sparked debate over public finances, taxation, the process of law, personal rights and liberties, property, and exchange. After Charles was beheaded, the Cromwellian commonwealth and protectorate followed, thus capturing the essence of the era's controversies: the nature of authority and the institutional forms of governance and law.

The English civil war (1642–1648) was a violent protest against Charles's seemingly capricious and tyrannical exercise of his royal authority. In broad terms, groups fought over the nature and features of society and the place, form, and foundations of authority within that society. To be specific, it was a conflict over the king's expansive view of royal prerogative. Before the war it was clear that the authority to enact statutes rested with the king-in-Parliament. Statute-making authority, legislative sovereignty, or sovereign authority—call it what you will—was an integrated balance between the two institutions (Pocock, 1980:7; 1987:312). The civil war ripped them apart, thus destroying the constitutional balance and vitiating the rule of law. In legal terms, a belligerent monarchy had violated the (social) contract bonding society. Authority no longer controlled the common law upon which society was grounded. Indeed, with authority crumbled and the social order razed, citizens had to act anew and alone to recraft political authority and society. Legal discourse provided the tools and the means.

The Ancient Constitution and the Common Law

The foremost feature of common law culture was the assertion by jurisprudents, theorists, and activists of an "ancient constitution" (Pocock, 1957, 1987). In turn, the existence of an ancient constitution rested on their assumption that all English law was common law representing timeless, immemorial custom. Such custom was reinforced by consistent practices persisting through the infinite stretches of time, back to time beyond the memory of humans (Pocock, 1957:ch. 2). Common law was the unwritten and uncodified law, the *jus non scriptum,* that provided the foundation and justification for statutory enactments. Law was the mirror of custom, the record of agents' practices. But it contained a paradox: The common law did not treat citizens in common.

Law is a citizen's property and privilege. As property, the law confers rights and therefore duties and obligations. As privilege, the law offers a means to resist royal prerogative. Privilege complements prerogative. As royal prerogative represents an exclusive right, privilege conveys advantageous rights or immunities. Rights became balanced: One's rights extend only so far as they infringe upon the rights of others. Benefiting from legal privilege were the populace in general, any individual citizen, and Parliament as a representative institution. The notion of mutual obligation reduced prerogative and expanded privilege. Royal prerogative should extend only so far as the citizens' property (rights) to and privilege in the common law. The etymology of *privilege* as private law (from *privus* + *leg* or *lex*) makes the point. Thus, the monarch enjoyed unique prerogatives and unrivaled authority, but neither was sufficient to confiscate property without permission, according to Parliament's *Petition of Right* (1628) and later Locke (see Tully, 1980:135–142).

It was paradoxical but not unusual that the law was both universal and exclusionary. The common law (and common law culture) sought to protect the liberties and properties of citizens against the possible excesses of royal authority. As the common law was founded upon and comprised persistent practices pertaining to real property, the common law was fundamentally reducible to real property law (Pocock, 1987:292). Yet the distribution of land clearly made the liberty to exchange it far from universal. Thus, Pocock (1987:320) remarks on "a consciousness universal among Englishmen that property was the distribution of land by law and law the distribution of land as property." The common law emphasized, reinforced, and further exaggerated class distinctions. The impoverished, marginalized, small landowners, and those who owned no land could not avoid the practical realization that the law excluded them. Law represented the custom of the aristocracy, and it served their (landed) purposes (Harding, 1966:244–247). Consequently, justice was an instrument of social control wielded by the aristocracy and rising gentry. As I noted earlier, rules yield rule, which always embodies forms of domination. Property and practice provided the foundation for the common law, yet they also provided the means for oligarchic rule and the means for elite groups and institutions to contest the location of sovereign authority.

In the 1620s Sir Edward Coke, Sir John Davies, John Selden, and Matthew Hale forthrightly argued that the ancient constitution blunted unrestricted royal prerogative. They sought to protect citizens' rights and property by employing both common law and custom as political slogans and legal concepts (Harding, 1966:239). In their view, royal prerogative summarizes the rights of monarchical authority, not the rights of the person of the monarch. By this view the ancient constitution rested squarely upon common law, itself resting upon the law of real property. The common law, as law, thus directly protected citizens' rights and property. It indirectly buttressed citizens against royal acts by delimiting in law the Crown's authority to act in ways that might curtail property and liberty.

Jurists argued that royal prerogative existed but that it flowed from the common law's ancient foundations in practice. In short, royal prerogative could not violate the spirit of the common law nor exceed customary practice.

These forceful views expanded the concept of custom, particularly the persistent practice of legal reasoning. Prevalent practices conditioned such reasoning, but certainly very different forms of legal reasoning prevailed. What they shared was a legal worldview. The heightened status of statute increased significantly the power of judges because statutes had to be interpreted (Harding, 1966:231). The judge rendering decisions in his court was much like the king exercising sovereign reason in his parliament. Thus, common law culture sought to embrace statute and add it to the use and custom (*usus et consuetudo*) foundation of the common law (Pocock, 1987:269). In so doing, it introduced the construction of law rather than the mere acknowledgment of persistent practices: As judges interpreted and construed the law, they created or constructed it (Harding, 1966:232).

Indeed, in contrast with Filmer's later defenses in *Patriarcha* of absolute royal prerogative, other jurists and historians investigated the origins of statutory law and the king's authority. Thirteenth-century political struggles between the king and the baronial aristocracy were resolved by acknowledging that the king could issue some (feudal) orders only upon the concurrence of a council of barons. In return the barony recognized Henry II as the custodian of community customs. His orders, called statutes, would henceforth be issued in the name of "the community of the realm." As time passed, statutes became more like outright legislation expressed as statements of "future custom" (Harding, 1966:224–227).

If statute was indeed a subordinate or derivative element of common law, the king's many courts and jurisdictions provided him with ample opportunity to exercise royal prerogative. On logical and practical grounds, many jurisprudents, theorists, and activists advocated restricting the law-*making* role of Parliament (Pocock, 1987:270–271). The common law sufficed in their view; law need not be made, only interpreted.

> Ancient usage gave the law its antiquity and thus much of its authority, yet usage would have no meaning without the constant workings of reason in courts and parliament. (Pocock, 1987:271)

Both Sir John Davies and Sir Henry Spelman understood that the English common law arose out of conflicts with other systems of law (Roman and feudal, for example) and that it often took shape in courts (Pocock, 1987:260, 263, 266). For example, Davies was sent to Ireland to bring its laws into accord with English custom. His *Irish Reports* of 1612, comparing English common law with Irish brehon law, make clear he knew his enterprise was to purposefully destroy Irish customs and convert them into common law (Pocock, 1987:266). Pawlisch (1985) calls the effort "legal imperialism." Nevertheless Davies persistently defined common law as the "common custom of the realm," the common uses among the people.

With the renowned judge Sir Edward Coke, Davies was the foremost spokesman for common law culture. Davies understood the consequences of discrepant practices but could not understand the practices as incompatible with immemorial custom. Spelman, however, questioned the entire edifice of immemorial customary common law. Still, such disputes and disquiet did not make a substantial mark upon political debate for decades. Indeed, they little affected actual legal practice, much less the codified law, until very late in the century.

Royal Prerogative and Coordinate Sovereignty: The Late Constitutional Crises

England's seventeenth century witnessed attempts to restrict the royal prerogative of the king. Variations on this theme included the *Petition of Right* in 1628, the civil war, and the Exclusionary Controversy auguring the Glorious Revolution in 1688. Actors during the era saw each of these episodes as, among other things, a legal controversy. They acted in accord with the apparently legal nature of these affairs. More specifically, juristic theorists and advocates made these crises intelligible as controversies over the character and range of property rights held by the monarch and the subjects.

While the restoration of the monarchy in 1660 resolved the immediate constitutional quandary, it raised new problems and failed to address old ones. Both Charles II and James II ruled as "determined autocrats" (Kenyon, 1978:263), resurrecting the issue of royal prerogative. Yet challenges to their rule or to royal prerogative in general represented challenges to the foundation of authority, threatening to precipitate chaos anew. Such assaults provoked what have become standard defenses of authority: Monarchs rule as a consequence of a balanced constitutional foundation set by the authority vested in the law of conquest. The alternative, of course, held that the king ruled by authority of law: While the law legitimized royal rule, law was the property of the citizens. The common law specified the rules pertaining to property and was therefore a statement of citizens' significant (property) rights and privileges vis-à-vis the monarch.

The move was balanced, however. To challenge royal prerogative is to challenge royal authority, but the purpose in this instance was not solely religious toleration or civil liberties: Royal prerogative threatened commerce. In cases as early as 1602 and 1615, Judge Coke demonstrated a remarkable prejudice against the regulation of trade, perhaps primarily

> because he feared the royal prerogative which was the instrument of this regulation, but also because he was a member of a class which was grasping the opportunities of untrammelled economic enterprise. (Harding, 1966:223)

By threatening the balance between prerogative and privilege, the monarch threatened the law directly and thus the law of land and land tenures. He also threatened exchange. For example, English monarchs occasionally interrupted commerce through port towns to levy fees, fines, or taxes. Indeed, chronic national financial problems could spark the monarch to interfere with local and national finances. Forest fines and ship money were two notorious exactions. Such decisions illustrate that the legal disputes over royal authority directly impinge on property rights, statecraft, and capitalist commerce.

In this context arose debates over "coordinate sovereignty" (Weston and Greenberg, 1981), the sovereignty jointly shared by Parliament and the Crown. Both sought to win control of the law. The debates were less about *constituting authority* than about *instituting sovereignty* (Harding, 1966:228; Nenner, 1977:ch. 3). Many individuals regarded a sovereign authority as necessary to protect the self-property of personal liberty and the material property and prosperity of capital exchange. Thus, the common law worldview represents "an ideology as well as a practice" (Pocock, 1987:279). Indeed, the ideology and practices were becoming modern.[6] "If England was ceasing to be medieval by 1642, law played its part in the change, along with religion, trade, and government" (Harding, 1966:252). These changes are more dramatic by the Glorious Revolution of 1688.

Over the course of the seventeenth century, the common law and property comprised an ideology and a vocabulary that helped to constitute social relations and practices. In the crucible of the midcentury constitutional crises, actors invoked the common law to construct relations of authority and market exchange. These became the distinct social spaces we call politics and economics; each is conceptually grounded in changing understandings of property rights that actors constructed through legal discourse.

The common law was Janus-faced (e.g., Harding, 1966:217; Pocock, 1987:274–275, 287). Common law practitioners looked back and forth between custom and statute as the foundational elements of the common law. Yet on the side of custom they saw ambiguity because again they could look in two seemingly opposite directions, perceiving either immemorial, unchanging practices or adaptability. Then, too, common law practitioners saw both conquest and contract as foundational sources. However, no matter what direction the law faced or what it saw, it apprehended property. Common law jurisprudents—indeed, anyone possessing a common law worldview—made sense of statute and custom, immemorial customary practices and flexible responsiveness, and conquest and contract through some concept of property. Jurists employed property to define and delimit the common law and vice versa. Through property and common law, jurisprudents made sense of other concepts embedded in the relevant conceptual constellations. They similarly attributed meaning to the practices embedded in social interactions. The conceptual and practical links with authority then become more evident.

By institutionalizing authority, English actors constituted the state and sovereignty. Simultaneously, the construction of a separate realm of market exchange involving wages and possibly alienable labor constitutes the conceptual foundation for a distinct economic system. Thus, by approximately 1700 the conceptual crosshairs are in place, though not yet fully recognized. Actors have constituted the foundations of a modern ideology.

NOTES

1. Speaking and writing are social acts. Through speech and script—or, more generally, through language—one makes and makes sense of the world. Through words comes the world, though the choices and range of latitude is never boundless because individuals are always embedded in specific social and material contexts. Similarly, what we say, no less than what we do, makes us what we are. The following quotation, a statement of principles of sixteenth-century theatre acting, keenly illustrates discourse as a social activity with cultural consequences:

> Who I am is the stand I take, and the stand I take is that *I am my word.* . . .
> I have thoughts, but I am not my thoughts; I have emotions, but I am not
> my emotions; I have a body, but I am not my body. Who I am is what I am
> saying, and *my essence and existence lives* not in my thoughts, emotions,
> or body, but *in the speaking and listening.* (Robbins, 1997:2; emphasis
> added)

Robbins (p. 2) mistakenly adds that "such speaking is completely uncharacteristic of our age." I would instead say that such speaking characterizes all speech because speech is necessarily performative, thus constitutive. Yet our age and culture do not typically *recognize* these characteristics.

On language and discourse as forms of action, see Searle (1969) on "speech acts," J. L. Austin (1961, 1965) on "performative utterances," and Lakoff and Johnson (1980) on "metaphors we live by." Jürgen Habermas (e.g., 1984) is the towering contemporary theorist of the performative and constitutive character of language and its implications for social life. See also Ball et al. (1989) and citations therein. More generally, see Wittgenstein (1968) and Pitkin (1972) on the performative character of language. Wittgenstein's insights helped trigger the "linguistic turn" in twentieth-century philosophy. See in particular Wittgenstein's action-oriented view of language in his discussions of "language games" and "forms of life": "The speaking of language is part of an activity, or of a form of life" (quoted in Pitkin, 1972:132).

This view readily lends itself to forms of structuralism, historical sociology (e.g., Abrams, 1981), cultural anthropology (e.g., Geertz, 1973; Darnton, 1984), structuration (e.g., Giddens, 1984), and the agent-structure problem (Wendt, 1987).

2. On liberalism and law, see Hart (1955), Nozick (1974), and Lowi (1979). Edgerton (1985) considers rules, laws, and rights. On norms and morality, see Nardin (1983), D'Amato (1984), and Raz (1990). Prominent work in critical legal studies includes Unger (1986), Kennedy (1986, 1987), and Koskenniemi (1989).

3. Recall that Macpherson (1962) and others argue that property rights were alienable. However, Tully (1980) and others claim that property rights were merely exclusive but not by the late 1600s fully alienable. The difference is not crucial for my case, since I argue that changes in property rights by 1700 promoted and reinforced notions of exclusivity and alienability. These two features contribute to the conceptual crosshairs that constitute the social "spaces" of the modern world(view).

4. Recall Tuck's (1979:3) comment that as early as the fourteenth century one could "argue that to have a right was to be the lord . . . of one's relevant *moral* world" (emphasis added). Such claims, particularly in the context of medieval Christian theology, contrast with seventeenth-century assertions about the political and social character of property rights. Land was the conceptual battleground.

In this regard Pocock (1957:65–66) writes of transformed conceptions of property rights in land. Courts recognized land as privately owned and therefore inheritable. Lost were the feudal relationships underlying land tenure and the contingent character of *seisin,* representing the possession of a freehold estate in land or chattels. Yet freeholds were variable land tenures. They included fee simple (heritable), fee tail (restrictably heritable), or for-life-only tenures. Feudal land tenures depended specifically upon the *manner* in which land was granted by lords and received by vassals, contingent upon due and appropriate homage, the performance of specific or implied duties, and the concomitant and varied nature of justice between the parties.

Two etymological trails illustrate these points. First, the root of *fee* is the same as that for *fief, feudum, feudal,* and so on. *Fee* derives from Germanic languages and means "property," "money," or "cattle."

Another example involves the words *servant* and *sergeant.* The latter is a contemporary spelling of an Old or Middle English word *serjant,* which is itself a variant on *servant. Servant* shares the same Latin (from Etruscan) root as *serf,* both of which mean "those which serve others as a slave." There is no etymological difference between *servant* and *serjant;* contextual differences suggest the key distinction involved only the type of service (another word with the same root) one rendered. Servants, the more servile, performed in the home; serjants worked in the stables with the horses and livestock. Hence serjeanty was a form of personal feudal service, or servitude, distinct from military tenure or socage (agricultural) tenure.

5. I thank Alice Colwell for bringing this point to my attention.

6. My comment about capital exchange recalls another scholarly controversy. Tully (1980:ch. 6) cites several notable sources to argue that capitalism as a "mode of production in England" did not arrive "until at least the late eighteenth century" (p. 140). It is clear that this dating depends upon the definition of capitalism.

Macpherson (1962:60), for example, differently defines capitalism in terms of the right to alienate labor in exchange for a wage. Debates between those who define capitalism in these two terms, emphasizing production or exchange, occupy a prominent place in Marxian scholarship. I raise the point to illustrate again that definitional and disciplinary premises greatly color historical interpretation. I also want to be clear: I am not arguing that capitalism arose in the seventeenth century. Rather, I seek to demonstrate that in the seventeenth century actors constructed the conceptual foundations for the modern world and the international system. These include the crosshairs that constitute distinct political and economic spaces or systems—a system of states and a system of capitalist, market exchange—as well as distinct national and international domains. Such a worldview constitutes an international political economy as an element of the modern world(view). Consequently, I do not attend in great detail to the controversies over dating or defining capitalism as a material historical event.

5

The Agents of Statecraft

As seen from 1600 or so, the development of the state was very contingent; many aspiring states crumpled and fell along the way. . . . Both the primacy and the ultimate form of the state were very much in doubt.

Charles Tilly (1975:7)

Throughout the period [of the seventeenth century] intervention by the state in economic and social affairs in the interests of the community as a whole was generally considered to be both natural and desirable, and both government ministers and parliament devoted a great deal of time to such matters.

C.G.A. Clay (1984b:203)

This chapter turns from the practices informed by the legal worldview to the property-related practices of policymakers. I argue that these practices were inextricably related to the activities of entrepreneurs, merchants, and bankers because polity and economy were neither independent nor distinct in the seventeenth century. The result was a coherently unified but nascent institutional-legal-economic order. Institutional rule marks a transition from personal dynastic authority to the sovereign state. The Thirty Years' War effectively marks this transition on the Continent; in England the civil war and execution of Charles I mark the same. Yet the construction of protostates occurred in tandem with innovations in legal and economic institutions that yield a coherent set. For example, joint-stock companies spearheaded commercial and financial revolutions and fueled the development of national economies, currencies, legal codes, and national administration. These companies ignited capital accumulation and helped stabilize the national order. Thus, as actors constructed authority and administrative control in the seventeenth century, they also simultaneously and inextricably constituted bureaucratic offices, politically authoritative joint-stock companies, banks, and national legal systems.

Moreover, early modern actors did not conceive the structure(s) of civil society as distinct from the practice(s) of promoting the state and promoting exchange. In short, the social structures were not distinct, social practices were not distinct, and structures were not distinct from practices. The seventeenth-century actors did not yet possess a conceptual framework that disaggregates these phenomena (Walzer, 1984). Rather, they understood the process and flux of social construction. Yet from the modern worldview born of liberalism's analytic, positivist vantage point, the social relations of polity and economy appear distinct and separate. As above, I explore the elements by exploring practices concerning property.

By approximately 1700, actors had constructed many modern practices and structures as elements of a complex, integrated, institutional system: Depersonalized civil authority, coordinate sovereignty, bureaucratic administration, a professional army and navy, modern banking practices, insurance coverage, regularized national taxation, national currencies, fiat currencies, institutionalized instruments of credit, pooled resources for investment, infrastructures and capital plant, capital accumulation and reinvestment, and much more. For each of these, one might construct an elaborate conceptual history. By investigating property as a constitutive principle, I harvest elements from the diverse fields that surround these various histories and activities. I hope to make clear how closely the histories of authority, sovereignty, and capital(ism) are tied to each other by property and property rights relations. Vocabulary remains a problem, since I argue that many contemporary terms applied to seventeenth-century phenomena are inapt.[1]

While the term *the state* was not much used in the seventeenth century, the terms *polity* and *commonwealth* had for ages suggested civil society. The concepts governance, government, authority, and sovereignty are clearly related. I use the infelicitous phrase *institutional-legal order* to avoid conceptual and definitional squabbles and to reflect more accurately the subject of this chapter. By this phrase I mean enduring relations of governance and rule, specifically, the institutional-legal order managing political, social, and economic relations (Benjamin and Duvall, 1985). Actors in the seventeenth century crafted such arrangements to be *national* institutional-legal orders. In hindsight, theorists and historians call these sixteenth- and seventeenth-century innovations by the name *states*. I do not because the word connotes too much and too little: The word *state* connotes too much institutional stability but too little of the legal and economic components necessary to administer, govern, and rule. Political scientists' attention to authority blinds them to the latter, but attention to institutions of governance misleads them in the former direction. In exploring the relation of, to put it crudely, polity to economy and society, I require a different vocabulary. To invoke polity, economy, and society (and their reputed synonyms) is to misrepresent the relations, prejudge the outcome, and prejudice the analysis. I hope to keep contexts and uses clear.

To be clear: Before the seventeenth century, civic authority was located primarily in personal rule, not the institutional apparatus of a state. Jackson (1990:51) makes the point when he qualifies himself: "The earliest modern states such as France and England *or rather Francis I and Henry VIII* were palpable political realities internally and in their neighbourhoods" (emphasis added). I explore how actors constructed the palpable realities of the transitions from "Henrys" to "Englands."

The commercial activities of the era similarly lacked recognizable labels. Today we call the activities of bankers, merchants, and entrepreneurs economic. Yet I argue that only in this era did actors of significant status and numbers begin to conceive a distinct realm of social relations. I argue further that they conceived it as a realm of mobile property rights exchanges. Although this was later called an economy, to use the term in the seventeenth-century context distorts both the analysis and the historical conditions. Thus, I use the term *economy* and its cognates in a general sense. I also use *capitalism* generically to capture the production and exchange relations at issue. My goal throughout is to illustrate the early social construction of institutional-legal-economic orders that possess national character and characteristics.

I begin by considering views on sovereignty and authority before turning to the practices of policymakers in the hostile and competitive contexts of domestic turmoil and foreign threats. Efforts to constitute authority in response to social disarray turned on instituting sovereignty (Harding, 1966:228; Nenner, 1977:ch. 3), which in turn hung on property rights and law. For example, could the monarch through royal prerogative confiscate personal property and interfere with commercial relations? In the next chapter, I explore commercial actors in the same competitive contexts. By separating policymaking (Chapter 5) from commercial activity (Chapter 6), I do violence to their inextricable character as they existed in the early modern era. Yet the break improves the exposition and reinforces an understanding of their contributions to seventeenth-century events and to my larger argument.

RULE, RIGHTS, AND RESOURCES

Coherent Practices

Myriad social conditions affected state-building in north and west Europe. National histories of England, France, the Netherlands, Spain, and Portugal attest to the variety. They share one compelling factor, however: Amid the turbulence of the century, it became "rational" to constitute a secure site of authority and stability. Several senses of rationality apply. First, a central-ized authority was a rational or logical solution to the problem of social disorder. Second, Cartesian philosophy advanced reason and science as modes of thought preferable to theology and scriptural interpretation. Third, secular authority based on reason rather than divine right offered the prospect of tolerance rather than the undecidable controversies and chronic internecine warfare that divided Christian denominations. Thus, to disman-tle and replace the murderously feudal worldview held by European rulers seemed to require the certainty of central authority (Toulmin, 1990:69–75, 97–104). The idiom of certainty held vast appeal in a period of insoluble violence and theological dogmatism (Toulmin, 1990:70).

Foreign threats to each nation provided further incentives to centralize national authority. Actors conducting the same policy calculus acted in slightly different ways in each nation to achieve the same goal: The con-struction of institutional-legal orders that helped agents of civil authority extract, command, and direct valued resources. The personal, dynastic, and religious frictions that sparked European competition gradually trans-formed into national rivalries. Thus, it became important to develop stable national institutions and impersonal bureaucratic power (Tilly, 1975:chs. 1–4, 7–9). Governments or states must extract and control resources to maintain social stability. This is state-building and statecraft. Such efforts also constitute society and preserve and secure civil authority. These are not perfectly congruent activities, but they are deeply related. The more efficiently authorized agents control resources, the more efficiently they can stabilize society and prevent infringements by foreign actors. Of course the same logic quickly engulfed foreign policy conflicts: Bring resources under the jurisdiction and authority of the national institutional-legal order, then direct the resources into advantageous purposes.

Actors crafted national institutional-legal orders to address these con-cerns. Institutionalized authority made the task easier but still required inextricable interactions between rulers and merchants. Grounded in insti-tutions, the resulting order embraced classical elements of political authori-ty yet also comprised commercial actors, activities, and relations. Grounded in reason, arguments encouraging institutional-legal-economic innovation drew from changing philosophic judgments and worldviews. In an era racked by irreconcilable controversy and era-shaking decay, a for-mal, rational theory based on abstract, universal, timeless concepts offered hope for salvation. Yet for most seventeenth-century actors, timeless princi-ples were embedded in law. How did legal and philosophic doctrine address the prospects of personal rule becoming institutional? Would efforts to reconstitute society and authority in the face of domestic turmoil and for-eign threats privilege rule, rights, or resources? Indeed, in a clash over (property) rights to (property) resources, would the ruler's rights prevail over subjects' rights as stipulated in law? Who could decide, and how? At issue was the character of sovereignty rather than sovereigns. As Jackson (1990:34) remarks, "sovereigns preceded sovereignty."

Personal Versus Institutional Rule

Jean Bodin bridges the chasm separating medieval and early modern thought on sovereignty. Bodin asked novel questions that built from the "difficult terrain" of earlier disputes (Pennington, 1993:37): What limits constrained the prince's power? Could the prince expropriate the property of subjects? Could he act arbitrarily? Did the prince's power have limits? Bodin's contribution to political thought was to ask these questions and write a systematic tract on sovereignty (Pennington, 1993:283). A long but worthwhile quotation ably describes the difficult terrain and Bodin's place in it:

> If we may draw a long and continuous line from the twelfth to eighteenth centuries when we discuss the development of juristic ideas governing due process in judicial proceedings, the lines delineating the evolution of *potestas absoluta* and juristic definitions of sovereignty are neither neat nor agreed upon.
> During the sixteenth century, jurists described the authority of the prince with the same terminology that their predecessors had used since the thirteenth. The prince had "plenitudo potestatis," "potestas absoluta," "ordinata," and was "legibus solutus." Historians cannot agree, however, on whether these terms shifted their meanings in the sixteenth century. The key issue is whether medieval jurists attributed "true" sovereignty to the prince and whether sixteenth [and seventeenth—KB] century jurists interpreted these terms as granting the prince absolute power, untrammeled by any limitations. (Pennington, 1993:275)

Pennington (1993:275) suggests a "limited comparison of medieval and early modern definitions" that avoid the "grim detail." Building upon treatments in Chapter 3 that explore property and sovereignty in several seventeenth-century authors, I consider Machiavelli, Bodin, Hobbes, and Locke below.

The Machiavellian-Italian tradition of statecraft conceived a personalized state directed from highly personalized rule. While Machiavelli coined the term *state* (*lo stato*), his interest in *The Prince* (1513) is in rulers rather than in institutions (de Grazia, 1989:chs. 10–12). His concept of *lo stato* represents a locus of authority, the politico-military and administrative apparatus at the ruler's command (Mansfield, 1983). The perspective remains personal. In this light, almost sixty years later, Bodin (1576/1992:1) reflects on sovereignty because "no jurist or political philosopher has defined it," yet it is "the chief point . . . that needs most to be explained in a treatise" on political life. For Bodin (1576/1992:4), only God is greater than or superior to a sovereign. The concept sovereignty represents

> the absolute and perpetual power of a commonwealth (*civitatis*), which the Latins call *majestas;* . . . and the Italians call *seignioria,* a word they use for . . . those who have full control of the state. [I think *governance* is a better translation of the last two words—KB] (Bodin, 1576/1992:1)

According to Bodin, sovereignty is thereby reducible to "the highest power to command" (p. 1) and thus to the authoritative power administering a commonwealth.

In Bodin one hears republican echoes of Machiavelli's authoritative Prince. In harmonic counterpoint one hears afar Hobbes's corporate Leviathan and Locke's "Absolute Arbitrary Power" (Locke, 1690/1965:405). While in *The Prince* Machiavelli levels his attention upon the personal character and characteristics of rulers, Hobbes and Locke look to rulers and to the institutional apparatus of government they command. The law is particularly important. Thus, Hobbes (1651/1958:143) refers to the "commonwealth by institution" and the subordinate "body politic" comprising agents, ministers, bureaucracies, and such (ch. 22, p. 181). Moreover, for Hobbes as for Bodin, sovereign authority need not be a single person (Hobbes, 1651/1958:144; Tuck, 1989:65). Thus, by the seventeenth century sovereign authority is a decidedly corporate, not corporeal condition, as Hobbes (1640/1994) comments in *De corpore politico*. Still, the character of states, statecraft, and sovereignty are uncertain in this era (Mansfield, 1983; Tuck, 1989:72). Bodin links these eras and views.

Bodin's subject is the prerogatives of political authority by which a commonwealth is governed. He is clear that a commonwealth is a civic association, a relationship between society and government. He investigates the authority relationship between them, so, following tradition, he notes three forms a commonwealth may take: monarchy, aristocracy, and democracy. In his judgment, in any stable polity only one of the three possesses sovereignty (Bodin, 1576/1992:89). As a matter of preference, Bodin was a monarchist. As a matter of analysis, Bodin suffers "serious confusions" when he concludes that sovereignty is indivisibly housed in a supreme monarch (Bodin, 1576/1992:49–51, 103–104; quotation in Franklin, 1992:xx). Conditions argued otherwise. For example, Bodin was clearly familiar with the practice of addressing monarchs as "sovereign," although they typically required the consent of legislative or advisory bodies to conduct affairs. Simultaneously, however, the Crown's vast authority assured that no significant decisions could be made without the monarch's approval. Seventeenth-century theorists called this condition coordinate sovereignty (see Weston and Greenberg, 1981). In Bodin's era jurisprudents had little scrutinized the ideas of shared sovereignty, balanced government, or federation. Only with difficulty could Bodin imagine absolute sovereign authority functionally divided among ruler, legislature, and ministers. Still less imaginable would be a republic on the U.S. model (Onuf and Onuf, 1993).

In pursuing the location and limits of sovereignty, Bodin parts company with Machiavelli. Yet Bodin's attention to absolute and perpetual power and to the power of command taps a rich reservoir of thought extending to twelfth-century Europe. For example, Frederick Barbarossa (ruled 1152–1190), the most powerful European ruler of the age, sparked several centuries of jurisprudence and political philosophy by justifiably asking if he was "the lord of the world" (Pennington, 1993:ch. 2; quotation on p. 16). Bodin (1576/1992:13) similarly asks, "Is the prince not subject to those laws of the land that he has sworn to keep?"

Twelfth-century answers understandably varied: The prince could well be lord of the world, yet simultaneously "he was not lord over private property" (Pennington, 1993:16). Bodin, Hobbes, and Locke offer similar answers. Monarchs may rule absolutely, but they do not possess absolute power. They are bound by customary and moral law and should not, for example, confiscate private personal property (Bodin, 1576/1992:31–32, 39–42). Bodin writes boldly:

> For if we say that to have absolute power is not to be subject to any law at all, no prince of this world will be sovereign, since every earthly prince is subject to laws of God and of nature and to various human laws that are common to all peoples. (p. 10)

Within these confines, however, the sovereign possesses unrivaled authority. "Persons who are sovereign must not be subject in any way to the commands of someone else. . . . [Thus] the prince is not subject to the law" (p. 11). Here Bodin refers only to positive law, the law as command or edict from the ruler. As the unrivaled authority, Bodin's sovereign may change rules and laws as he or she sees fit, so long as the changes are for just cause, in the interests of the subjects, and do not derogate from contracts. Thus, the "prince is not subject to his own laws or to the laws of his predecessors, but only to his just and reasonable contracts" (p. 14).

> It is essential, therefore, not to confuse a law and a contract. Law depends on him who has the sovereignty and he can obligate all his subjects [by a law] but cannot obligate himself. A contract between a prince and his subjects is mutual; it obligates the two parties reciprocally and one party cannot contravene it to the prejudice of the other and without the other's consent. (Bodin, p. 15)

On the sanctity of private property, thus limits on sovereign authority, Hobbes and Locke concur, though Locke is more forceful in his conviction. Hobbes (1651/1958:199) writes that the property "which a subject has in his lands consists in a right to exclude all other subjects from the use of them, and not to exclude their sovereign, be it an assembly or a monarch." This sounded to many ears like a strikingly arbitrary extension of royal prerogative, yet Hobbes qualifies the claim. If the sole function of the Leviathan is to promote "the common peace and security," and the monarch is the sole judge of interests and threats, then whatever the monarch decides will necessarily be just and fair. For sovereigns to do otherwise by pursuing their passions would breach the law of nature and the bonds of trust (Hobbes, 1651/1958:ch. 24, p. 199). So while "the sovereign . . . is not subject to the civil laws" (ch. 26, p. 211), civil and natural law form reciprocal parts of each other (p. 212). The Leviathan becomes subject to natural law once it is expressed as positive law in a commonwealth. Indeed, Hobbes (p. 215) reduces natural law to a single sentence, the Golden Rule: "Do not that to another which you think unreasonable to be done by another to yourself."

In contrast to Hobbes's subdued attention to private property and royal prerogative, Locke (1690/1965, paras. 137–138, pp. 405–406) proclaims that

> whatever Form the Common-wealth is under, the Ruling Power ought to govern by *declared* and *received* laws, and not by extemporary Dictates and undetermined Resolutions. . . . The *Supream* [sic] *Power cannot take* from any Man any part of his *Property* without his own consent. . . . The Law of the Community [declares] that no Body hath a right to take their substance, or any part of it from them, without their own consent; without this, they have no *Property* at all. (emphasis in original)

Locke's comments are a stunning landmark. In the transitions from Machiavelli to Locke, we see the world change. Actors and scholars constructed it anew from familiar elements. In Locke's work we see that institutional rule has eclipsed personal rule. Actors constructed sovereignty, distinct from sovereigns, so also constructed social relations in law, in a novel institutional order, and in distinctive economic conditions. While Machiavelli wrote *The Prince* to ingratiate himself to the Medicis, Bodin wrote *The Six Books of the Commonwealth* as a systematic account of public law and absolute sovereignty in an era of dramatic social change. Similarly, Hobbes and Locke wrote to address the turmoils arising from the social decay and political (re)constitution that pocked their eras. Hobbes and Locke confronted judicial, administrative, and legislative units developing as a national set. Such conditions emerged in inchoate form in France in the late sixteenth century and in England in the seventeenth century. In

France the king retained enormous personal power over the administrative apparatus, often to Bodin's frustration (Franklin, 1992:x–xi). Indeed, in France the burgeoning institutional-legal order became for over 100 years an attribute of personalized, sovereign power. Writing in 1632—and demonstrating the heightened influences of rationality, science, and Bodin—the political and legal scholar Le Bret proclaims that sovereignty is "no more divisible than the point in geometry" (in Bonney, 1978:26). Sovereignty was an attribute of the monarch, but the *manifestations* of sovereignty were the administrative and bureaucratic institutions. Thus, "when Bodin spoke about the unity of sovereignty, the power he had in mind was . . . the ordinary agencies of government" (Franklin, 1992:xiii). Authority retains a personal face, but the apparatus of rule and governance become institutional. As part of such institutional development, questions about the source and limits of sovereign authority understandably arose, as did questions about the constitutive and regulative character of law. These questions became particularly pointed when, in the throes of institutional innovation, monarchs claiming royal prerogative laid claim to private property.

The blend of republican and modern ideas is telling. Personal, republican rule becomes recast as institutional authority. This becomes a modern institutional order with an impersonal, corporate character. Bodin conveys republican elements by emphasizing the need for a strong government to secure and enhance citizenship. Similarly, Machiavelli writes of the *uno solo*—the "prince new" as "one man alone" and unrivaled—that his strength comes from acting as God's agent for the good of the broad population beneath his authority (see de Grazia, 1989:236–240, 268). However, such rule remained personal and noninstitutional early in this era (Pocock, 1975:236). The authority of a commonwealth is absolute, perpetual, and impersonal; rule is also absolute but not perpetual and not yet depersonalized (Bodin, 1576/1992:8, 31–34). Rule remains a feature of the person of the mortal ruler. Such rule is hierarchical—sovereign command—but is tempered by the heteronomous requirements of diplomatic reciprocity and contractual arrangements.

In similar circumstances the term *sovereignty* emerges in English political and legal discourse. Hobbes marks the significant change. His views on rule and authority decisively differ from the Machiavellian, republican tradition. For Hobbes, the state was a corporate entity, though ruled by a powerful individual. Yet rule—the exercise of sovereign powers—stands distinct from the ruler, no longer necessarily a person. Through Hobbes the conditions of the state and rule lose their personal character. By Rousseau's era (1712–1778), some 100 years later, the transformation in Europe is complete. The personalized state is gone and liberal, individualized, alienated politics has displaced the personal tradition. It is no contradiction, however, that Anderson (1974) calls this the age of absolutism. Sovereigns ruled absolutely, but not without restrictions. Bodin, Hobbes, and Locke would agree.

> Definitions of princely authority in the early Middle Ages were descriptions of rank, legitimacy, prerogatives, or privilege. Those jurists who studied canon law concocted and adopted terms defining power, like "plenitudo potestas," "auctoritas," or "plena potesta," but neither they nor these terms described the prince's relationship to the law. (Pennington, 1993:9)

By the early modern era, however,

> "Princeps" was . . . a multicolored cloak whose colors shifted hue and intensity at different times and with different owners. . . . Paradoxically, the title could grant independence, arbitrary authority, and *limited power.* (Pennington, 1993:36; emphasis added)

All claims to sovereignty, dominion, *dominium,* or authority locate the prince within the law and thus enmesh him in the institutions of governance and society.

As Hobbes marks a watershed in political theory, Sir Edward Coke marks a similar divide in English jurisprudence, the English civil war marks one in practice, and Descartes and Grotius mark them in philosophy and law. The rise to prominence of the common law and common law culture occurred only after the precedents of local courts overcame customary practice. Concerning these changes, Coke collected and penned, with assistance, an extensive set of treatises called the *Institutes of the Laws of England.*[2] However, by the restoration of monarchical rule in England in 1660, Parliamentary statute law had won ascendancy over local precedents and practices, thus inaugurating an era of national law and national identity. Only in this circumstance did the "nation" come into being. Heretofore, a man's greatest loyalty had been to the local community—his *patria* or country or county—because that was the jurisdiction, and in all likelihood the unique code of law, from which *he* acquired justice; women rarely possessed legal standing (Harding, 1966:251). By wresting control of the common law and sovereignty from the Crown, Parliament not only decentralized authority and circumscribed royal prerogative but also fostered a national consciousness. Simultaneously, parliamentary control of statutory common law promoted "national" communal sensibilities and responsibilities. It also made administering them more efficient. Statutory law is more focused than customary law and therefore a better instrument of policy. Customary law was simply too incoherent for the administrative needs of an expanding institutional infrastructure (Harding, 1966:218) and too regionalized and inconsistent for expanding commerce.

By William and Mary's arrival in 1688, then, a British national consciousness was forming and a legal order for administering and governing it was taking shape. This institutional order possessed sovereignty, though a sovereign monarch ruled. Thus, in the seventeenth century sovereign authority increasingly meant an individual and surrounding institutions for ruling and administering. Originally such authority was vested overwhelmingly in the person of the ruling monarch; governing occurred, but government was derivative. Slowly, conflictually, and uncertainly during this century, actors constituted governing institutions with a measure of independence from the monarch. Such structures would become enduring in succeeding decades and centuries. The next section surveys the personal rule of monarchs and their close ministers. It suggests how the exigencies of the day helped develop a relatively coherent, institutional-legal, administrative apparatus.

STATECRAFT POLICYMAKERS

Creating an Institutional-Legal Order

The English civil war eventually replaced Charles I with a more institutional form of rule. By the reign of William and Mary, English society had crafted a coherent, stable institutional order. The Glorious Revolution was less a political transformation than a widely appreciated constitutional fiction (Pocock, 1957; Nenner, 1977; Kenyon, 1978:256–260). In the aftermath William and Mary confronted three fundamental challenges. First, they acted quickly to reconstruct constitutional authority and to recraft relations between society and monarchy. Second, so that the newly constituted authority relations could better wage war and endure crises, William and Mary established a stable institutional infrastructure (Clay, 1984b:222–250). Third, they organized and administered their postrevolutionary government to foster social prosperity through economic success; this required the participation and support of the merchant class. I consider these three challenges below, two in the following sections and the third in the next chapter.

Recrafting Civil Authority:
Coordinate Sovereignty and an Institutional-Legal Order

When William III assumed the English throne, leaders in Parliament sought a constituent convention to constitute society and civil authority anew. They demanded William call a convention to preserve religion, rights, laws, liberty, and property and to establish "such sure and legal foundations, that they may not be in danger of being again subverted" (quoted in Kenyon, 1978:254). Parliament obliged William to promise to govern England according to parliamentary statute and the laws and customs of the realm (Kenyon, 1978:261).[3]

The constituent convention and coronation oath declare Parliament's institutional superiority over the monarch. The monarch governs but is not the government. Government exists independent of the monarch, but the monarch is the most important governmental official, a sovereign authority ruling by absolute right. The declaration and oath (a set of promises) also indicate the victory of Parliament's control over the common law, recognized now as the superiority of statute law over custom. This victory consolidated decentralized and depersonalized authority. It also transformed authority into the ability to make rules rather than exercise power. This fundamental but oft-overlooked distinction defines coordinate sovereignty (e.g., Pocock, 1975:481).

Coordinate sovereignty in England was "government" only in the narrowest sense. Although it represented authority, it had not yet proven it could administer affairs. Thus, the challenge to reconstitute authority and social stability was pressing. Since effective administration was a legal, social, and political concern, reconstituted authority must craft an institutional-legal order that coherently arranges elements of authority, rule, and administration. These elements include what current vocabulary calls government, public administration, law, bureaucracies, bankers, and entrepreneurs. As part of the newly crafted social contract, William, his ministers, the coterie of Dutch intimates, and Parliament were obligated to form the necessary institutions to protect law, liberty, and property. Although property was still conceived primarily in terms of land, personal possessions, and (self-proprietary) property rights, protecting property remained key since property rights were the foundation of the law. The new "government" had now to protect personal, landed, and commercial property. William was also obligated to protect the rule of law itself, which protects property and the liberties as matters of property rights.

The Crown and Parliament struggled over control, even possession, of English law and society. The pitched contest conceptually located authority, royal prerogative, and citizens' property rights within the developing worldview and institutions. William and Mary also had to marshal coalitions for setting broader public policy. Beyond establishing stable domestic authority and institutions, the monarch confronted systemic concerns, including war and foreign policy. The difference between "domestic" and "foreign" realms remained always unclear.[4]

Establishing Stable Institutions: Confronting War and Financial Crises

William and Mary's second significant challenge was to organize and administer the government apparatus in order to address pressing war and trade issues (Clay, 1984b:203–222). Coordinate sovereignty made waging war and conducting foreign policy a troublesome enterprise compared with the greater latitude and relatively unencumbered prerogative earlier rulers enjoyed. If authority and rule dominated domestic concerns, then authority and administration were necessary for efficient, competitive statecraft.

English seventeenth-century foreign policy marks the transition from primarily religious and dynastic controversies to commercial rivalries (Howat, 1974:1). The same transition occurred across Europe, as destructively and decisively illustrated by the Thirty Years' War. Tudor rulers— from Henry VII (1485–1509) to Elizabeth I (1558–1603)—advanced foreign policies intended to secure their dynasty against threats from Catholic Spain. Hanoverian rulers—from George I (1714–1727) to Victoria (1837–1901)—conducted a confrontational foreign policy to constrain French and later German military and trade might. Stuart and Cromwellian foreign policy in the intervening seventeenth century was unusual and unfocused. It lacked the clear purpose of the preceding and succeeding centuries, in large measure because of the transitional nature of the century, domestic preoccupations, desires to avoid the vortex of the Thirty Years' War, and absence of an overwhelming enemy. Of course English armies and navies battled the Scots, Irish, Dutch, and French during the seventeenth century, and fears of intrigue and invasion by Catholic Spain endured throughout the era. Yet these matters were not the central concerns of English foreign policy.

Although by the mid-1500s actors used advances in production and exchange to serve religious and dynastic controversies, by the mid-1600s competition over production and exchange became an end in itself. In keeping with this trend, by the late 1600s British rulers were preoccupied with commercial competition. For example, James I (1603–1625) formulated policies primarily to address religious and dynastic concerns. Not until midway through his reign did his courtiers recognize that Dutch commercial supremacy seriously challenged English interests. Charles I (1625–1649) was also too deeply embroiled in controversies over religion and rebellion, especially concerning Ireland and Scottish Puritans, to devote careful attention to commercial rivalries. Late in his reign he temporarily tempered military hostilities with the Dutch, but he did not forestall their commercial challenge to England and Europe. However, Charles did act to protect English and Scottish fishing and shipping interests.

With the Cromwells (1649/1653–1659), religion again returned to the European and English center stage. They ardently promoted an alliance of Protestant rulers against Europe's Catholics. The result was predictably unsuccessful, since the bloody mayhem of the Thirty Years' War ended with the Peace of Westphalia, just a year before Charles's beheading. The Thirty Years' War began as a political-religious rivalry of Austria's Catholic

Hapsburgs against a coalition of northern European Protestant armies. When the Catholic Bourbons of France intervened in 1630 on the side of the Protestant alliance, the war ceased to be a religious struggle and became a titanic political contest. Continental rulers in midcentury saw the Cromwells' foreign policy as an attempt to revive the religious bigotry and intolerance calmed by the Westphalian treaty in 1648.

Yet with Charles II (1660–1685) and James II (1685–1688), efforts to counter Dutch commercial and financial supremacy became national priorities. However, when William and Mary accepted the English throne in the bloodless revolution of 1688, an English-Dutch alliance became secure. William was a noted Dutch leader and a distinguished general in the campaigns to defend the province of Holland against French armies. Under William and Mary, English political, military, and commercial rivalries with France dominated policy matters. William, in advance of the Hanoverian rulers, threw English resources into an immediate and enduring war with France that spanned most of the period from 1689 to 1713. Indeed, English-French military conflict for political, commercial, and colonial supremacy marked fifty-six of the years between 1689 and 1815.

Stuart rulers and the leaders of the Protectorate were in general far abler and more comfortable with domestic political and religious concerns, but "none of these rulers could ignore the impact of trade on foreign affairs. The three wars fought against the Dutch were basically economic in origin. . . . Their alliance of 1678 confirmed the growing common fear of French political and economic hegemony" (Howat, 1974:5). William secured this alliance and brought to it an enduring animosity toward France. Thus, certainly by the end of the seventeenth century, English rulers confronted a hostile, competitive international realm. Hostility was a European standard, but commercial competition entailed novel dynamics. To compete more effectively, William had to address several domestic matters and secure the stability of the new institutional order.

William confronted immediate security threats. He worked quickly to quash an Irish rebellion and an invasion of Scotland by the deposed James II, who was backed by Louis XIV of France. In upholding his coronation oath, William acted on these threats in the name of protecting sovereign territory and extending his control over the English Isles. By protecting territory, property, and law, he stabilized the institutional-legal order. William assumed sole responsibility for the prosecution of the war and the conduct of foreign policy (Kenyon, 1978:270). He exercised his personal property right in the Crown—that is, his constricted royal prerogative—by acting as the singular agent of political authority. Although Parliament's ministers increasingly regarded themselves as policy initiators rather than inhibitors, Parliament's foremost obligation immediately following the revolution was to check royal prerogative. However, Parliament was not yet in a position to affect royal *foreign* policy initiatives. Thus, while the constitution of society had been recrafted, the authority to conduct foreign policy remained largely unchanged.

Last, William recognized that the continued stability and effectiveness of the English institutional-legal infrastructure was best measured against that of foreign foes. With most citizens content with the reconstituted authority (Pocock, 1957; Nenner, 1977; Kenyon, 1978:256–260), the measure of long-term stability depended upon favorable comparison with *systemic* rivals and allies (Kenyon, 1978:281). Again, the Thirty Years' War provides a benchmark and clear lessons: English rulers must avoid dynastic absolutism. As the Dutch proved, commercial success was necessary but insufficient in systemic rivalries. Military might was also insufficient, as the French were proving. Moreover, military prominence came at great cost but could be temporarily decisive. How decisive was uncertain, since the French—the biggest winners in the thirty-year ravages—seemed poised for continental domination but unable to achieve it. Indeed, France, too, was racked by national financial woes of monumental proportions.

Thus, William sought to promote a competitive, efficient order able to exercise influence and control both at home and abroad. To this end, he and others fashioned an institutional structure as a vehicle for his authority. Indeed, they crafted a competitive protostate through which a leader could effectively command and direct resources in the turbulent domestic circumstances and in the hostile international environment. A leader of secure national institutions could advance the commercial, financial, and military policies necessary to advance the nation's interests. That is, rulers commanding efficient institutional-legal structures could advantageously direct resources. As observers, we return to authority, rule, and administration as foci. In the formation of national units, we see as well the formation and recognition of an *international* system.

Amid clashing conceptions of rule, rights, and resources, English actors in the mid-seventeenth century depersonalized authority by creating sovereignty from sovereigns. By century's end they had constituted a novel, stable institutional-legal order capable of shaping a national identity and pursuing national interests. William and Mary, as heads of this institutional set, succeeded in two of their challenges: They helped to recraft civil authority into coordinate sovereignty, and they established necessary institutions to confront the perils—war and financial crises—of Europe's transformation into a system of competing nation-states. The Treaty of Westphalia (1648), ending the Thirty Years' War, gave this system some formal sanction.

To erect and maintain these national institutions, William and Mary and other European national leaders had to acquire resources. This meant extending property rights, whether the goal was to foster social prosperity or acquire resources from abroad. We turn to this third challenge in the next chapter. The effort requires that we, as observers, recognize commerce and banking as indistinguishable from statecraft.

NOTES

1. A brief conceptual history of the term *capital* illustrates tangled relationships. The adjective *capital* derives from the Latin for *head* (thus derive *decapitate* and *per capita,* for instance). Over time *capital* acquired the meaning of "chief importance, influence, or value." This meaning extends to the words *capitaine* (French) and *captain* (the commander, or "head," of a body of troops and therefore the most important). *Capital* quickly acquired the sense of "advantage or gain." The word *chattel* derives from these meanings. *Chattel*—a corruption of the spelling and pronunciation of *capital*—means "property distinct from real estate." (The etymology of *estate* and *state* winds through and around these same concepts.) In particular, chattel refers to any movable or immovable personal, freehold property distinct from land. Ownership of such property was "advantageous."

From capital through chattel derives *cattle*. Thus occurs the expression "head of cattle," which conveys the three senses of capital, chattel, and cattle. *Cattle* is easily understood as capital stock or as capital in the stockyard—that is, as "accumulated goods or value" from which one derives "advantage or gain." (*Stock* was originally a variation on *stick,* referring to the wooden posts, timbers, or slats used to construct the fencing and pales to pen animals.) Cattle comprise a distinct form of chattel property, however, because they are living, or *livestock*.

2. In legal vocabulary, "institutes" are names occasionally attributed to textbooks that systematically compile elementary principles of jurisprudence. The *Institutes of the Laws of England* (sometimes called the *Institutes of Lord Coke*) entail four volumes. The first was published in 1628. The other three, originally confiscated by the Crown, were published in 1644 by order of Parliament (White, 1979:10). These four volumes are justly famous in legal scholarship, but citations, especially in the seventeenth century, are often inconsistent because the *Institutes* were frequently revised and reprinted by numerous sources and in varied editions after 1644. (Coke died in 1634.) A consensus has developed in the intervening centuries (Bowen, 1957: 565).

The first volume comments extensively upon a treatise on land tenures written by Judge Littleton during the reign of Edward IV (1461–1483). Coke's comments collect a wealth of common-law decisions drawn from ancient reports and Year Books. This, the most famous volume of the *Institutes,* is often cited in legal texts as "Comments on Littleton," "C. Litt.," or "1 Inst." This volume (Coke, 1628/1986) was essential reading in the legal curricula of the Untied States and Great Britain until the late 1800s.

The second volume (Coke, 1644a/1986) comments on old acts of Parliament. The third (Coke, 1644b/1986) is a methodical treatment of pleas of the Crown. Volume four (Coke, 1644c/1986) depicts several types of court. These volumes are often identified in legal citations as 2, 3, or 4 "Inst.," without any author's name (*Black's Law Dictionary,* p. 800).

Thanks to David Langenberg and Richard K. Burch, Sr., for assistance with the bibliographic material of this note.

3. Late Tudor and early Stuart monarchs heightened their power and authority by directly issuing greater numbers of edicts. They also granted commissions, monopolies, and patents at the expense of enacting statute law and often in contravention of such law. These activities represent the dominance of directive- and commitment-rules rather than instruction-rules (see Onuf, 1989). Instruction-rules— roughly synonymous with custom—epitomize the relations and circumstances being eclipsed. Yet by the late 1600s statutes, directives, and promises had eclipsed custom and instructions as the medium of social relations. I suggest in the sketchiest possible terms that the modern state develops as an institution for enforcing directive-rules. This is the practice of Stuart statecraft. Commitment-rules reflect the circumstances when personal promises convey more significance than institutional promises. For example, one may describe the common law—with its emphasis upon (property) rights and duties—in terms of commitments and promises. These forms of rule developed at roughly the same time to augur the emergence of modern practices and relations. See Scheingold (1974:ch. 1) on the place of promises and rules in contemporary Western law and state practice. Hobbes remarks extensively on promise-making in chapters 14 and 15 of *Leviathan*.

4. I reservedly distinguish *domestic* and *foreign* but nevertheless employ them here to focus attention on the location of other relevant actors. By *domestic* I mean within national jurisdiction; by *foreign* I mean beyond national jurisdiction.

6

The Agents of Commerce

[A] new means of governing was very slowly to emerge. The structures left tottering . . . had been felled: the rebuilding could now commence.

Ronald Hutton (1989:380)

What was the origin of such [novel] strength? It was the result of three steps in a sequence: One, productive and commercial strength in the world-economy created the basis for sound public finances. Two, sound public finances combined with a worldwide commercial network. . . . Three, productive and commercial strength . . . brought in remittances, which enabled [the government] to live off productive surplus.

Immanuel Wallerstein (1980:57)

The previous chapter tells the story of how English leaders constituted an institutional-legal order to address domestic woes and foreign rivals. This chapter completes that story by illustrating how English leaders addressed their third challenge—fostering prosperity—by enlisting the aid of merchants, bankers, and entrepreneurs.

In the late seventeenth century, governance in France, the Netherlands, and England was relatively stable. Louis XIV ruled France as an absolutist monarch. The United Provinces of the Netherlands had won their independence from Spain and formed an effective confederation. Coordinate sovereignty in England was workably efficient and socially desirable. It had to be to confront the persistent threats of war and the chronic lack of financial resources. To maintain stability and effectively pursue necessary policies, English rulers transferred property rights. They did so to secure influence and acquire resources. Indeed, the king and his ministers acted to defend and extend merchant property rights claims, even abroad. Merchants then introduced valuable resources and commodities into the realm, which the monarch deployed against foreign and domestic rivals. Further, beneficial relations with merchants helped relieve pressing financial burdens.

William had few alternatives to extending property rights to merchants. Waging war costs money. Indeed, only insufficient funds and resources curbed English aggression in this era (Hutton, 1989:ch. 9). Ending rebellions in Ireland and Scotland and battling France on the Continent proved especially expensive. Throughout this era a chronic money shortage threatened the newly established foundations of civil authority; a general shortage of capital (Scott, 1912/1968a:344–345) marks the era, as it had for several centuries. For example, in 1662 Charles II married a member of the Portuguese royal family in order to obtain the £500,000 dowry. Also during his reign, Charles II sold the city of Dunkirk to Louis XIV of France for a sizable personal sum.

Parliamentary ministers' appallingly poor fiscal management exacerbated matters. In 1666, for example, during a brief maritime war against the Netherlands, the Dutch fleet gained tremendous advantages because most of the British fleet was in port; Parliament had not allocated money for maintenance and provisions. The following year a small Dutch fleet sailed unhindered up the Thames to burn or capture docked British ships! From spring 1665 to spring 1666, English public revenue fell by more than half while Parliament allocated less than one-third of previous amounts. In the following year, national revenue fell to one-third of the mournful 1665 levels (Hutton, 1989:231, 242). In February 1667 the English Navy Board reported an outstanding debt of almost £149,000 to suppliers and £790,000 to sailors. It was also short £500,000 necessary to outfit the fleet (Hutton, 1989:242). By war's end in 1667, England had spent the unprecedented sum of £5.25 million, but the Dutch spent the equivalent of £11 million, and the French were enjoying a temporary but tremendous annual *surplus* of £9 million (Hutton, 1989:249). In despair, Charles II secretly signed the Treaty of Dover in 1670, pledging to withdraw from the Triple Alliance against France on condition that Louis XIV pay Charles a generous personal subsidy (Hyma, 1928:151). Although European rulers confronted a constraining, conflict-riddled international system, "the English monarchy was simply priced out of the market of sustained European warfare" (Hutton, 1989:249).

William faced similar woes. Parliament curtailed his royal revenue, the sum from which the ruler had to pay the costs of administration. Parliament authorized £1.9 million annually for James II, yet William, the "Great Deliverer," was allocated less. Indeed, Parliament niggardly apportioned the monies to William in three-month intervals, as if the ministers lacked confidence that William and Mary's reign would last (Kenyon, 1978:266–267). Some members also sought to provide a separate, concurrent revenue for Mary's sister Anne, as if to impugn William and Mary's rule. Between personal resentment and Parliament's reluctance, William had good reason to be concerned about the apportionment of monies and the administration of national revenues. Indeed, Parliament occasionally forgot or failed to reauthorize tax collections and/or disbursements.

Parliament also drastically underestimated the costs of war. In 1689 Parliament apportioned the woefully inadequate figure of £2 million for the war against France. The following year it authorized £1.2 million. A committee authorized by Parliament concluded in 1868 that the costs of war between 1688 and 1697 actually exceeded £49 million (Kenyon, 1978:266, 272–273). Further, Parliament provided insufficient funds for William to pay regularly his soldiers and administrators. Parliament also collected insufficient taxes to pay William and his high-level ministers (e.g., Kenyon, 1978:280). Financial management had not much improved by 1712, when a discrepancy in the national accounting revealed that £36 million were unaccounted for. Historians suspect that bribes to members of Parliament make up most of the missing funds (Scott, 1912/1968a:385).

With the clearly deficient organization of government—or, more specifically, the deficient coordination of sovereign authority—William had to extract, command, and commandeer resources by other means. To this end he developed a militaristic monarchy, established a set of governmental programs, relied upon the merchant class for financial and political support, and exercised governmental patronage (Kenyon, 1978:271–274, 288; Pocock, 1985:66–67). With the expanding geographic scope and national commitment to war against France, now recognized as the foremost threat to England, the patronage opportunities available to government administrators expanded as well, whether to bestow military rank, government contracts, or political office (Kenyon, 1978:274).

By the 1690s a distinct, integrated institutional-legal order combined recrafted authority, rule, and administrative efficiency with a burgeoning commercial mission. This institutional order promoted social stability, advanced individual liberties (particularly citizens' property rights), and sought to protect the nation from external threats and internal rebellion. Yet the means to act on these responsibilities were lacking. The financial and productive underpinnings of the order were profoundly weak. The new order required prosperity and growth. Thus, William faced a third serious challenge: to promote English production, trade, and financial relations in order to spark English commercial growth and stabilize the institutional order. Indeed, this was a challenge to all new "modern" institutional arrangements.

FOSTERING SOCIAL PROSPERITY

By 1693 the financial situation was desperate. National finances were shattered. War financing left a stunning national debt and a painful precedent of deficit financing. Similar conditions prevailed in France. Several of William's key government members were now cooperating to draft financial legislation for Parliament's review. However, the financial crises worsened. Scandal struck. In a thoroughly modern twist, the secretary of the treasury and the speaker were removed from office for accepting bribes to expedite military contracts (Kenyon, 1978:277–278). At the same time, the public learned that the lord president of the Privy Council was unscrupulously involved with the East India Company. Parliament was paralyzed.

The Roles of Merchants, Bankers, and Statecraft

Under these grave financial circumstances, Charles Montague, chancellor of the exchequer, suggested that some of the merchants of London found a bank in order to extend loans directly to William as the ruler of England. Some London merchants garnered enormous wealth from the commercial revolution of the 1670s (involving primarily the reexport of goods imported from the colonies) and the financial revolution of the 1690s (involving credit and other financial instruments). Following these successes, they founded the Bank of England in 1694 to help William finance administrative needs and the continuing war with France.[1] Recall that these needs were two of the three policy challenges confronting William and Mary. The Bank of England also served three purposes for the merchants: It promoted commercial and financial stability, supported an advantageous institutional arrangement or infrastructure, and was likely to turn a handsome profit. Obvious mutual advantages accrued to merchants and monarch alike.

In exchange for founding the Bank of England and extending loans, government ministers concluded lucrative contracts with these merchants to provide war materiel. The merchants of London supplied the government with uniforms, food, arms, munitions, transportation, and ships (Kenyon, 1978:286). As we have seen, officials were not loath to accept bribes, skim funds, or participate in conflicts of interest. In these circumstances money makes money. Money as credit helps drive statecraft, just as successful statecraft opens money-making opportunities.

In response to the merchants' Bank of England, a large group of powerful landholders established a rival Land Bank. They hoped to attract government contracts as well but sought primarily to earn interest revenue. Land taxes were exacting a heavy toll on the landholders. Warfare strained the national budget, as we have seen, so Parliament members responded in a time-honored manner: They taxed property, particularly landholdings. Parliament assessed a land tax in 1692. It remained permanently.

The burden (not to mention the irony or unfairness, depending upon your view) was unbearable. Landholders' taxes were funding the national budget, while merchants were making enormous profits. Yet the merchants paid virtually no taxes. Parliament did not tax profits on interest earned from government repayments of merchants' loans (Kenyon, 1978:272–273, 284, 286–287). The land tax financed the repayments, of course. Profits on trade were little taxed, however. Other than deficit financing, Parliament funded government through customs duties on imports and consumption taxes, primarily upon goods such as wine, beer, vinegar, cider, tea, coffee, and the like. Traders and merchants passed on to consumers the costs of import and consumption taxes; the burdens of land taxes could not be forwarded.

The only other effort by Parliament to address the mounting fiscal crisis was to raise customs duties on imports. Unfortunately, just as in the 1930s, rising tariff walls served only to restrict imports and consequently drive down the revenue collected from customs (Kenyon, 1978:286). The immediate repercussions were borne by the landholders as land taxes became more onerous. The Land Bank was both protest and defense against these burdens.

It was short-lived, however. William encouraged the founding of the bank as another source of revenue for him, but it failed to survive the bullion or specie crisis of 1696, triggered when William decided to collect the silver coins of the realm to capture their commodity value (i.e., the value of their silver), then mint new coins. Once done, the public hoarded the new coins, also to retain their commodity value as opposed to their value as a medium of exchange. Thus, very little specie circulated. The unlubricated economy ground violently. Amid the friction William appealed to the banks, but only the Bank of England had sufficient resources to keep the government and the economy in motion. The Land Bank was dead, and the political significance of the merchant class as rivals and eventual successors to the landholders was assured.

The Institutional-Legal Order and Intangible, Mobile Property

Charging ethically inappropriate relationships between government officials and merchants, Parliament members launched a campaign against government "patronage" and corruption (Kenyon, 1978:287; Pocock, 1985:66–67). Members of Parliament identified patronage as a form of government property inaptly transferred to merchants. Similarly, actors were coming to recognize "profits," "surpluses," "interest," and so on as forms of property. Although clearly assets, they were neither landed nor chattel property. They had been socially significant for decades, if not for 150 years, but their late-seventeenth-century significance was to transform well-established social relations. Thus, it appeared to many observers that a new form of mobile property was emerging. In different terms, actors began conceiving a new concept: intangible, liquid property. Patronage and corruption were ethically unpalatable forms.

Governmental actors, especially William and his key ministers, recognized the value and strength of commercial power. They also saw the important contributions of intangible, mobile property to commerce and influence. Parliament members were aware of it primarily because it escaped their legislative grasp. The burdens of Parliament's inability to wrestle it into control fell upon the landholders, the possessors of the most tangible form of property. Merchants had for some time understood the advantages of intangible, mobile property and were enjoying sudden benefits.

The ruler, his ministers, and Parliament members came to recognize that the stability and efficiency of the institutional-legal order depended substantially upon commercial and financial considerations. Heretofore the relations between the Crown and merchants had been mutually advantageous. These relations were now mutually necessary. The significance of trade in bonding these new social relationships was becoming more obvious to actors throughout the century but became especially clear during the 1690s. In an effort to restrict merchants and draw trade within the purview of Parliament, members attempted in 1694 to establish a Council of Trade. William quashed the attempt, realizing that it threatened his policy latitude by restricting his opportunities to draw upon merchants' material and financial resources (Kenyon, 1978:279). Leaders recognized that the political problems of domestic stability and international conflict in a competitive system are intimately related to the problems of exchange, trade, and the circulation of intangible property. Successful trade demands political stability and the defense of property rights claims. In the years approaching 1700, such property was more widely understood as intangible and mobile, and not merely as tangible landed or chattel property.

By approximately 1700 landed property and intangible property were contributing to distinct yet related activities. In both England and France (Beik, 1985:288), the two forms of property unified into a striking single dynamic. English state-building was grounded upon the notion of property as landed and territorial, to which exclusive property rights were attached. Efforts by English rulers to maintain and extend statecraft became intimately, inextricably involved with English commercial ascendancy and hegemony. Commercial success rested squarely upon notions of intangible, mobile property.[2] These include licenses, charters, contracts, privileges, grants, and so on, all of which accomplish much the same result.

Such legal instruments or immunities represent grants of property rights, thus control over property. Yet the property the merchants controlled was not solely landed property, although colonial land grants and monopolies involved significant tracts. Rather, these grants were a variety of intangible property. Grants are one variety, government patronage another. Credit was the most significant, however. And it was credit that fueled English commercial ascendancy. Moreover, credit reaped its most stable rewards, if not also the greatest rewards, in the service of the government. The results were more striking as the institutional-legal order of the state became more secure, as was the circumstance at approximately 1700 (1690–1720).

By this era, English policymakers, commercial actors, and jurists were constituting a world and worldview through their understandings of property and property rights. Through these rules and practices, English actors constituted distinctive international relations based upon sovereignty and constructed separate political and commercial relations by the bifurcation of property into landed and mobile forms.

I turn now to the entrepreneurs. They knew that commercial success requires a stable institutional-legal order and that a stable order requires commercial success.

CAPITALIST AGENTS:
JOINT-STOCK COMPANY ENTREPRENEURS

> *Chartered companies have been founded to serve purposes so widely apart from one another as banking and the promotion of scientific research. [These] corporations . . . were brought into existence always, and necessarily, with the approval of the State, and frequently by its direct action, in most of the countries of Western Europe, for the encouragement of commerce and colonisation. In all cases they were endowed with some powers of jurisdiction and administration for the enforcement of the law and the maintenance of order. . . . They began to arise in the sixteenth century; they played their greatest part in the seventeenth.*

David Hannay (1926:1)

Even the greatest and most powerful European monarchs in the sixteenth and seventeenth centuries faced severe material constraints on their rule. Finances were viscous rather than liquid, limited rather than plentiful. Currency was unusual and enjoyed only restricted geographic and commercial circulation (Hannay, 1926:12; Heckscher, 1934; Schumpeter, 1954; Ekelund and Tollison, 1981). As one historian describes the situation, "Given the relative backwardness of the British economy and the serious problems that stood in the way of efficient tax collection, government tax revenue was plainly never going to expand sufficiently to cover more than a part of its expenditure" (Wilson, 1977:131–132). Such constricted finances greatly constrained policy choices (Scott, 1912/1968c:485–544). Circumstances compelled rulers to delegate limited authority and grant rights to subjects who would venture for themselves yet partially benefit the government. Monarchs granted privileges, property rights, even monopolies (Hannay, 1926:12; see also Hunt, 1986:4, and Freedeman, 1979:4, on France). In short, they constituted mobile property and associated social relations. These relations constituted a social sphere of production and exchange.

A brief comparison with France and the Netherlands makes the point about deficient resources and the relationship to developing institutional orders. French rulers had faced a painful lack of resources since at least the Hundred Years' War (1328–1453). In desperation King John II called the Estates-General in 1356 to ask for taxes to fight England. Seizing the opportunity, the Estates-General demanded a measure of control over royal use of taxes and allocated monies, sought supervisory roles, and also demanded regular meetings of the Estates-General. John relented, but emboldened by his decision, several members of the Estates-General steered the body toward open revolt against the Crown. By 1360 the future Charles V reestablished royal authority and crushed the opposition. Several years later he exacted from the Estates-General a nearly perpetual right of taxation, thus permanently wresting control of French national finances from the legislative body and into the embrace of the royal treasury. Not for another 400 years would France see a representative assembly. Thus, in France the Hundred Years' War confirmed royal absolutism.

By the seventeenth century, French national finances were administered by royal agents. The duke of Sully diligently managed finances under Henry IV. The national treasury had been depleted by civil wars, painful loans, and gifts to nobles in exchange for their compliance. Sully promoted industry and advanced agriculture to such a degree that the treasury showed a surplus by Henry's assassination in 1610. It was so quickly squandered by the successor that the Estates-General was hastily convened in 1614. Petty bickering reduced the body to uselessness, and it was quickly abandoned, not to be called again until 1789.

Cardinal Richelieu, the power behind the weak midcentury monarchs, and his protégé and successor, Cardinal Mazarin, each poorly administered French finances. Each also vigorously supported royal absolutism. Richelieu effectively abolished or crushed wide-ranging (property) rights, especially political and military privileges. The Huguenots in particular were persecuted as a symbol of the futility of resisting royal authority. Yet Richelieu did introduce elements of an institutional-legal order by inaugurating a system of civil servants called *intendants* to administer select provincial affairs. Mazarin maintained this system, often by using violence, as when he confronted in 1649 and 1650 the two open revolts against absolutism.

In 1661 Colbert, the finance minister for Louis XIV, inherited from Mazarin and earlier monarchs a national debt equal to 50 percent of annual revenue. As a reformer, he eliminated corruption, reduced expenditures, and increased revenues. Indeed, by 1667 his mercantilist policies showed a stunning surplus, as noted above. His tariff policies effectively excluded all imports into France. In 1664 he introduced a Dutch model of international commerce by founding two large joint-stock companies. However, his successes were rapidly squandered by the opulence and excess of Louis XIV's personal lifestyle and the extravagance of his foreign wars.

In short, lacking an effective institutional balance against absolutist royal authority, French monarchs could retract or abolish citizens' political, religious, and property rights, though they could upon royal sufferance retain limited civil rights. Thus, property rights remained a central issue, but they were not extended so much as restricted. Royal prerogative was little checked, so fiscal insolvency followed profligate spending. By late in the century, as initiatives by Richelieu and Colbert illustrate, even the French monarchy was compelled to consider innovations in administration and commerce to strive to create an institutional-legal order that could govern, promote prosperity, and compete abroad.

The Dutch encountered different circumstances. Since the fifteenth century, the Netherlands had been a set of separate provinces, each with its own laws, administration, Estates-General, and governor. Although a comprehensive States-General had existed since before 1500, it held only limited power. Rather, the Netherlands functioned as a loose confederation. In the early 1500s, Charles V introduced elements of an institutional-legal order to administer select activities such as police and justice, but he did not severely limit the independence of the provinces. He also created a Council of State to administer specific matters affecting military affairs and policies with neighboring kingdoms. Most important, however, Dutch institutions and prosperity arose dramatically during the long revolt against Spanish rule, beginning in 1566. By 1579 the seven northern provinces united under the Union of Utrecht, a document that effectively served as the Dutch constitution. Two years later they declared their independence from Spain, saw it recognized in 1609, and formalized in 1648.

The Dutch political situation was unique, since they consistently rebelled against royal absolutism and governed themselves in more local than imperial fashion. Remarkably similar to the Swiss confederation, the Netherlands firmly advanced provincial rights. The Dutch consistently sought to extend property, civil, and other rights to citizens and entrepreneurs because their livelihoods depended so fundamentally upon doing so. Three factors balanced Dutch structural inefficiencies. First, the political prominence of the province of Holland gave it clear leadership in the national States-General, thereby avoiding an ineffectual or incapacitated body. Second, the revered status of the princes of the House of Orange gave the Dutch republic de facto national leaders. Third, lacking natural resources, the Dutch national republic and its provincial republics were necessarily commercial entities. Indeed, they were impressively wealthy entities. Property rights were already extensive; commerce reigned; an institutional order existed but required more formal unification in order to compete effectively with other countries and their merchants.

Dutch and Spanish recognition of mobile property is traceable to as early as 1569. In that year the duke of Alva, the head of the Spanish force sent to the Netherlands to end the original revolt, enacted a staggering tax to pay for his campaigns. Doing so, he distinguished real from mobile property. He imposed a 1 percent tax on all real and personal property and a 5 percent tax on the sale of all land. He also imposed a 10 percent tax on the sale of all movable goods, which meant, of course, all tangible trade-able commodities. Nonetheless, the conceptual distinction is evident; mobile property was recognized. The tax was so onerous that it sparked widespread opposition and violent reaction. By 1573 Alva relented and was replaced, but by then he had galvanized the Dutch into nominal unity and a long campaign for independence.

However, rather than form a unified government to overcome the difficulties of confederation, Dutch leaders preferred instead to promote commerce. They created in 1602 the Dutch East India Company. The company, receiving a monopoly grant from the States-General, functioned as the Dutch government in the Indian and Pacific Oceans and served as an institutional source for unified commercial policy. Since commercial policy dominated foreign concerns, this arrangement worked quite well. Until the Peace of Westphalia in 1648, Dutch commerce overwhelmed its European rivals by employing familiar administrative and organizational features: Property rights, a stable institutional order for effective governance, and the inextricable character of statecraft and commerce.

The English situation is comparable. As in France, the English king had to call Parliament to ask for funds and taxes to meet expenses incurred during the Hundred Years' War. Indeed, Edward III (1327–1377) called Parliament forty-eight times during his fifty-year reign. Edward exchanged royal concessions to Parliament for needed funds. Over time, royal concessions became privileges held by Parliament. These concessions then acquired the character of rights possessed by Parliament and embodied in the customary, ancient law. By 1399 Parliament was the principal source of law. For centuries after, English monarchs dueled Parliament for authority and finances. By the 1600s English rulers had for several centuries been financially strapped and often insolvent.

Attempts by the English government to generate revenue in the seventeenth century included coercing heavy loans from citizens (e.g., Kenyon, 1978:37–41); borrowing from foreign individuals, governments, and enterprises (Clay, 1984b:269–281); and imposing more and heavier taxes (Wilson, 1977:134). Perhaps the most significant innovation was to employ the resources of joint-stock companies, "one of the most important inventions in business organization of all time" (Clough, 1959:152; similarly, Scott, 1912/1968a:v):

> I weigh my words when I say that in my judgment the limited liability corporation is the greatest single discovery of modern times, whether you judge it by its social, by its ethical, by its industrial, or, in the long run,— after we understand it and how to use it,—by its political effects. Even steam and electricity are far less important than the limited liability corporation, and they would be reduced to comparative impotence without it. (N. M. Butler, quoted in Freedeman, 1979:xiii)[3]

Joint-stock companies, the precursors of modern corporations and multinational enterprises, were the largest commercial or economic enterprises in existence. In an era of small family businesses, the joint-stock companies dominated and transformed the social landscape. They possessed a distinct legal personality that made them independent of the persons who owned or managed them, their permanence transcending the lives of individuals and family enterprises. Their size dwarfed any private entities for production or trade. Indeed, their size and influence outweighed many countries and monarchs (de Vries, 1976:131–132). The unique character of joint-stock companies as corporations—as nearly corporeal entities—gave them a legal standing that made it possible for them to accumulate capital on a vast scale. Merchants created joint-stock companies to marshal capital for savings and investment. Such capital bolstered national governments and financed state-building, infrastructure development, warfare, and expansionist foreign policies (see Nef, 1934; J. H. Parry, 1966:88–90 and *passim;* de Vries, 1976:131–143; Wilson, 1977:135–138; Hadden, 1979:110; Cipolla, 1980:ch. 7; Clay, 1984b:74–82, 182–212). Corporate investments also financed massive projects like digging canals, laying railway track, building sailing ships and steamships, and producing goods in factories. The Dutch created a commercial republic from such companies, but the English created formidable corporations and a stable, centralized government. These features were essentially indistinguishable. The resulting English institutional order eclipsed the Dutch and outpaced the French.

English monarchs encouraged, used, and participated in joint-stock companies to achieve personal and national ends they could not attain alone. Indeed, the development of corporations from partnerships parallels the development of depersonalized government from personal rule: Each represents the development of perpetual or continual existence (and administration) apart from that of members and personalities (see Hunt, 1986:3; Holdsworth, 1922–1926, vol. 8:203). Joint-stock companies were "quasi-public institutions" (Freedeman, 1979:4) that complemented and completed the institutional-legal order.

Thus, a brief examination of joint-stock companies completes a look at the institutional nexus of law, governance, and production/trade.

Acquiring Property Rights and Authority

The history of joint-stock companies is inseparable from the rise of commerce and modern government. Such a history traces the unusual though indispensable relations between corporations and the government (Scott, 1912/1968a:440). The Crown solicited, promoted, and often created large companies in order to address chronic destitution.[4] Commercial and financial leaders saw the benefits of a stable institutional arrangement and pried property rights advantages from the Crown. These were almost always exclusive, monopolistic rights stipulated by royal grants or charters.

While companies with similar features existed as early as 1485 (Hannay, 1926:3), joint-stock companies rose to prominence in England, Spain (Fehrenbach, 1968:19–20), and the Netherlands at the same historical moment in the early sixteenth century. French joint-stock companies arose in the 1660s. By the 1550s wealthy merchants in England had organized large and socially significant joint-stock companies that immediately became a means for mustering funds for maritime expansion and colonizing. Then, from about the time of the Protectorate to the Glorious Revolution, they provided the means for extending and securing shipping trade sites and routes. From 1550 to 1690, "the progress of the joint stock companies is inseparably connected with British naval and maritime progress" (Scott, 1912/1968a:440). By pooling available capital and extending credit, joint-stock companies also became the instrument for corporate and national capital accumulation (Hadden, 1979:110).

Since the medieval era, commodities and specie had dominated economic relations, therefore little money circulated. Consequently, extracting and storing bullion were important Crown activities that influenced the conduct of foreign policy and the health of production and trade. This is the material basis for mercantile practices. Yet, as noted, lack of funds and crushing debts had crippled English rulers—indeed European rulers generally—since the late medieval ages and earlier. However, by the 1500s, and especially by the Thirty Years' War, dynastic and religious controversies engulfed most European rulers. To defend themselves and exercise influence over others, rulers became more concerned with extracting resources from their citizens and territories (North and Thomas, 1973; North, 1981). Joint-stock companies proved remarkably effective. From William's reign until about 1720, joint-stock companies helped the Crown accumulate capital. One method was to expand greatly the pool of available credit, since only joint-stock companies had the institutional and material resources to do so (Scott, 1912/1968a:441, 462).

Merchants recognized that privileges dispensed by the Crown could valuably help collect and employ their capital. The Crown, however, enticed or pressed merchants and joint-stock companies to perform tasks that the Crown wanted done but could not perform itself. Thus, the Crown extended property rights and other advantages to the companies to give corporate directors incentives to act on behalf of the ruler's interests. The Crown granted monopolies, patents, charters, and other benefits, including exclusive licenses to trade or restrict trade, copyrights, privileges in manufacturing, and immunities or reductions on tax or customs duties (Scott, 1912/1968a:105–128; Hannay, 1926). In short, the Crown extended property rights on the condition that the joint-stock company abide by legal, contractual obligations to perform duties or services. In each instance, however, the Crown sought to extend sufficient property rights advantages to make the investment risk acceptable. By relying on the long-standing legal principle that rulers cannot derogate from contracts they create, monarchs make themselves attractive partners. Said differently, the Crown had to address the opportunity costs of alternative ventures the joint-stock company might undertake.

As I note below, while the returns on joint-stock ventures could be extraordinary, the costs for long-distance trade and colonizing were similarly enormous. Two examples illustrate why entrepreneurs and investors thrilled at compensatory advantages from the Crown. Company directors from the English East India Company financed its initial voyage by selling shares totaling £68,000. Yet by the third voyage, manned shortly after 1600, the cost rose dramatically to £1.63 million (Clough, 1959:153). This figure exceeds the total annual revenue of the English economy in each year of the Commonwealth (1654–1658) except one (Wilson, 1977:132, table 5.22). Also, in the early years of operation, the East India Company lost one-quarter of all ships it sent to sea (Clough, 1959:149). Similarly costly were voyages by the Dutch East India Company: Over the company's history, only one-third of all sailors who began the five-year voyages to Asia survived to return to Europe.[5]

While the Crown entered into innumerable relationships with a wide variety of companies and individuals, the bewildering diversity of these practices is nonetheless coherent because in each instance the ruler transferred property rights. Moreover, in addition to granting property rights, the Crown granted authority. Corporate governorship acquired many of the characteristics of civil government. Indeed, corporations became essential elements of the institutional-legal order (Scott, 1912/1968b:38).

> In brief, in return for a trade monopoly, the Company was given the task of performing all the acts of government in those regions under its jurisdiction . . . the right to exercise in this region all the privileges, prerogatives, and powers usually held by sovereign states—to seize and defend territories within its sphere of action, to make peace, to levy taxes, to administer justice, and to make local laws. (Clough, 1959:153)

Corporate officials also received the power to arrest debtors, to seize the property (and split it with the Crown) of grant violators, to take possession of unclaimed territories in the name of the Crown, and to extend their grants to those lands "not commonly frequented" by Englishmen (Scott, 1912/1968b:38). Dutch and French joint-stock companies enjoyed similar grants of privilege from their rulers (Ergang, 1954:304–306, 464–465).

Company directors and stockholders reaped enormous rewards, but they confronted other obligations as well. Defending monopoly claims was expensive, administrative costs were high, and waging war entailed heavy losses of men and materiel. English investors were well aware of the agonies of the Spanish and Portuguese attempts to defend their long-distance trade routes, because pirates and English privateers had dealt crippling blows (Thomson, 1994). Consequently, joint-stock company directors petitioned the Crown for greater authority and more extensive property rights transfers. All actors saw the prospects for mutually advantageous practices.

The Crown extended such property rights and granted privileges primarily to induce companies to act on behalf of foreign policy interests and to meet needs for national infrastructure, domestic consumption, or the national interest. Through joint-stock companies, English monarchs confronted foreign rivals and domestic needs. For example, the Crown might grant privileges in exporting, importing, producing certain commodities, or conducting these activities in particular locations. The Crown might also grant property rights to extensive land claims or mineral deposits. Two examples among countless include the tobacco monopoly granted by charter to the Virginia Company and the monopoly proprietorship extended to seven noblemen for what would become Fairfax County, Virginia (Scott, 1912/1968a:121; Netherton et al., 1978). Similar monopoly land grants by the Spanish government set the legal and material basis for Latin American *encomiendas*. In exchange for offering attractive grants or property rights as incentives, the Crown attained desired goals and acquired revenue by taxing the imports, production, and/or consumption of the goods. To specific merchants the advantages of joint-stock ownership were obvious. While no individual would undertake full entrepreneurial liability, a group of individuals acting in concert could provide the required funds and minimize individual risk by forming a corporation (Scott, 1912/1968a:461). Moreover, by these efficiencies, joint-stock companies were effective economic and political vehicles likely to attract royal favor.[6]

Joint-Stock Companies and Foreign Policy

Two of the first such companies—the Guinea (later Africa) Company and the Russia Company, both founded in 1553—directly served the Crown. The Russia Company was to open diplomatic and commercial relations with the czar; the Guinea Company was to outflank and impede Portuguese and Spanish trade in Africa to open the way for English slavers. In exchange, the companies received special dispensations from the Crown. For example, the Russia Company received a grant of monopoly from Queen Elizabeth for all imports into Russia and all exports from Russia into England. The Crown taxed the imports to earn revenue, but the profits of sale accrued solely to the company investors. Also, the Russia Company could import goods necessary to English shipbuilding, such as timber for masts and planking and pitch for sealant, with lower customs duties (Scott, 1912/1968b:37–40).

In the 1580s, as a matter of public policy and financial investment, the Crown backed privateering raids against Spanish shipping, especially in hopes of commandeering bullion from the New World. The returns could be astronomical. From an initial outlay of approximately £5,000, Francis Drake captured bullion estimated at between £1.5 million and £1.75 million (Scott, 1912/1968a:446). Out of this total, each of the five investing adventurers received about £250,000—a profit of approximately 4,600 percent—while the Crown collected about £300,000 in untaxed bullion. The Crown used this profit to handle pressing obligations and to assist the Netherlands against the Spanish and French. Given the success of these raids, the Crown provided considerable financing for other privateering excursions, often acting as one of the principal backers. In the twenty-six years from 1558 to 1584, privateering tripled the wealth circulating in England, much of it going to the Crown (Scott, 1912/1968a:84, citing the treasurer of the navy, 1584).

To challenge rival European powers, other companies colonized and cultivated abroad and established or enhanced foreign trade (Scott, 1912/1968b).

Joint-Stock Companies and Domestic Needs

The Crown similarly granted charters, patents, monopolies, and other bene-fits to companies to entice them to enhance England's national production and infrastructure. Such companies constructed and maintained aqueducts; built bridges; erected and maintained streetlights; constructed metalworks; delivered mail; made paper, linen, wool, silk, other cloth, soap, glass, and porcelain; formed banks and insurance houses; and conducted other activi-ties (Scott, 1912/1968c; Hadden, 1979:110). The Crown chartered mining operations, notably the Mineral and Battery Works, to mine ore and fashion it into ship cannon for the navy. The company also made metal-teethed fiber cards for combing and drawing cotton fiber for the linen trade (Scott, 1912/1968a:440; 1912/1968b). The Mineral and Battery Works delivered to the Crown one-tenth of all desirable metal it mined; the Crown further reserved the right to purchase all the gold, silver, and copper it wanted at slightly below market price (Scott, 1912/1968b:384). This provision little concerned company directors, however, since the Crown had few funds for such purposes.

In a notable case brought by a grant recipient, the Court of Exchequer held in 1566 that all gold and silver mines within the realm, even those pre-dominantly but not entirely of gold and silver, belonged to the Crown (Scott, 1912/1968b:386). This ruling is significant for two reasons. First, it illustrates that the property rights were held by the Crown and extended to grant recipients at the sufferance of the Crown, unless otherwise stipulated in the legal documentation of the charter, grant, or contract. Second, it holds that all mines within the realm—that is, within all territories falling under royal jurisdiction—were owned by the Crown. Similarly, land grants in North America often transferred all rights and property to the recipients, except those trees suitable for mastheads (to fell these was to risk death). This suggests the range of sovereign authority and royal property rights: Dominion was as extensive as it was intensive.

Joint-Stock Companies and National Finances

Government officials, ministers, and the monarch often participated as principals in joint-stock companies. In one instance concerning the African trade, Queen Elizabeth participated as an individual, not as monarch. She provided four ships and several hundred pounds sterling for provisions and was then due a proportion of the surplus over expenses commensurate with her investment (Scott, 1912/1968b:4–6). Additionally, Queen Elizabeth was a major individual shareholder in the company organized to finance Francis Drake's privateering. One story holds that the queen, excited about the enormous profit on her investment, knighted him immediately upon his return (Clough, 1959:152, note 10).

Similarly, James I offered to participate in the East India Company in 1624 by sending out company ships under the royal flag. For this participation, he expected a principal's share, yet the company directors coyly protested that such an arrangement made James a partner, and no citizen could be an *equal* partner with the *supreme* sovereign (Nenner, 1977:55). Charles I held shares in the Africa Company, and James II held stock in the East India Company. James II also personally founded a joint-stock company to engage in trade in Africa. In many other instances, English monarchs extended royal protection in exchange for personal reward (Scott, 1912/1968a:321, 1912/1968b:13, 109–110, 149).

One reason for monarchs' personal involvement in joint-stock companies was the sorry state of national and royal revenues. Extending property rights advantages greatly spurred trade and generally improved Crown finances, both directly and indirectly. Participation by the monarch or the government in a successful venture earned often grand rewards. Even without direct participation, the Crown earned tax income on most imports and sales. The enormous success of most enterprises contributed substantial sums. For example, between 1609 and 1613 the annual profit for the East India Company fluctuated between 121 percent and 234 percent. From 1608 to 1615, the Russia Company distributed 339 percent; in 1613 and 1614, it paid annual dividends of 90 percent (Scott, 1912/1968a:141, 145–146). Similarly, the Dutch East India Company earned such vast returns that for almost 200 years it paid annual dividends ranging from 12.5 percent to 50 percent (Ergang, 1954:305). Conversely, the French companies conducting trade in the East Indies were so poorly managed that they lasted fewer than twenty years before failing in the early 1680s (Ergang, 1954:465).

Taxation was often onerous since financial circumstances were grave. However, merchants could pass on the costs of taxes and other obligations to consumers. For example, in 1635 the Crown exacted £80,000 in obligations from a particular group of traders. In order to pay this obligation, the merchants increased the price of the imported goods and earned additional profits of between £200,000 and £300,000 (Scott, 1912/1968a:208–210). The Crown earned revenue and the merchants made profits, but consumers were squeezed.

While the Crown sought to extract advantage at every opportunity, it consistently incurred budget deficits. As mentioned earlier, chronic financial crises dated back to at least the Hundred Years' War (1328–1453) and especially since Henry VIII's reign (1509–1547). The deficits became especially pronounced in the late seventeenth century, when the demands upon the Crown, then government, grew dramatically. The government ran a consistent deficit from 1688 to 1815 (Wilson, 1977:132, esp. table 5.21). The French monarchy suffered similarly crushing deficits. Over the same period, English merchants earned handsome profits. By about 1680 some joint-stock company directors were forming small banks to loan money to other joint-stock enterprises. They were especially eager to lend to well-established ventures. Thus, credit circulated rather freely and routinely among joint-stock companies. The East India Company could borrow at 3 percent, for example, yet the English Crown often had to pay upwards of 10 percent, and in the 1660s the French Crown accepted loans at 25 percent interest. With their accumulated surplus, merchants also began to develop other ventures, such as insurance companies (Scott, 1912/1968a:299).

By the 1690s financiers and merchants were forming an enormous number and range of joint-stock companies. In the seven years following James II's flight from England in 1688, approximately 85 percent of the 150 existing joint-stock companies were established (Scott, 1912/1968a:327–328). Much of this activity may have been sparked by a celebrated company that in 1688 returned profits to its investors of about 10,000 percent (Scott, 1912/1968a:326). Of the total estimated capital of £4.25 million of these joint-stock companies, a full 50 percent was controlled by three huge firms: the East India Company, the Africa Company, and Hudson's Bay Company (Wilson, 1977:136). Of similar scope and influence was the Dutch East India Company, which by the late seventeenth century was employing 12,000 full-time workers (de Vries, 1976:132). In its two centuries in operation, the Dutch company sent more than 1 million sailors to Asia (de Vries, 1976:131).

By the 1690s European actors had nearly completed constructing a discernibly modern world. More indicative, the English institutional order and English society were poised to take advantage of war with France, a war best understood in systemic terms. By 1690 many English joint-stock company directors hoped to profit from the war with France by providing stocks, munitions, and loans to the government. At the same time, the Crown was directing joint-stock operations to develop a national infrastructure to stabilize and secure the institutional-legal order, to compete more efficiently with France, and to outstrip the Dutch.

CAPITALIST AGENTS: BANKERS

This section examines the ties between the English government and the Bank of England to illustrate practices blending policymaking and entrepreneurship. Without a better accounting of finances, banking, and fiscal-monetary policy (e.g., Ardant, 1975; Braun, 1975), the union of statecraft and capitalism may appear suspect. Credit more so than money made production and exchange liquid and dynamic. Credit also strengthened the institutional order and the fledgling state. Indeed, credit's intangible quality as property was decisive.

The English institutional-legal order was inefficient. Traditional forms of command and authority often obstructed burgeoning market relations, and traditional exercise of royal prerogative led to abuses of power. In contrast, distributing property rights to joint-stock companies was attractive, efficient, manageable, and palatable. Nevertheless, finances largely eluded governmental control. In despair, the Crown often levied the most easily enforceable and collectible taxes it could enact; citizens endured customs duties and consumption taxes because tax collectors could monitor trading ports, stores, pubs, and inns with relatively little difficulty. However, revenue remained fairly consistent because inefficient tax collection posed a continuing problem.

One measure of the Crown's frustration was its effort to collect taxes in kind or in valued commodities. While this assured collecting consistently high value, commodities are not liquid and so are not easily exchanged for other valued goods. Alternatively, the government could collect taxes in bullion or currency, but bullion was scarce. Currencies, bank notes, and bills were uncommon and had notoriously unstable value. Indeed, few bank notes or currencies actually circulated. Those that did were issued from many sources (Keynes, 1953a:14–16; Lewy, 1975:163). Not until the eighteenth century did practices constitute anything approaching a national economy in either England or France. Keynes (1953a:16) dates the appearance in England of a uniform monetary standard at 1844. If, as Keynes believed, commodity money dominated throughout the eighteenth century, then it was certainly so in the 1690s, when taxes were typically collected in commodity coins. People value commodity coins for their content, such as the gold and silver in the coins, rather than for their denominated value. Two vestiges of commodity coins in the United States, dating from the colonial era, remain in popular speech: The expression "pieces of eight" and the counting meter "two bits, four bits, six bits, a dollar." U.S. citizens frequently sliced Spanish silver dollar coins into eight wedge-shaped pieces to use for exchange because they distrusted unbacked state or local currency and the demeaned value of British coins. Thus, a quarter coin is still often called "two bits."

Under William, the English government issued new silver coins but encountered an old problem. Individuals shaved away slivers of the coins, thus devaluing them, or hoarded the coins to retain the value of the silver, not the denomination—a recurring fate of commodity money. The debased coins illustrate Gresham's law that bad money drives out good. Over a century earlier, Sir Thomas Gresham (1519–1579), Queen Elizabeth's financial expert, was empowered to help relieve the Crown's chronic financial despair. He was reduced to "forcing merchants to lend to the crown by methods that were akin to holdups" (Schumpeter, 1954:342, note 4). One pressing problem he confronted was the lack of circulating money to lend as individuals hoarded commodity money. Thus, "bad money"—that is, money containing lesser-quality metal, debased metal, or more generally, money of lesser reliability—is used for exchange and payments, and good money disappears from circulation (Schumpeter, 1954:343; Clough, 1959:105, note 1). Over time the debased coins become worth less than their denominated value, thus fueling inflation. For example, if the government levies taxes in coins, then the higher the taxes, the greater the incentive to debase. Thus, the government can purchase fewer goods with its revenues. If the government raises tax and customs rates to enhance purchasing power, then the population further debases the coins.

The clear alternative is to issue fiat currency such as paper bills or notes, which are virtually costless to produce and possess no intrinsic value yet serve as markers of value and as mediums of exchange. In contemporary terms, fiat currencies are unbacked monies, meaning that they are not necessarily tied to any standard, typically gold, silver, and/or securities. This was not the exact case in the 1690s, but English officials were devising instruments with similar characteristics. They sought to issue notes with high exchange (face) values and negligible production costs.

Parliament achieved this in 1694 when it granted a charter to a group of financiers in exchange for a loan to the government of £1.2 million at 8 percent interest. The charter extended to the financiers the property rights to accept deposits, trade in bullion and other precious metals, transfer funds, and issue bank notes. Upon these terms the merchants formed the Bank of England. It could issue notes up to a total of £14 million by holding first-class securities as backing. To issue notes in excess of this total, the bank had to hold an equivalent sum of bullion. These rules limited the supply of paper money in circulation (Clough, 1959:193, 356). Yet the limit was unrestrictive since, according to Wilson (1977:131, table 5.20), the entire national debt in 1697 was £14.5 million. The sum of £14 million also represents 42.8 percent of the total income of the Crown from 1688 through 1697 (Wilson, 1977:132, table 5.21). In short, Parliament extended to the directors of the Bank of England the right to cover the national debt! Yet individuals had no reason to regard the bank notes as valuable unless they expected other actors as well to regard the instruments favorably. This raises questions about individuals' faith in what backs the notes. Monetary theorists argue that faith in money depends upon faith that the issuer will not induce inflation by issuing more notes, thereby demeaning their value. In other words, individuals must remain confident that the issuer will preserve the value of the notes.

This is the tragedy of the original French central bank and a telling contrast between British and French institutional innovation. The French bank was established in 1716 upon principles much like those for the Bank of England. Yet the Law Bank (named after its Scot founder, John Law) issued an enormous volume of bank notes and invested in speculative enterprises. By 1720 it had issued almost 2.7 *billion* livres worth of notes, a tragic case of overissue (Clough, 1959:194).

The bank was insecure in other ways. In 1718 the Law Bank ceased being a joint-stock bank. The king became the sole shareholder and directed it to make heavy investments in government securities. He then discovered that only one-fourth of the bank's initial capitalization had been paid in; the rest of its capital comprised weak and dubious government bonds. To attract revenue and secure capital, the bank extended large loans to trading and colonizing companies, especially to the Mississippi Company. Yet in a monumentally scandalous turn, the Mississippi Company was founded and directed by John Law. When the trading company failed to earn, the value of shares in both the Law Bank and the Mississippi Company plummeted. As people rapidly lost confidence in the bank's notes, both institutions collapsed. France was financially crippled for several generations. Only in 1776 was another central bank established in France, though it was greatly restricted. However, it collapsed in the revolution thirteen years later (Clough, 1959:193–194). By the 1780s, French banking and commercial institutions were eighty years behind the English and 175 years behind the Dutch.

While such concerns are significant, two others may have been equally important to actors in the late seventeenth century: That the issuing authority remain both stable and unconquered. These tangible fears unnerved English citizens, who had already experienced chronic financial crises, civil war, and invasion attempts. On the Continent the ravages of the Thirty Years' War raised other grave fears.

Leaders in several countries were drawing similar conclusions. Since only a *national* currency can satisfy the monetary demands for security, stability, exchange value, and circulation, then a stable, secure institutional-legal order becomes valuable. Thus, the national government must eliminate local currencies and limited-issue notes. However, to create a national fiat currency, the government must ascribe monopoly rights to the issuer of the currency, else there is no assurance that individuals will value the fiat money. If individuals refuse to use the fiat currency, the government loses its ability to raise revenues by creating money. As should be clear, only a strong central government can issue and back a currency, circulate it nationally, and eliminate local notes.[7]

English actors created an embryonic national currency in the 1690s. The Bank of England was not technically a central bank in the modern sense, but it performed some of the same functions. In particular, it held a monopoly property right to issue bank notes. Issuing a national currency is advantageous to the national government because it provides another means for extracting resources. This is called seigniorage. It arises from acts of arbitrage: With government-issued currency the government can always extract resources from society at *virtually no cost* simply by printing more money and acquiring resources with it (e.g., Fisher, 1911/1931; Keynes, 1953a,b). The government spends little to print money, but it immediately acquires goods. The central bank (or issuing authority) always has arbitrage opportunities. Recall that the Bank of England was unrestrictively limited to circulating no more than £14 million worth of notes. Alternatively, the government could float debt by selling bonds, but the government would have to pay a positive nominal interest rate; it pays no interest when it issues money. However, the option to float debt was essentially unavailable to the English government in this era because it was already crippled by outstanding debt. To attract buyers, the government would therefore have to pay a hearty interest rate. Yet many investors thought the government unlikely or unwilling to honor even its existing debt obligations (Kenyon, 1978:284).

The government had few options for extracting resources. Parliament had amputated royal prerogative. Direct taxation was inefficient. English officials and merchants jointly recognized the many advantages of seigniorage (the revenue earned from arbitrage) over direct taxation. Under similarly bankrupt and war-torn circumstances, Louis XIV of France resorted to brutal direct taxation by heavily armed brigades called *démons déchainez* ("unchained devils") (Bonney, 1978:214–215, and chs. 9 and 10). As a less repressive alternative, exercising arbitrage options and issuing currency were reasonable, thoughtful policy choices, but they required a secure institutional-legal order as a prerequisite.[8]

Neither law nor arbitrage offered advantages in the competition among European powers. Conquest and expanding commerce provided the best means for extracting resources. Colonies were especially valuable because they were subject to three extractive options: Legal coercion, financial manipulation, and military pressure. English actors, by establishing a unique institutional-legal order and by exchanging property rights, established a foundation for competitive success. The establishment and maintenance of this institutional-legal order required the related contributions of a market society, commerce, and banking. Influential actors similarly constructed the British Empire. Joint-stock companies provided the capital and credit necessary for trade, colonizing, and empire-building. With its vast colonial empire, the English state could extract valuable resources relatively easily.

Across the globe, England modeled, dispersed, and imposed these coherent practices. These relations help constitute the modern world, a world born in part of practices understandable in terms of property and property rights.

SYMBIOSIS

In the seventeenth century, prominent actors realized that governmental success was necessarily a function of commercial success. The national institutional order administered, arbitrated, and organized social life, yet institutional stability depended considerably upon the success of corporations. Commercial enterprises contributed resources, revenue, and credit that national agents required to perform their responsibilities. Further, commercial activities contributed directly to foreign policy. Commercial agents often performed tasks on behalf of the government. Indeed, joint-stock companies acted as quasi governments or governmental agencies.

In turn, corporate directors and stockholders realized that commercial success depended to a significant degree upon the stability and success of the institutional-legal order. An unstable government or unchecked authority could interfere with commerce in untold ways. For example, nearly unchecked royal authority in France consistently undermined potential advances in production, trade, and banking. In the Netherlands the loose confederal system worked admirably while Europe's powers struggled with one another, but once they turned their sights on Dutch commercial power, the Dutch republic was no match in military or, ultimately, commercial terms. A strong and relatively secure government in England, by contrast, distributed resources and advantage, enforced contracts, and achieved a measure of domestic prosperity and systemic security. Foreign concerns also affected the development of the newly constituted government: Warfare, threats of invasion, intrigue, interrupted trade, privateering, tariffs, and the like directly influenced not only production and exchange but also the stability of the institutional order.

William Scott's reports, *The Constitution and Finance of English, Scottish, and Irish Joint-Stock Companies* (1912/1968a,b,c), illustrate how commerce deteriorated when public authorities were uncertain or insecure, whether from financial or political concerns. A few enterprises enjoyed enormous good fortune, however, after receiving property rights transfers from the Crown and then taking commensurate risks. When commercial ventures were unsuccessful, the Crown endured hardships as well.

Joint-stock companies played central roles in conducting war, conquering and colonizing, developing and stabilizing national institutions, promoting national production and trade, accumulating and circulating capital, and fostering international trade. By shielding individual investors from excessive risk, joint-stock companies offered wealthy individuals a way to reap rich reward. Property rights grants from the Crown offered the prospect of tremendous fortune. Thus, de Vries (1976:133–134; emphasis added) writes that the

> formation of joint stock companies enjoying a trade monopoly in some part of the world may have been necessary to mobilize the resources required for highly speculative trade in distant places. But it is unlikely that they would have arisen from the competitive, small-scale trading structure that characterized most European trades had it not been for the *intervention of the state.*

Governmental actors intervened in great measure by dispersing and specifying property rights. Scott (1912/1968a:456–457; emphasis added) writes that only "joint-stock companies *with far-reaching privileges*" could have conducted special foreign trade, if it was to occur at all. Having received property rights privileges, joint-stock companies provided individual investors and the Crown with several advantages. While some individuals were earning vast wealth, national advantages were accruing through rising commodity imports, corporate contributions to national revenue, and developing national industries. Each of these advantages improved England's competitiveness with European rivals. No wonder, then, that "*all the leading European countries* [or rulers or governments] agreed in carrying on certain branches of foreign commerce by means of joint-stocks" (Scott, 1912/1968a:455, note 4; see also Beik, 1985:289–290). This is Macpherson's market society at work in the international system.

Many seventeenth-century citizens invoked the vocabulary of rights and liberties to assail the consequences of the far-reaching privileges enjoyed by joint-stock companies and other grant recipients. The centralization of wealth and influence was a common target. For example, Sir Edwin Sandys declares in *Instructions Touching the Bill for Free Trade* of 1604 that comprehensive property rights grants lead to monopolies, concentrated wealth, and violations of natural rights. He levels his condemnation in the familiar vocabulary of property, property rights, burgeoning market society, and reconstituted social relations:

> All free subjects are born inheritable as to their land, as also to the free exercise of their industry, in those trades whereto they apply themselves and whereby they are to live. Merchandize, being the chiefest and richest of all other and of greater extent and importance than all the rest, it is against the natural right and liberty of the subjects of England to restrain it into the hands of some few; . . . yet, apparent it is, that the governors of these companies, by their monopolizing orders, have so handled the matter, as that the mass of the whole trade of the realm is in the hands of some

200 persons at the most, the rest serving for a shew and reaping small benefit. (Scott, 1912/1968a:120, quoting Sandys)

The "small benefit" for England—by 1604 not yet anticipated, much less attained—ultimately included liberalism, globally dominant trade and production, and global hegemony. The histories of the Africa Company, the East India Company, the Greenland Company, Hudson's Bay Company, the Kathai (Cathay) Company, the Levant Company, the Massachusetts Bay Company, the Merchant Adventurers (privateers), the Mineral and Battery Works, the plantation companies, the Russia Company, the South Sea Company, the Bank of England, and other organizations collectively make up the history of England's rise to commercial, colonial, and political dominance. These enterprises mark the transition from England's medieval circumstances and religious preoccupations to its early modern status as a stable state and global hegemonic power directing the global capitalist economy and serving as the engine for its expansion. That both England and France sought to follow the Dutch lead in organizing joint-stock companies illustrates the widespread appeal of this innovation. That joint-stock companies arose to augment or function as governmental institutions illustrates the broader notion of singular, coherent worldviews in the years approaching 1700.

By 1700 policymakers and merchants had constituted a union of statecraft and capitalist practices. Actors conceived these as a unity, but to constitute the unity they also constituted a pair of conceptual crosshairs that dominate the modern worldview and practices. Thus, seventeenth-century actors constructed a relatively efficient institutional-legal-economic order bound by the practices and relations of property rights. Actors worked to transform far-flung colonies into empires. English rulers and merchants had already battled and then allied with their foremost seventeenth-century rival, the Dutch. Less than a century later, by 1763 and the conclusion of the Seven Years' War, English forces had defeated the French; English rulers dominated the global capitalist economy. Such success almost immediately fostered the Industrial Revolution and England's truly global hegemony. By the mid-1800s, "the sun never set on the British Empire" and England was the "workshop of the world."

CONCLUSION

I make the simple claim that institutional-legal orders and market society form an inextricable union. Actors forged this union in the fires of European great power competition and domestic turmoil. These institutional-legal orders ultimately became states. To function effectively, these protostates needed specific goods, services, and finances. To acquire them and to stabilize nascent institutions, policymakers granted property rights to merchants. Some grants actually duplicated the rights and responsibilities of governments. With these incentives and possessions, merchants engaged in wider trade, introduced more and varied goods into the national economy, paid greater taxes, and contributed to institutional stability and economic liquidity.

Merchants required the official sanction and necessary resources to better conduct their affairs. Without property rights grants, most merchants lacked incentive to undertake many risky enterprises. Yet without stable government, merchants could not depend upon the continued viability of corporate and commercial law. By encouraging and promoting a national government, merchants expected to enjoy future benefits. The revolutionary legal innovation of the corporate person provided a legal foundation for limited liability and forms of capital accumulation. Bankers contributed to accumulation and stability by issuing bank notes and extending necessary loans. Since the early seventeenth century, the ability of English rulers to govern the nation and wage war depended upon the political support and financial contributions of merchants, bankers, and financiers.

The development of joint-stock companies and banks from independent merchants and lenders mirrors the development of depersonalized, institutional rule from personal monarchies and dynasties. This trend toward bureaucratic organization illustrates Max Weber's argument about the rationalization of modern society. I amplify the argument by illustrating that rationalized political administration, economic production, and trade occurred simultaneously as a set. In my judgment they were rationalized and institutionalized as a union, as the modern world.

Conceptual innovations sparked these institutional innovations. In particular, the concept sovereignty constituted national relations of authority. Sovereignty also constituted the state as the premier social actor. Further, sovereignty divided national social relations from the international system. This conceptual threshold remains socially definitive (e.g., Walker, 1993; C. Weber, 1995). Equally significant, the development of mobile property provoked the social construction of bifurcated meanings of property and property rights. Rights to mobile property helped constitute the conceptual foundations for a system of mobile exchange, which further established the framework for market society and capitalist exchange and production. Thus, distinct political and economic social relations emerge.

These distinctions are not absolute, however. I do not want to suggest that national affairs remain clearly separate from international relations or that economic behavior stands absolutely removed from political life. Rather, I am highlighting a *conceptual framework* through which actors conceive their world. These conceptual bifurcations constitute a *worldview,* not a particular world of affairs. Even Adam Smith and contemporary conservatives envision occasional governmental intervention in the economy to respond to market failures. Again, I draw the distinctions conceptually, not concretely. Yet note the vocabulary we use in everyday language. We say the "government [political actor] intervenes [by crossing a threshold, entering a different space] in the market [the economy]." The conceptual framework endures, although social life is a mix, indeed a unity.

NOTES

1. However, these merchants founded the Bank of England on suspect practices. Scott (1912/1968a:344–345) reports that the Bank of England and other prominent endeavors "all carried on business without any working capital provided by the members." The total commitment of stockholders to the bank was £720,000, but upon its founding the bank extended a loan of more than £1 million to the government of England. Although the bank's charter authorized it to deal in bullion and bills, to issue bank notes, and to extend loans on the security of merchandise, the bulk of the loan and all working capital were provided by depositors. By this suspect practice, the bank issued loans in excess of its bullion reserves and did so by issuing its own paper currency (Scott, 1912/1968a:344–345, 1912/1968c:205–207; Kenyon, 1978:284–285).

2. The extreme version of the landed property argument was its extension to the high seas. Could a nation claim the high seas as it could claim landed territory? Grotius and Selden debated the issues and the related logic of *jus conquestas* (Tuck, 1979:chs. 3 and 4; Grotius, 1609/1916; 1625/1957; 1625/1949).

3. In contrast, Cipolla (1980:194) argues that commercial and financial developments in medieval Italy were the most telling for capitalist development. To "avoid boring the reader" (p. 195), he devotes little attention to seventeenth-century developments! De Vries (1976:133) calls joint-stock companies a "superficial" innovation. However, Hadden (1979:110) admonishes Tigar and Levy (1977) for overlooking joint-stock companies.

4. The Crown's financial woes are a recurring theme in accounts of joint-stock companies. For example, Scott (1912/1968a), Howat (1974), and Kenyon (1978) turn often to this subject.

5. Valuable and extensive information on the Dutch and English East India Companies appears in Davis (1962), Chaudhuri (1965, 1978), Furber (1976), Steensgaard (1982, 1990), Prakash (1985), and Israel (1989, 1990).

6. Scott (1912/1968a:461) adds that joint-stock companies also arose to conduct foreign trade and privateering, colonize, develop inventions, and introduce manufactures already established abroad. This welter of activity raises public goods dilemmas: How to procure or produce them; how to prevent free riders; how to establish initial cooperative behavior; and how to create norms, rules, practices, and institutions. Indeed, the rise of joint-stock companies offers a historic microcosm of many neorealist concerns in international relations and international political economy, including collective goods, regimes, hegemonic stability, and burgeoning norms. See, for example, Olson (1965), Kindleberger (1973), Krasner (1983), and Keohane (1980, 1984, 1989).

7. Keynes (1953a:3–7) begins his monumental book by illustrating the rela-

tionship of law, the state, and finances as he discusses the origins of modern money. He first distinguishes "money" from "money-of-account." Debts and payments create money-of-account. Debt represents a contract for deferred payment; prices are offers to enter into contracts for sale or purchase. Money represents the medium of exchange by which debts are paid.

> Now by the mention of contracts and offers, we have introduced Law or Custom, by which they are enforceable; that is to say, we have introduced the State or the Community. Furthermore it is a peculiar characteristic of money contracts that it is the State or Community not only which enforces delivery, but also which decided what it is that must be delivered as a lawful or customary discharge of a contract which has been concluded in terms of the money-of-account. The State, therefore, comes in first of all as the authority of law which enforces the payment of the thing which corresponds to the name or description in the contract. But it comes in doubly when, in addition, it claims the right to determine and declare *what thing* corresponds to the name, and to vary its declaration from time to time. . . . This right is claimed by all modern States. . . . [Thus,] the doctrine that money is peculiarly a creation of the State . . . is fully realised. (Keynes, 1953a:4; emphasis in original)

Keynes argues that the state must enforce contracts by establishing a legal infrastructure and determining what constitutes the medium of exchange, whether shells, beads, wooden nickels, bullion, coins, paper, or something else. Yet Keynes ignores one other enormously important power of the state; since he assumes prices to be sticky or relatively stable, he does not much consider inflation. However, the state can control the volume of money in circulation simply by issuing more or stipulating that additional items constitute a medium of exchange. In short, Keynes ignores arbitrage opportunities.

Keynes (1953a:7–11) goes on to discuss commodity money, fiat money, and a hybrid of the two called managed money. These three make up what he calls "state money." The only other instrument of exchange is "bank money," which is an acknowledgment of debt rather than money proper. We know, however, that bank money will be held and circulated by the central bank. We know further that in the 1690s the English government acted to create the Bank of England and to use it much like a central bank by employing its resources and privileges.

8. Arbitrage also illustrates a telling difference between sovereignty and seigniorage. Seigniorage is the consequence of engaging in arbitrage; it is the short-run revenue or purchasing power the government collects by minting commodity coins with a significant difference between their face value (denomination) and metal value. In the case of fiat currency, seigniorage is the revenue earned, resources acquired, or debt paid upon printing additional money. The English words *seigniorage* and *seigniory* derive from the French *seigneur,* a feudal title. In French, *seigneury* conveys the power and authority of a feudal lord, his lordship and dominion. One of the lord's most significant rights is the right to coin money. Yet *seigniory* and *seigneury* also indicate the territory over which the lord holds jurisdiction or controls governance. However, we typically understand *sovereignty* to convey the sense of supreme jurisdictional control over territory and, secondarily, one who possesses "supreme authority within a limited sphere."

Seigniory and *sovereignty* are synonyms, except in their adjectival forms (*seigniorial, sovereign*). *Seigniory* better conveys the senses of authority, (property) rights, territory, and jurisdiction that political scientists intend to represent with the word *sovereignty*. Further, *seigniorage*—the term economists embrace—indicates one of the particular privileges of authority: The monopoly right to coin money and print currency (or the right to grant such privileges). Seigniorage is also one means by which authority was exercised and modern institutional-legal structures emerged from feudal practices. This brief etymology indicates that the practices at issue were inseparably, coherently unified through property rights.

PART 3
PROPERTY AND CONSTITUTION

7

Constituting Sovereignty, Political Economy, and a Modern Worldview

Simple answers cannot describe the complex evolution of Western theories of sovereignty.

Kenneth Pennington (1993:284)

Once constituted and instituted, sovereignty—understood as depersonalized authority or coordinate sovereignty—becomes the conceptual division between national and international. The international system comprises conceptually distinct political and economic systems, claimed by the fields of international relations and international economics, respectively. Scholarly efforts to explore their interrelationships fall to international political economy (IPE), which privileges either political or economic premises, so skews analyses (e.g., Gilpin, 1987:8–12). In this sense, IPE is an ideology that characterizes the international system in distinctively modern, typically liberal terms. Thus, IPE is a cultural artifact of modernity. Indeed, I hold that IPE, liberalism, and modernity share the same ontological framework. Although scholars characterize modernity in different dimensions, similar premises prevail.

For example, Walker (1993:13, 25) writes that the "sovereignty of states is often taken to be the most important fact of life in a world of more or less autonomous authorities," making sovereignty "the key feature of modern political life." Alternatively, Habermas (1973:51–54) defines the modern era in terms of the separation of politics from economy. Actors in the seventeenth century constituted these horizontal and vertical premises as a grid of social systems separated by a pair of crosshairs. Here I explore the social construction of these crosshairs, first briefly reviewing earlier material to label the elements and connections in the argument.

	POLITICAL	ECONOMIC
INTERNATIONAL		
NATIONAL		

Figure 2   The Conceptual Framework of the Modern World(view)

In seventeenth-century western Europe, social actors constructed and reinforced these crosshairs as a defining element of the modern world(view). Subsequent social theory and IPE address the content, character, and relations of the basic categories and cells. Little dispute arises over the framework itself. Indeed, liberal-modern premises are so pervasive and seem so self-evident that one is "not conscious of their being assumptions at all" (Arblaster, 1984:6). However, one can reasonably ask, "How and why [did] economics and politics bec[o]me separated in the first place" (Tooze, 1984:3)? How did sovereignty become "a fundamental source of truth and meaning" (Ashley, 1988:230)?

Some scholars (e.g., Philpott, 1995) attempt to reckon sovereignty as the conceptual overlap of the intersecting contexts of authority, power, legitimacy, law, supremacy, and territory. I construct no figurative Venn diagrams. Instead, I investigate sovereignty and the conceptual split between politics and economics through the single, comprehensive subject of property and property rights. Attention to property rights conceptually and practically coheres the overlapping concerns (e.g., North and Thomas, 1973; Levi, 1987). Such attention also illuminates the crosshairs as the constitutive elements of the ontological framework. For example, sovereignty as a property right conveying authority distinguishes the "inside" state from the "outside" system (Walker, 1993). Property rights also distinguish the economic world from the political by proscribing the use and disposal of possessions, hence production and exchange. In short, by exploring property rights I "live on borderlines" (Ashley, 1989). As the crosshairs constitute IPE, liberalism, and modernity, individuals constitute the crosshairs through property rights in the interplay of social events and circulating ideas. The context is seventeenth-century Europe and the transition to the modern era. The focus throughout this book is seventeenth-century western Europe: The time and place in which coalesced many of the ideas, practices, and actors that have come to dominate the planet. This chapter constructs the crosshairs, so to speak, from previously collected elements.

In the following three sections I offer answers to the questions posed by Tooze and Ashley. The first introduces several definitions by which to orient questions concerning the crosshairs created by politics, economics, and sovereignty. The second illustrates how disputes, practices, and conceptual changes involving property rights constitute state sovereignty. I argue in the third section that social practices and the bifurcation of property into real and mobile forms constituted the conceptual split and ideological premise separating politics from economics.

IPE, MODERNITY, IDEOLOGY

By *social construction* I mean the process by which social agents, social structures, and shared meanings are co-constituted, resulting always in a form of social rule involving domination. In reconstituting authority in the seventeenth century, actors constituted social relations and roles by reflecting and acting in terms of rules. Rules yield rule, as the disputes over sovereignty illustrate. As communities of individuals make the world—materially and conceptually—they make sense of it; the making and the making sense are the same. To organize the social turmoil they confronted, actors constituted sovereignty and sovereign relations. Language was the medium: "The limits of one's language mark the limits of one's world" (Ball et al., 1989:2). And as Doty (1996:25) reminds us, "behavior has no meaning at all outside of discourse." In these terms, language is a medium of social action. Indeed, language shapes and animates ideology (Thompson, 1984:5). The constitutive, performative, and animating character of language is most evident during social turmoil as actors attempt to gain control, impose order, and rescue meanings (Doty, 1996:13, 16). Hence, the imploring, recurring question—Is a prince subject to the law?—is a question about securing foundations. As such, it is a question about rule, rules, domination, authority, the law, ideology, social actions and relations, and language. The question reduces to a conceptual dispute: What do we mean when we say *sovereign?* In this sense I take concepts, the units of language, as basic ontological elements. Conceptual histories of significant concepts, constitutive principles of society, illuminate changing meanings. Conceptual histories of property and property rights tell us much about the constitution of the international system and the modern worldview.

Recall that property rights comprise those rules allocating access to and control of resources (Waldron, 1988:31). Such rules establish social relations and domination. This is social construction in practice. To secure advantages over rivals, individuals create rules and deploy resources in accord with yet other rules. "Resources are nothing until mobilized through rules; rules are nothing until matched to resources to effectuate rule" (Onuf, 1989:64). Property, the resource at issue, is an aggregate of rights relevant to every thing or resource that is or may be owned. Indeed, a property right is "the highest right a person can have to anything" (*Black's Law*

Dictionary). In the modern world, it is difficult to divorce property as "owned object" from "rights to property." This becomes a central ideological claim.[1]

By *ideology* I refer to philosophical foundations, not to a doctrinaire program of political change. An ideology comprises the fundamental, socially created meanings that are sufficiently coherent and comprehensive to constitute a way of life and an outlook on life (Geertz, 1973:12–14; M. Hamilton, 1987:38). A coherent ideology constitutes a culture and its worldview (McLellan, 1986; Carver, 1995) because ideological-cultural patterns "provide a template or blueprint for the organization of social" activities (Geertz, 1973:216). That is, cultures and ideologies make "politics possible by providing the authoritative concepts that render it meaningful" (Geertz, 1973:218). In this neutral sense, an ideology is a coherent system of thought and practice grounded upon the ontological categories and concepts of a worldview and the epistemological premises about how one understands the world. However, this loose conception of ideology does not help identify which social groups and ideologies are socially relevant (Thompson, 1984:126). Thus, one may critically conceive ideology as a worldview that sustains relations of domination, though often unintentionally (Thompson, 1984:5). Dominant meanings are often mobilized through legitimation, reification, and rebutted or deflected critiques. These efforts inexorably entwine ideology with language and concepts (Thompson, 1984:ch. 3, esp. 127–132).

By *modernity* I refer to the congruence of "the modern era" and "the project of modernity." The development of the state, state system, and capitalism in western Europe in the sixteenth and seventeenth centuries marks the dramatic social transition to the modern era. Equally profound is the development of rationality and a philosophical quest for certainty. These constitute the project of modernity, scientific inquiry, and the Enlightenment (Habermas, 1987; Harvey, 1990:10–39; Toulmin, 1990:140–145; Onuf, 1991:425–429). The crosshairs were constituted in the events precipitating the modern era; the quest for certainty reinforces the crosshairs' seemingly certain or natural character. Thus, liberalism (Arblaster, 1984; Gray, 1986:90; Rapaczynski, 1987:25–28) and positivist-empiricist rationality (Bernstein, 1976:3–54; 1983:1–16) are the premier cultural and conceptual embodiments of modernity.

The modern world(view) rests atop three defining premises: state-centric organization, rational state behavior, and power-seeking. Keohane (1986:163) describes these as the "three most fundamental Realist assumptions." Arblaster (1984:ch. 6) traces identical premises—individual actors, rationality, and interests—as essential to liberalism. Macpherson (1962:3) similarly identifies bourgeois society. By declaration and inference, these premises constitute the character, content, and "spaces" of social life. They make up a modern worldview.

PROPERTY AND SOVEREIGNTY

Scholars in political philosophy, law, and history mightily contest the meanings of sovereignty (e.g., Merriam, 1900; de Jouvenal, 1957; Hinsley, 1986; James, 1986). Yet understood as "final and absolute political authority in the political community" (Hinsley, 1986:26), sovereignty was long ignored by students of international affairs. To explore the modern constitutive character of sovereignty requires attention to its medieval idioms. Sovereignty played crucial roles in political disputes over authority, property, and social organization in the transition to the early modern era (see Onuf, 1991; Kratochwil, 1995). In these disputes sovereignty drew from ancient Greece and Rome the "classical idiom of power and prerogative [and] became the modern idiom of statecraft" (Onuf, 1991:429). In broader terms, significant shifts in understandings of property rights constitute the simultaneous seventeenth-century emergence of sovereignty, the state, liberalism, and modernity as a constellation of ideas and practices (e.g., Agnew, 1994).

Before these transitions, European feudal life comprised densely layered, overlapping obligations and rights. Hinsley (1986:75, 77) describes a "medieval proliferation of overlapping and conflicting communities and authorities . . . [yielding] a prolonged bedlam of incomplete and conflicting arguments." Ruggie (1983) calls feudal life "a form of segmented territorial rule [that] represented a heteronomous organization of territorial rights and claims." Rather than an absolute authority or power, a sovereign was one of many feudal statuses or titles in the "great chain of duties" (de Jouvenal, 1957:171) implicated in the Great Chain of Being.

Sovereign, seigneur, suzerain, sire, sir, sieur, monsieur, and *monseigneur* are feudal terms sharing etymological roots from Latin meaning "superiority," "supremacy," or "seniority." As adjectives, these superlatives refer to undisputed rank or status or to unrivaled quality. When wedded by practice to power (*potestas,* potency), majestic bearing (*majestas*), and rule, the notions of superiority surrounding the term *sovereignty* give us its modern sense of "supreme authority" (Onuf, 1991). Applied to territory, notions of supreme jurisdiction follow. Yet territory suggests more. Sovereign territories were landholdings or estates. Yet *estates* comprise not real estate but the full range and bundle of rights (*status*) possessed by anyone. One's estate is most clearly manifest in rights over land. Thus, *state* is an etymological hybrid, combining roots from *estate* (land, property, rights) and *status* (authority, standing, rights). In early modern idiom, the state represents the territorially grounded object of the property rights of sovereign monarchs. The set of such specific rights was called *dominium* (thus, domain and domination), *proprietas* (property), or simply sovereignty. Thus, Kratochwil (1995:25) concludes that sovereignty represents "the quality of a claim to authority," so is therefore "inherently limited."

As a practical matter, early modern rulers endured severely limited authority. They were poorly equipped and positioned to be obeyed, lacking substantial physical resources and personal influence along the overlapping edges of fading feudal loyalties. For example, European rulers could scarcely avoid convening advisory assemblies, especially if they required resources from the bodies. "The crown had never been sovereign by itself, for before the days of parliament there was no real sovereignty at all: Sovereignty was only achieved by the energy of the crown in parliament" (quoted by de Jouvenal, 1957:177). Thus, while sovereigns were many, sovereignty was rarely known.

Feeble public finances strained rulers and encouraged centralized authority. After ascending to the throne, a monarch acquired a specific estate (property rights and assets) from which to satisfy public functions, but the resources rarely sufficed (de Jouvenal, 1957:178–180; Wilson, 1977:131–132; see also Howat, 1974; Kenyon, 1978; and Hutton, 1989). With only limited rights and authority, monarchs confronted foreign foes, institutional rivals, and powerful domestic agents. Monarchs invited subsidies, but those who were asked to make financial contributions negotiated for favorable conditions or reciprocal rights.

The interlaced practices of royal families, privileged elites, and restless merchants transformed the monarchy into the Crown, then into the crown state, when rulers transferred property rights to merchants, the bourgeoisie, and others as part of an institutional alliance. Royal property rights and political need allowed rulers to dispense commercially advantageous property rights in politically beneficial ways through grants and monopolies (Burch, 1994). Thus arose the modern inclination to unbundle property rights from the narrow but workable conception of title versus possession to the multiple and overlapping property rights that currently construct social life. The decisive (rhetorical and political) move allied bourgeois elements with those advocating a centralized, more resolute sovereignty. The bourgeoisie, now more free of feudal bonds and increasingly able to participate in the commercial revolution, sought to protect their property and rights by buttressing public authority as a weapon against remaining feudal ties (de Jouvenal, 1957:181). Real property set the foundation for the claims by states' rulers to be territorial rights-bearers—that is, landholding sovereigns. Mobile property and natural law underscored merchants' claims to be rights-bearers, too—that is, to be citizens possessing personal sovereignty and liberty. The stage was set for an era-shattering clash of powers, prerogatives, and rights.

The result is two forms of sovereignty and two forms of property. A monarch exercises sovereignty over a state; an individual exercises limited personal sovereignty over herself and her possessions. Indeed, in the view of many, a ruler may exercise sovereignty over a subject population of citizens on condition the monarch respect private, personal property (*potestas in re*) and personal liberty (*potestas in se ipsum*). As Kratochwil (1995:25) notes, "Sovereignty became a distinct institution when the claim to supreme authority was coupled with a specific rule of allocation for exercising this authority." To rule required rules or implicit norms recognizing property (rights) as landed *and* mobile. Most important, claims to the absolute, exclusive character of personal liberty and property—and the economic system it constitutes—delimit the supreme quality of the monarch's unique royal prerogative. In this sense it becomes clear that absolute or unqualified sovereignty as a matter of political authority never existed. Instead, these were *claims* of rights and authority; they were political ploys or practices.

Yet the quality of a claim to authority depends directly on the quality of the property rights held by the claimant. How might one reasonably claim absolute sovereign authority? How might others entertain the claims?

As a property right, sovereignty is the highest, most complete right of ownership (*dominium*); it combines both perfect title and possession. Such rights are variously called *proprietas plena* or *plenitudo potestatis* or full property. To label the rights *absolute sovereignty* in the seventeenth century connoted not absolute power or authority but absolute (pure, uncontested) *claims* to property. *Absolute sovereignty* is a redundancy intended to clarify and emphasize a legal claim to land or property. However, to translate these property rights into rights of authority, governance, and rule required unique conceptual and historical circumstances. Such circumstances arose in the seventeenth century. Moreover, these circumstances created incentives for vesting royal authority with greatly enhanced political power and status. Only in this situation do the *political* connotations of absolute sovereignty emerge, though the rights and powers remain far from absolute.

A widespread need to reconstruct authority grew out of the significant crises of the seventeenth century: Prolonged economic crises, widening poverty, sociopolitical chaos, and violent religious intolerance. Observers now view the century as "among the most uncomfortable, and even frantic, years in all European history" (Toulmin, 1990:16). Reconstructions centralized authority. Legal discourse became the means for discussing and enacting social change. Throughout the century actors used legal language to formulate virtually every important controversy and justify every position (Nenner, 1977:ix; also Little, 1969/1984:vii). In justifying sovereign *politi-*

cal authority in terms of relatively exclusive (rather than conditional) *property* rights, imperial notions of sovereign authority and liberalized notions of exclusive rights entered the popular vocabulary. Ultimately, absolute sovereignty (the quality of a property claim) metamorphosed into political claims of nearly absolute authority and political supremacy (a condition of rule). Fundamentally, claims to absolute sovereignty encouraged a stable, workable, tolerable social order. Guarded recognition of supreme authority on the basis of absolute sovereignty was a socially advantageous fiction because the claim to authority satisfied many domestic groups and interests.

In crafting domestic order, hegemonic claims—whether advanced by warring families, warring religious groups, or warring philosophical factions—proved insufficiently compelling to become truly dominant ideas.[2] Profound social disaster followed. However, burgeoning heteronomous ideas were also insufficiently rooted, although rapidly blooming among commercial classes. As a form of rule, only hierarchy remained. It was feasible, it drew from well-established idioms, and it could be erected upon existing social rules, especially property rights. Better still, the hierarchical form, though nominally absolute, would never be so in practice. As noted above, monarchs had to recognize the personal, exclusive rights of individuals. As such, hierarchically secure monarchs exchanged reciprocal promises (heteronomy) with the protobourgeoisie. The promises legitimized the developing liberal worldview and its practices as a potentially hegemonic set of ideas. Thus, actors constructed the specific hierarchy of absolute sovereignty in part to obscure inchoate hegemonic ideas and relations. They rule today in liberal-modernity, constructed in the seventeenth century in conjunction with the reconstitution of authority.

In England in particular, political authority had collapsed by the mid-1600s, yet God had not revealed alternatives. Each individual had to "rediscover in the depths of his own being the means of reconstituting and obeying" social authority (Pocock, 1985:55; also 1975:348; 1977:15; 1980:10–11). A retreat to theology promised renewed sectarian conflict. Reconstituting authority necessarily begged questions about the title (property rights) by which political personality could be constituted. On what basis can authority (*status,* standing) be claimed or recognized? On what basis should individuals obey? What property rights (civil liberties) would citizens possess? Monarchs possessed the proverbial nine-tenths of the law, that is, they had absolute sovereignty over their personal, landed possessions. The adage illustrates a centrally important legal principle: "Every claimant must succeed by the strength of his own title, and not by the weakness of his antagonist's" (*Black's Law Dictionary*). As monarchs possessed the strongest titles, their success seemed most likely. Bourgeois citizens exacted an exchange.

Unless men inherited or acquired property, it was hard to see how they acquired an obligation to obey the laws of society. . . . Freedom must have a material base: that a man must own himself if he were not to be owned by another. (Pocock, 1977:27)

Myriad actors—policymakers, public officials, feudal nobles, merchants, bankers, financiers, entrepreneurs, lawyers, judges, philosophers, theologians, millenarians, citizens, and others—engaged in cumulative, conflicting efforts to reconstitute society as a whole. In political and cosmic senses, the institutional-legal order emerged as an agent of stability and reason. Individuals in seventeenth-century Europe generally conceived "authority and magistracy [as] part of a natural and cosmic order" mirrored in national social life (Pocock, 1985:55). In the terms that Bodin, Hobbes, and Filmer used: "What God is to Nature, the King is to the State" (Toulmin, 1990:126–128, quotation on p. 127). In this sense, the history of sovereignty is inextricable from the history of administration and state-building (de Jouvenal, 1957:179). The history of sovereignty is similarly entangled with cosmic renewal.

Only in the context of the state does sovereignty's fusion of idiomatically different ideas become a constitutive principle. At the dawn of the seventeenth century, a prominent French jurist declared that "sovereignty is entirely inseparable from the state. . . . Sovereignty is the summit of authority, by means of which the state is created and maintained" (quoted in de Jouvenal, 1957:180). To this degree, states and sovereignty are distinctively and solely modern (Onuf, 1991:426). Thus, states, sovereignty, possessive individualism, reconstituted authority, and liberalism are each socially constructed elements of the transition to modernity. Sovereignty becomes central to "reorganizing reality" into modernity (Bartelson, 1995:ch. 6). Knowledgeable, conflicting actors constituted the elements through practices derived from bifurcating property rights. In short, "properties are the foundation of constitutions" and, I add, of constituting (quoted in Macpherson, 1962:139).

In the social tumult from the late 1500s to the mid-1600s, Grotius and Pufendorf argued for exclusive property rights; Bodin and Hobbes advocated unchallengeable lawmaking authority. These arguments erected the elements for institutionalizing depersonalized sovereignty and the emergence of modern relations. Hobbes's citizens fear not the Leviathan but the social chaos unleashed by ruthlessly self-centered, atheistic individuals. Political necessity demanded that to centralize reconstructed authority into the institutions of the sovereign state required the expansion and protection of personal sovereignty and individual liberty. In turn, the establishment and defense of personal liberty called for a powerful authority. In this era bourgeois individualism and commercial society seemed to require an unassailably sovereign authority who creates law by his or her commands and who creates order through law. In this rhetorical move, sovereignty-in-itself—a sovereignty not possessed by a sovereign—enters the stage (de Jouvenal, 1957:198). Sovereignty-in-itself was then located within governing institutions. Corrupted as the doctrine of state sovereignty, it simultaneously absorbed the rights of the ruler and the rights of the community (Hinsley, 1986:126). Thus, the modern era and worldview arrive because sovereignty-in-itself constitutes the state, the state system, and state-society relations.

By the seventeenth century, the subject of politics is no longer the cultivation of the good life. Instead, politics represents the achievement of security and prosperity within an orderly, rational society (Habermas, 1973:43). Modern "politics" becomes (domestic) "domination" in which "society" subsumes "polity" and "economy." As a result, "the *dominium* of the princes becomes sovereign and the *societas* [is] privatized under the administration of territorial states" (Habermas, 1973:49). These changes occur in part because the "point of departure of the Moderns is how human beings could technically master the threatening evils of nature" (p. 51), notably physical attack, starvation, and cosmic uncertainty. "This practical necessity requiring technical solutions marks the beginnings of *modern social philosophy*" (Habermas, 1973:50–51).

This view of property rights and concomitant social relations suggests that the origins of the modern state as a territorial entity are based not solely upon sovereignty (Ruggie, 1983; Kratochwil, 1995) but upon specific property rights, of which sovereignty comprises a distinct set. Sovereign property rights simultaneously yield states and the state system as a matter of definition and social practice (Kratochwil, 1995:25). The conditions and social practice of sovereignty-in-itself construct and rule modernity as they divide discrete national realms of sovereign authority. Yet this is only part of the story, since the political system of authority was itself separated from a system of exchange (of rights). Again, property rights help us see the split.

PROPERTY AND THE SPLIT
BETWEEN POLITICS AND ECONOMICS

> *Political economy requires analysis of the way in which ideas about what constitutes the political and the economic have emerged historically.*
>
> Stephen Gill and David Law (1988:xviii)

In western Europe prior to 1600 there was no clear distinction between the state system and capitalism, no distinction between political and economic activity in the relations among nations. These relations made up a unity. By approximately 1700, however, commercial expansion, transferable entitlements, and diverse social practices created distinctly real and mobile forms of property, hence novel applications of property rights (Pocock, 1957; Burch 1994). During the 1600s, states and a state system developed and capitalism's distinct socioeconomic relations emerged from politics. At one extreme are the early Dutch and English joint-stock companies, founded in the 1550s, and the establishment of the Dutch central bank in 1605; at the other extreme is the founding of the Bank of England in 1694 and the failed French attempt in 1719 to create a central bank modeled on the English example.

Attempts to define, control, and constitute property rights were key. Monarchs extended property rights to other actors in order to reinforce royal rule and domination. Rulers also realized that the institutional needs of burgeoning states required resources that were effectively attained by promoting mobile property and capitalist exchange. Simultaneously, beneficiaries profited from the social stability provided by effective rule. Bargains were struck.

The bifurcation in property (rights) established the conceptual division between the state system (real, tangible property) and the capitalist system (mobile, intangible property). Upon this conceptual foundation, and with the development and recognition of mobile property, capitalism becomes a system of fluid exchange. For example, perceptions of the market built substantially upon the public's earlier perception of credit (Pocock, 1985:69). Thus, property rights contribute to the constitution and singular coherence of capitalism and the interstate system (e.g., Chase-Dunn, 1981); differences between real and mobile property contribute to the differences between the two systems. Crucial to this development is the interplay of ideas and practice.

As a matter of ideas, seventeenth-century disputes over property were inextricable from contemporaneous disputes over rights generally, whether expressed as natural versus positive rights or contingent versus exclusive rights. Sparking the controversies was the growth of market society and capitalist relations, and with them "massive revolutions" (Shapiro, 1987:71) in law, roles of the state, morality, authority, commerce, philosophy, and worldviews. England was the crucible (Tuck, 1979:81; Shapiro, 1987:71, and 23–79 more generally). For example, partisans in the English civil war used elements of Grotius's earlier advocacy of a strong (property) rights theory both to defend absolutism and to defend individual property and resistance to absolute rule.

One doctrine, the jurisprudential tradition of legal interpretation, encouraged in two ways the emergence of (so-called) distinctly economic activity. First, the juristic view conceives social life as relations between individuals and objects. Rights characterize the relations. Indeed, the concept of rights thoroughly imbues the liberal, modern worldview (cf. Arblaster, 1984; Rapaczynski, 1987; Shapiro, 1987). However, rights quickly transform into conceptions of use, with decidedly economic connotations that directly introduce production, exchange, and accumulation, thus promoting trade, profit, and savings. Second, the juristic tradition's emphasis on property rights ultimately undermined political participation as the key social activity. This emphasis augured the crucial separation of political and economic realms: Property was a legal term long before it acquired economic meanings (Pocock, 1985:56). Similarly, efforts to distinguish political theories of property raise conceptual problems because property is simultaneously a legal, economic, and political institution (Reeve, 1986:10). Yet the modern world erects walls and partitions that divide social life. The social world was not always divided so. Property rights play a key role in maintaining those walls and in overcoming the barriers so we might see as related the divided spaces and concerns. By focusing on property rights, however, we can see the divisions as part of a larger social-conceptual edifice.

New conceptions of property rights transformed the political world and laid the foundation for an economic realm that sprang from household or manorial production to become society's prime mover. Economics relates individuals to objects in the service of marketable production. These relations eclipse the political relations among people (Pocock, 1985:105). Market society vanquished the classical view of participatory politics and replaced it with alienated politics (e.g., Marx 1844/1964). As a result, politics no longer involves the relations among equal individuals but instead the relations of authorities to subjects, a situation entirely analogous to the property relations between individuals and possessed objects. The new economics was crafting a political world in its own image, though the shadow of a hierarchical system of domination never faded.

As a matter of practice, by promoting mobile property rights sovereign authority could then through rules and rule marshal resources to establish social order and challenge foreign foes. Systemic competition and domestic pressure spurred bureaucratic development in England, France, and the Netherlands. The exercise of sovereign property rights sparked the drive to global capitalism and the competitive state system as it also became the means of directing the state toward acquisitive and aggressive ends. Acquiring material and monetary resources posed a particular difficulty, so policymakers fostered institutions that could do so. Again, the practice and ideas involved property.

Rulers use rights over mobile property to service competition with other states. Such competition opens opportunities to accumulate capital. Monarchs specifically solicited, promoted, and often created companies to redress the problem of chronic national insolvency in the period 1500–1800 (e.g., Wilson, 1977:131–132). State leaders not only encouraged but also co-opted successful companies. Merchants understood the circumstances so looked to profit by extending high-interest loans to the Crown.

In turn, the Crown extended property rights—as grants, monopolies, charters, use rights, exemptions, and many other benefits—primarily to induce companies to bear most of the investment risk, to act on behalf of foreign policy interests, and to meet needs for national infrastructure and consumption. Against European foes, rulers used trading companies to advance colonial claims and used the credit extended by newly created central banks to finance military operations (e.g., Polanyi, 1944; McNeill, 1982; Andrews, 1984). In general, in exchange for property rights the Crown promoted social order and received necessary resources, goods, services, and specie.

Joint-stock companies date to as early as 1450, became prominent by the 1550s, and became prime movers by roughly the 1650s. They were essential elements of the institutional-legal-economic order. In the last half of the seventeenth century, England developed an institutional infrastructure that appeared more modern than medieval. The English state comprised an institutional-legal order wedded to joint-stock companies, which received monopoly concessions.

Thus, the development of central banks, joint-stock companies, and an institutional-legal infrastructure in England, France, and the Netherlands occurred at similar times and under similar circumstances. Whether told as stories of state-building, interstate rivalry, capitalist expansion, mercantile commerce, or colonization, these experiences were understood and conducted in terms of property rights. Indeed, the uncertain seventeenth-century distinction between statecraft and economic activity illustrates the degree to which the separation of politics from economics is an ideological premise that coalesced in the following century. After 1700 the development of liberal thought and modern practices further encouraged the view of these as conceptually distinct realms.

This conception of politics and economics suggests that their character and separation were constructed in the tumult of the seventeenth century as a consequence of social discourse and practice concerning property rights. One distinguishes politics from economics by the character of the property rights appropriate to each. The emergence of distinctive economic rights heralds the arrival of the modern era and liberal market society.

CONCLUSION

Through the bifurcation of relatively exclusive property rights into real and mobile forms, individuals constituted sovereignty and the split between politics and economics. These crosshairs serve as the foundations for modernity; cohere in the prevailing ideology of liberalism; constitute the state, state system, and capitalism; and are exemplified in conventional IPE. The conceptual bifurcation of property links the unfolding of the modern era and the development of liberalism. As social rules, actors use property rights to conduct the practices of sovereignty, modernity, and IPE, and to maintain the border dividing politics from economics.[3] Unique forms of social rule and social and material domination result.

NOTES

1. Consider eminent domain, the government's right to take private property for public use. Governments often invoke eminent domain when they build sidewalks, widen streets, or construct highways, for example. Although eminent domain remains "the highest and most exact idea of property remaining in the government," private property owners must receive "just compensation" in exchange for the government's claim (*Black's Law Dictionary*). That is, the sovereign (state) remains supreme, its claims the most eminent or exalted within its domain or dominion, yet the sovereign authorities must recognize and respect private property rights.

2. See Chapter 1, note 10 for a lengthy discussion of rules and rule, including contrasts among hegemony, hierarchy, and heteronomy.

3. On sovereignty as a social practice, see Ruggie (1983), Walker (1993:154), and C. Weber (1995). On the social practice of creating and maintaining the border between politics and economics, see Ashley (1983) and Burch (1994). On liberalism as a social practice, see Arblaster (1984:91) and Burch (1995). On modernity as a social practice, see Harvey (1990:38, 63, 111–113) and Giddens (1990:1). On IR and IPE as "knowledgeable practice," see Ashley (1989:287).

8

Conclusions and Implications

Classificatory schemes often serve to naturalize and hierarchize by placing human beings into stereotypical categories presumably designated by nature.

Roxanne Doty (1996:37)

As social rules, property rights simultaneously constitute social conditions and regulate activities. Actors make choices by deciding to obey, modify, or condemn a rule. Seventeenth-century actors had to decide whether or how to obey the diverse rules invoked to reconstruct society: Royal prerogative, papal infallibility, parliamentary sovereignty, coordinate sovereignty, sovereignty-in-itself, the "ancient constitution," and the law of reason, among others. Actors' choices always, if imperceptibly, affect rules, so reshape society and the condition of rule (Onuf, 1994).

Each form of rule was prominent in the seventeenth century, but changes in the relative significance of each were apparent. With monarchs' sovereign authority transforming into institutional sovereignty, hierarchical domestic rule is reinforced because a monarch *commands*. As rulers *assert* sovereignty, interstate relations become subject to a hegemonic set of ideas—that is, they become subject to a prevailing worldview in which sovereignty is a dominant idea. At the same time, heteronomous commercial practices are also vying for cultural and social hegemony. Heteronomous relations prevail among agents exchanging rights in a market because contracting parties *promise*. Yet the appearance of hegemonies hides international hierarchies *commanded* by great powers. (We confuse ourselves to talk of a hegemonic actor that dominates the global hierarchy, as the currently mistaken vocabulary puts it.)

In short, because actors had reestablished the foundations of social order in the tumult of the seventeenth century, no set of ideas could claim new or renewed hegemonic dominance by 1700: Traditional ideas had not yet faded and novel ideas had not yet proved their durability. Although heteronomous ideas (liberal rights and duties, contractual promises) were reshaping national societies and international relations, they were not yet fully dominant ideas. Indeed, as heteronomous relations became prominent in the seventeenth century, they eroded the overpowering hegemony of hierarchical social relations, most dramatically expressed in the rank and status characteristics of monarchical rule. Yet neither traditional hierarchies nor burgeoning heteronomy could prevail alone. Sovereign authorities perched atop hierarchically arranged societies found themselves advancing heteronomous ideas.

Thus, the seventeenth-century institutional-legal order in Britain, and elsewhere to differing degree, blends hierarchy and heteronomy. Social order seemed to require centralized authority and hierarchical rule, but that authority would be absolute in name only. Individuals and legislatures recognized monarchs as possessors of sovereignty (the familiar pinnacle of hierarchical rule), yet these allegedly absolute sovereigns recognized that individuals and legislatures, especially the British Parliament, possess exclusive rights. This "social contract" thereby institutionalizes the reciprocal exchange of rights, duties, and recognitions (definitive features of heteronomy). The society of states comprising the international system was similarly arranged, though the hierarchies were more informal, except in the case of colonial possessions.

In the eighteenth and nineteenth centuries a novel, modern hegemony developed that places heteronomous relations at its center. These heteronomous ideas were exported globally by the supremely hierarchical mechanism of European colonization campaigns. This conflation of the principles and practices of heteronomy and hierarchy inform the prevailing body of globally hegemonic ideas. The twentieth-century premium placed on heteronomous relations is evident in efforts to liberalize international trade and introduce democratic values throughout much of the world. The reliance upon hierarchies of power and influence are equally evident in U.S. leadership during Desert Storm and the expansion of NATO membership, the lack of U.S. leadership concerning Bosnia and Rwanda, and U.S. criticisms of the UN and its reform efforts.

Property rights, as rules and practices that constitute systems of rule and domination (e.g., Waldron, 1988:31), inform and illustrate these social changes, ruled relations, and the prevailing hegemony. Indeed, "hegemony involves the very production of categories of identity and the society of which they are a part" (Doty, 1996:8). I hope I have made clear the significance of property rights in such matters. The changes in property rights visible in the seventeenth century are especially significant because "the hegemonic form of politics becomes dominant only at the beginning of modern times, when the reproduction of the different social areas takes place in permanently changing conditions" (Doty, 1996:8–9). Set within the crosshairs, the patterns of rules and rule comprising social relations become clearer.

	POLITICAL	ECONOMIC
INTERNATIONAL	great power hierarchy legal, formal heteronomy of interstate treaties practical heteronomy of interstate relations cultural hegemony of modernity	corporate hierarchy commercial and social heteronomy cultural hegemony of commercial exchange
NATIONAL	administrative hierarchy of institutional- legal orders political heteronomy of rights-bearing "possessive individualism" social hegemony of burgeoning nationalism cultural hegemony of heteronomous relations, notably the reciprocal exchange of rights and duties in a liberal-constitutional institutional-legal order	corporate hierarchy commercial and social heteronomy of rights-bearing "possessive individualism" cultural hegemony of heteronomous relations, notably the reciprocal exchange of (commercial) goods in a market

**Figure 3   The Conceptual Framework of the
Modern World(view) and Patterns of Social Relations**

Similarly, since sovereignty and the split between politics and economics are also social conditions and practices (Walker, 1993:154), so, too, is the edifice of conventional IPE a social practice. Efforts to defend the constitutive crosshairs buttress both a discipline and a worldview. Yet the ideological stamp of conventional IPE goes generally unrecognized amid the striking durability of the ontological foundations depicted by the crosshairs and the consistent manner in which scholars, policymakers, and average citizens represent this framework. As Doty (1996:9–10) notes, echoing Michel Foucault, the unity and coherence of scholarly fields, social endeavors, and commonsense perspectives are found not in subjects, objects, concepts, or themes, but in a regular and consistent logic of representational (discursive) practices. Distinct but overlapping patterns of rule-bound relations reinforce the enduring foundations and representational practices. For example, IR and IPE offer description and stipulation. Conventional IR and IPE lack theories of the state, capitalism, and the global system. Also typically lacking are history, interpretation, socially contingent behavior, and attention to the emergence of historical structures. Gilpin (1987:10, note 1) stipulates his ahistorical foundations: "State and market, whatever their respective origins, have independent existences, have logics of their own, and interact with one another." That is, according to Gilpin, states and markets are unproblematic givens with histories irrelevant to their interactions. A deep premise holds that liberalism comprehends and coordinates states and capitalism. This premise reinforces popular acceptance of states and capitalism as the defining elements of the international system.

Alternatively, as Walker (1993:21) notes, "if the early-modern principle of state sovereignty that still guides contemporary political thought is so problematic, . . . [then] it is necessary to attend to the questions to which that principle was merely an historically specific response." By investigating the property rights debates impinging on sovereignty and the conceptual bifurcation of property, I offer answers that are richly textured, theoretically informed, and, I hope, creatively constructed. Indeed, my goal is to illustrate sovereignty and the politics/economics split through social construction. Although most social scientists offer parthenogenesis rather than generative theories, I seek self-consciously to build from Ruggie's challenge to distinguish descriptive structures from generative ones. The former are merely "abstract summaries of patterned interactions," but generative structures generate or constitute actors' identities and behaviors. In exploring generative structures, one seeks "to discover the underlying principles that govern the patterning of interactions" (Ruggie, 1983:266, note 16). In this vein, I introduce constitutive principles to advance this argument but link them to social rules to demonstrate that actors, in turn, generate or constitute the prevailing social structures. Thus, the perspective I advance in this volume is neither structuralist nor descriptive. In contrast, many social scientists—and most IR and IPE theorists—stipulate and describe social life in ideological terms rather than explain or interpret it. Individuals and groups define and construct the world through their worldviews and practices.

As an ideology, the ontological foundations of modernity constitute the framework of the global system and liberalism (e.g., M. Weber, 1958; Habermas, 1987:1–2; Toulmin, 1990:7–13; Seidman, 1983:14–18; Gray, 1986:7–15, 62–72). In one sense, the crosshairs constituting IPE's ontological framework situate the state, state system, capitalist economic activity, and domestic society. Prominent seventeenth-century actors hailed this framework as rational and virtuous. "The comprehensive system of ideas about nature and humanity that formed the scaffolding of Modernity was

thus a social and political as well as a scientific device: It was seen as conferring Divine legitimacy on the political order of the sovereign nation-
state" (Toulmin, 1990:128). Thus emerges our modern sense of domestic
and international politics, a separate system of economic relations, and the
centrality of reason and certainty as the measures of knowledgeable human
practice. Similarly, liberal notions of individual liberties and rights develop. Individuals discover that as sovereigns confront foreign threats and
domestic foes, sovereign authority protects (or usurps) individual rights.
Other individual rights are exchangeable in the market.

Though these social systems appear "natural," they were seventeenth-
century constructions built atop the fiction of *absolute* sovereignty, at least
of the unassailably absolutist variety imagined by Bodin, Hobbes, and west
European political theorists. Following the lead of such thinkers, the
renowned legal theorist John Austin (1790–1859) concludes that the law is
whatever the sovereign utters or commands. Austin (1832/1954:132) writes
that "every law simply and strictly so called is set by a sovereign person . . .
or (changing the expression) it is set by a monarch, or sovereign number, to
a person or persons in a state of subjection to its author" (see also Onuf,
1989:69–71). Indeed, for Austin a proper law must involve three characteristics: a "*command,* issued by a *sovereign* (superior to the subjects of the
law) and backed by a *sanction*" (Beck et al., 1996:56–57; emphasis in original). To this day most laymen continue to define the law in these narrow
terms.

Also, actors constituted from the landed confines of traditional politics
a seemingly natural economic world of fluid commerce. "The intellectual
scaffolding of Modernity was thus a set of provisional and speculative half-
truths" (Toulmin, 1990:116–117). As contemporary individuals now conceive the world in these terms—seemingly concrete but far from absolute—
they displace republican virtue and right reason for other social values.
Notably, these include the rational pursuit of self-interest through statecraft
and market exchange. In toppling one form of domination, others emerge.

Indeed, deeply implicated in these practices, as with all rule-based phenomena, are exploitation and domination. Imperial rapine, colonial impov-
erishment, capitalist underdevelopment, domestic coercion, and the daily
miseries of cheating and theft each testify to omnipresent modern exploitation. Actors justify and effect such behavior through systems of rules that
simultaneously privilege and dispossess as they also constitute conditions
and regulate behavior. Domination is not unique to modern life, but liberal-
modern domination is one version of a wider condition. So constructed,
IPE is also a political practice involving property rights and specific forms
of exploitation. For example, consider the deep normative and rule-based
implications of an apparently objective observation by Robert Gilpin
(1987:304):

> Like any Western predatory nation the NICs [newly industrializing coun-
> tries] have not hesitated to pursue policies that damage the economies of
> other Third World countries.

To explore the constitution of the modern international system is to
explore the constitution of a worldview or ideology, bringing to light the
simultaneous co-constitution of international social relations and social
actors. To examine these mutually constitutive relations is to examine constitutive practices, which in turn shift one's attention to the social rules that
are the medium of social behavior and choice-making. Thus, one must also
investigate the worldviews through which actors conceive rules, roles, and
relations. Worldviews set the conceptual context for actual practices.
Attention to property and property rights captures both worldviews (property as a constitutive principle) and rules (property rights).

For example, human rights advocates press their claims in the vocabulary of property rights (Hannum, 1990). Indeed, the UN hailed the 1948
Universal Declaration of Human Rights as an "international bill of rights."
Individuals "possess" these rights, which can be neither alienated nor
abridged. Governments seek to protect their "sovereign integrity" and
extend their sovereign rights in the same vocabulary of property rights (C.
Weber, 1995). Oppressive and suspicious governments use property rights
objections to protest international plans to intervene in their countries to
offer humanitarian aid, engage in peacekeeping operations, or end violence
(Lyons and Mastanduno, 1995). Despite the prominence of appeals to property rights, defeated or ignored governments often see their property rights
reshaped. For example, Germany was carved up after World War II. In
1989, U.S. troops kidnapped or "arrested" Manuel Noriega, the
Panamanian head of state. Similarly, since 1991, Iraq has endured a no-fly
zone imposed on its allegedly sovereign territory. The government of the
People's Republic of China eagerly awaited the return of its property rights
to Hong Kong. Note, however, that NATO forces will not violate Serbian
territory to arrest Radovan Karadzic for war crimes, nor did U.S. aircraft
"trespass" in Libyan airspace to deliver equipment to Operation Desert
Storm or relief supplies to Rwanda. In the 1980s the U.S. Air Force did
down a Libyan military jet and bomb targets in Libya, but proudly declared
that the U.S. planes had not entered Libyan territory. Clearly the rules and
principles are flexibly arbitrary. Yet even by the premises of power politics
evident in conventional IPE, political practice reconstitutes the crosshairs
of modernity.

Similarly, the advocates, adherents, and adversaries of high finance
and global trade press their views in the vocabulary of property rights. In so
doing, they retrace, if only slightly, the boundaries of sovereignty and the
divisions between economic, political, and social realms. So, also by these

market-oriented premises, actors' practices reconstruct the crosshairs and conceptual framework of modernity and the international system. Attention to property rights helps track these practices and their constitutive consequences.

The implications for sovereignty, the politics/economics dichotomy, and modernity merit brief attention. Scholars and pundits now commonly remark on the speed or severity of social change, whether to comment mundanely on "profound economic and technological transformations" (Camilleri and Falk, 1992:6) or to share the anxieties of "temporal velocities and incongruities," "the speed of dissolution [and] accelerative tendencies," and "unpredictable volatilities" (Walker, 1993:3). Observers typically gauge these dynamics in terms of the crosshairs I identify, rhetorically asking about "the end of sovereignty" or the era "beyond Westphalia" (Camilleri and Falk, 1992; Lyons and Mastanduno, 1995). Or one blanches at the prospect that economic matters will eclipse political and social ones, whether the subject is the speed or volume of high finance, the mobility of production or facilities, or the uncertainty of future conditions. Some, like Camilleri and Falk (1992:4–6), suffer both anxieties. It is significant, however, that these conceptual crosshairs continue to constitute the character and conditions of modern social life, practices, and outlooks.

Yet these crosshairs are not fixed. They never were. The spaces and divisions are not absolute. When Camilleri and Falk (1992:4), for example, assert "the extraordinary *penetration* of economic market relations into almost all aspects of human life" (emphasis added), they vividly convey the crosshairs and their contingent character. Switching the metaphor to frameworks, this view reifies a compartmentalized, segregated world(view) that encourages us to see "walls" rather than "relations." Walls must be penetrated or broken through for separated concerns to interact. This view connotes fixed, threatened frameworks buckling against irresistible forces, much as a beach house splinters against hurricane winds and tides. I exaggerate for effect, but I strive to make a contrary point in this volume. Humans construct and constitute these frameworks. While frameworks may imprison us, they need not. However, since these conceptual dividers are the load-bearing walls of the modern edifice, their change necessarily threatens collapse and precipitates anxiety. *Post*modernity may beckon. Our task, then, much as it was in the seventeenth century, is to recraft society. Indeed, in thoroughly constructivist terms, we always reshape society in the face of changing material and conceptual conditions.

In this context, one might better see (conceive) that sovereignty is neither a condition nor a characteristic. Rather, sovereignty is a social practice. Sovereignty is made, maintained, and exercised. Cynthia Weber (1995) writes that sovereignty is also represented and simulated. The same holds for the conceptual split between economics and politics and for the conceptual borders marking other allegedly distinct social realms: religion, culture, class, family, gender, public/private, home/work, home/homeless, and religion/school, for example. Each is staked and built from some sense of property and rights, just as sovereignty is. For these myriad reasons, Pennington (1993:284) declares that "simple answers cannot describe the complex evolution of Western theories of sovereignty." Accurate answers must be as rich and diverse as constitutive human practices.

Yet because these practices are constitutive, we never lack options. Botwinick (1983:37) shares a keen insight: "The existence of sovereign authority forms a precondition for our world as we know it, and therefore consent in the formation of sovereignty can be formally, rationally reconstructed." If we, as social members, regard sovereign authority as essential in some sense, then we may choose to preserve or reconstruct it. We may constitute functional equivalents. Or we may construct alternatives.

No matter what we choose and do, sovereignty gets reshaped and reconceived, if only imperceptibly. For example, efforts at national integration or economic union (such as the European Union and the North American Free Trade Agreement) dramatically erode anachronistic notions of absolute state sovereignty. Pat Buchanan repeatedly sang this theme during his recent U.S. presidential campaign. Similarly, developing notions of human rights erode sovereign authority by suggesting that some norms trump sovereignty. Wedded to notions of intervention, this combination disintegrates the fundamental principles of the international system as codified in positive international law. Alternatively, we might imagine that such challenges merely reconceive sovereignty rather than obliterate it. To entertain a conception of sovereignty that recognizes norms above and beyond national positive law is to recall a body of thought deeply rooted in Western philosophy, law, and history (Pennington, 1993:290). Such thought apprehends a more fluidly contingent and less concrete world.

In this sense, I hope this book contributes thoughtful critique to society and scholarship. Indeed, I seek here to contribute to the diverse bodies of critical theory and "critical social science" (Fay, 1987) by applying its themes to a specific case and empirical content. Cries for such demonstrations and applications have sounded from many corners (e.g., Biersteker, 1989:266–267; Goldstein and Keohane, 1993:26–27). In broader terms, I hope that this volume meets Bernstein's (1976) call for restructuring social and political theory by integrating empirical research, interpretation, and critique. Neufeld (1995) seconds this call and applies it specifically to IR theory. To highlight these related goals, I echo R.B.J. Walker's conclusions about apt foundations for social theory reflections on global life:

> First, I affirm the priority of history, and thus of approaches that stress interpretation, practice and the critique of reification. Second, I insist that

differences between approaches to contemporary world politics must be addressed at the level of basic ontological assumptions: the possibility of empirical research strategies is a significant but decidedly secondary matter. Third, I again suggest that the contemporary analysis of world politics poses fundamental questions of political theory—questions that remain interesting and provocative despite socio-scientific attempts to reduce them to problems of utilitarian calculation and empirical testing. (Walker, 1993:82)

Like Walker, I consider ontological foundations—for me, conceptual frameworks are basic ontological elements—in order to inform world-views, so to gain leverage on theory and policy, thus to address broad ethical and ideological concerns. By restructuring theory and locating critique within the scope of theoretical investigation and scholarly practice, I hope to open opportunities to reconceive and restructure social life.

By reconceiving society and ideology, I seek not only to inform their contingent character but also to reveal their constitutive relationship. If we view them in these terms, we more easily see that critique and culture have become indistinguishably entwined. This intermingling is "the defining characteristic of the postmodern" sensibility (Connor, 1989:12). It hails not a revolution in culture but a significant reconfiguration of power and domination within and across cultural, critical, and academic institutions. The scholarly practices of scientific inquiry and theoretical puzzle-solving are significant among such institutions. From this view, postmodernity questions and blurs boundaries, thus rendering indistinguishable the social and cultural, the political and ideological (Connor, 1989:61). Critical theory clearly shares these premises. So does this volume. In demonstrating the development of a set of conceptual crosshairs, I illustrate that the boundaries are always blurry, so must be arbitrarily erected and supported.

As a matter of theory, this book illustrates a constructivist approach and illuminates the constitution of the conceptual framework of the modern era. Regarding subject matter, I hope this book helps readers understand in a new light the transition from late feudalism to the early modern era. I intend to contribute indirectly to the literatures on the rise of the modern world system and the emergence of the modern state (e.g., Wallerstein, 1974a, 1980, 1989; Tilly, 1975; Mann, 1988; Thomson, 1994; Bonney, 1995). In particular, I will be pleased if readers now conceive the "transitions" in part as matters of changing understandings and practices rendered coherent by attention to property and property rights.

Concerning the conceptual subjects, I intend to show that one can effectively and insightfully measure social change in terms of conceptual change. Indeed, I hope this volume effectively demonstrates that conceptual histories valuably inform for us events, circumstances, and social change. Further, comparative conceptual histories are a unique and little used form of comparative analysis. I intend as well to reveal something of the significance and character of the concepts property and property rights that evade more traditional philosophic, legal, economic, and philological treatments. However, in the hands of masters like C. B. Macpherson, J.G.A. Pocock, and Richard Tuck, such investigations offer enduring rewards.

This volume also meets the challenges to compile genealogical and conceptual histories of sovereignty in order to reveal the "imposed interpretations which organize modern political reality as well as our understanding of that reality" (Bartelson, 1995:54). My purpose is to illustrate the sources of conceptual differentiation by demonstrating various components and facets of sovereignty as well as their social construction and cultural imposition. In this sense, my consideration of property rights helps inform "personal sovereignty" and its twin liberties: The negative liberty by which one enjoys freedom from interference and the positive liberty bestowing freedom to act in a self-directing manner (Berlin, 1969:ch. 3, and Jackson's 1990 application). Similarly, notions of "absolute sovereignty" correspond remarkably to the prevailing scientific and philosophical premises of scientific inquiry. For example, a cardinal premise holds that there exists a place or location from which to view affairs from on high, removed, objectively. This place or person is God-like, autonomous, and sufficiently powerful to preserve its status and self-identity across space and time. This is an absolute sovereign.

Last, I hope my endeavor is a creative success in two senses: For a thoughtful harvesting from diverse fields and for a thoughtful reconstruction of the elements into a constructivist account. I argue broadly that the constitution of the international system occurs as a function of the roles of property in statecraft, political theory, jurisprudence, national and international law, and international political economy. We recognize these patterns by adopting constructivist ideological premises that differ from the positivist-empiricist philosophical foundations that ground the international system and the modern world(view). To the degree that these constructivist foundations help us conceive and create alternative social relations, I will count my efforts here a success. Indeed, I also hope this research creatively advances critical theorists' efforts to "validate [our critical work] in terms of the lives of those to whom it is ultimately directed" (Neufeld, 1995:124). May we fare well in our constructive practices.

Bibliography

[Numbers in brackets indicate chapters in this book where the reference is cited.]

ABRAMS, Philip. (1981) *Historical Sociology.* Ithaca, NY: Cornell University Press. [1, 4]

AGNEW, John. (1994) "Timeless Space and State-Centrism: The Geographical Assumptions of International Relations Theory." In S. Rosow et al., eds., *The Global Economy as Political Space,* 87–106. Boulder, CO: Lynne Rienner Publishers. [7]

ANDERSON, Perry. (1974) *Lineages of the Absolutist State.* London: New Left Books. [1, 3, 5]

ANDREWS, Kenneth R. (1984) *Trade, Plunder and Settlement: Maritime Enterprise and the Genesis of the British Empire, 1480–1630.* New York: Cambridge University Press. [1, 7]

ARBLASTER, Anthony. (1984) *The Rise and Decline of Western Liberalism.* New York: Basil Blackwell. [1, 7]

ARDANT, Gabriel. (1975) "Financial Policy and Economic Infrastructure of Modern States and Nations." In C. Tilly, ed., *The Formation of National States in Western Europe,* 164–242. Princeton, NJ: Princeton University Press. [1, 6]

ARTHUR, C. J. (1970) "Editor's Introduction." In C. J. Arthur, ed., *The German Ideology,* by Karl Marx and Frederick Engels, 4–34. New York: International Publishers. [2]

ASHCRAFT, Richard. (1986) *Revolutionary Politics and Locke's Two Treatises of Government.* Princeton, NJ: Princeton University Press. [3]

ASHLEY, Richard K. (1983) "Three Modes of Economism." *International Studies Quarterly* 27(4) December:465–499. [1, 7]

———. (1988) "Untying the Sovereign State: A Double Reading of the Anarchy Problematique." *Millennium* 17(2) Summer:227–262. [7]

———. (1989) "Living on Border Lines: Man, Poststructuralism, and War." In J. Der Derian and M. Shapiro, eds., *International/Intertextual Relations: Postmodern Readings of World Politics,* 163–187. Lexington, MA: Lexington Books. [1, 7]

ASTON, T., ed. (1965) *Crisis in Europe: 1560–1660.* London: Routledge and Kegan Paul. [1]

AUSTIN, J. L. (1961) *Philosophical Papers.* New York: Clarendon Press. [1, 4]

———. (1965) *How to Do Things with Words.* Edited by J. O. Urmson. New York: Oxford University Press. [4]

AUSTIN, John. (1832/1954) *The Province of Jurisprudence Determined* and *The Uses of the Study of Jurisprudence.* Introduction by H. L. A. Hart. London: Weidenfeld and Nicholson. [8]

BALDWIN, James. (1955) *Notes of a Native Son.* New York: Dial Press. [1]

163

BALL, Terence, James FARR, and Russell L. HANSON, eds. (1989) *Political Innovation and Conceptual Change*. New York: Cambridge University Press. [1, 4, 7]

BARTELSON, Jens. (1995) *A Genealogy of Sovereignty*. New York: Cambridge University Press. [1, 3, 7, 8]

BECK, Robert J., Anthony C. AREND, and Robert D. VANDER LUGT. (1996) *International Rules: Approaches from International Law and International Relations*. New York: Oxford University Press. [8]

BEIK, William. (1985) *Absolutism and Society in Seventeenth-Century France: State Power and Provincial Aristocracy in Languedoc*. New York: Cambridge University Press. [1, 6]

BENJAMIN, Roger, and Raymond DUVALL. (1985) "The Capitalist State in Context." In Roger Benjamin and Stephen L. Elkin, eds., *The Democratic State*. Lawrence, KS: University Press of Kansas. [5]

BERLIN, Isaiah. (1969) *Four Essays on Liberty*. New York: Oxford University Press. [2, 3, 4, 8]

BERMAN, Harold J. (1983) *Law and Revolution: The Formation of the Western Legal Tradition*. Cambridge, MA: Harvard University Press. [4]

BERNSTEIN, Richard J. (1976) *The Restructuring of Social and Political Theory*. Philadelphia: University of Pennsylvania Press. [1, 7, 8]

———. (1983) *Beyond Objectivism and Relativism: Science, Hermeneutics, and Praxis*. Philadelphia: University of Pennsylvania Press. [1, 7]

BIERSTEKER, Thomas. (1989) "Critical Reflections on Post-Positivism in International Relations." *International Studies Quarterly* 33(3) September:263–267. [8]

BIERSTEKER, Thomas, and Cynthia WEBER, eds. (1996) *State Sovereignty as a Social Construction*. New York: Cambridge University Press. [1]

BLACK'S LAW DICTIONARY. (1990) 6th edition. St. Paul, MN: West Publishing Company. [2, 4, 5, 6, 7]

BODIN, Jean. (1576/1992) *On Sovereignty: Four Chapters from The Six Books of the Commonwealth (Les Six livres de la république)*. Edited and translated by Julian H. Franklin. New York: Cambridge University Press. [1, 3, 5]

BONNEY, Richard. (1978) *Political Change in France under Richelieu and Mazarin, 1624–1661*. Oxford: Oxford University Press. [1, 5, 6]

———. (1981) *The King's Debts: Finance and Politics in France, 1589–1661*. New York: Oxford University Press. [1]

———, ed. (1995) *The Origins of the Modern State in Europe, Thirteenth to Eighteenth Centuries: Economic Systems and State Finance*. New York: Oxford University Press. [1, 8]

BOTWINICK, Aryeh. (1983) *Hobbes and Modernity: Five Exercises in Political Philosophical Exegesis*. Lanham, MD: University Press of America. [8]

BOWEN, Catherine Drinker. (1957) *The Lion and the Throne: The Life and Times of Sir Edward Coke (1552–1634)*. Boston: Little, Brown & Company. [5]

BRAUN, Rudolf. (1975) "Taxation, Socio-Political Structure, and State-Building: Great Britain and Brandenburg-Prussia." In C. Tilly, ed., *The Formation of National States in Western Europe*, 243–327. Princeton, NJ: Princeton University Press. [1, 6]

BREWER, John. (1980) "English Radicalism in the Age of George III." In J.G.A. Pocock, ed., *Three British Revolutions: 1641, 1688, 1776*, 323–367. Princeton, NJ: Princeton University Press. [3]

BRUSTEIN, William. (1981) "A Regional Mode-of-Production Analysis of

Political Behavior: The Cases of Western and Mediterranean France." *Politics and Society* 10:355–398. [1]

———. (1985) "Class Conflict and Class Collaboration in Regional Rebellions, 1500–1700." *Theory and Society* 14:445–468. [1]

BRYANT, Arthur. (1934/1976) *The England of Charles II*. Facsimile of 1934 edition. New York: Ayer. [1]

BUCKLE, Stephen. (1991) *Natural Law and the Theory of Property: Grotius to Hume*. New York: Clarendon Press. [3]

BULL, Hedley. (1977) *The Anarchical Society: A Study of Order in World Politics*. New York: Columbia University Press. [1]

BURCH, Kurt. (1994) "The 'Properties' of the State System and Global Capitalism." In S. Rosow et al., eds., *The Global Economy as Political Space*, 37–59. Boulder, CO: Lynne Rienner Publishers. [1, 7]

———. (1995) "Intellectual Property Rights and the Culture of Global Liberalism." *Science Communication* 17(2) December:214–232. [7]

———. (1996) "Illustrating Constructivism: George Kennan and the Social Construction of the Cold War." *Swords and Ploughshares* 6(1) Fall:3–22. [1, 2]

BURCH, Kurt, and Robert DENEMARK, eds. (1997) *Constituting International Political Economy*. Boulder, CO: Lynne Rienner Publishers. [1]

CAM, Helen. (1962) *Law-Finders and Law-Makers in Medieval England: Collected Studies in Legal and Constitutional History*. London: Merlin Press. [1, 4]

CAMILLERI, Joseph A., and Jim FALK. (1992) *The End of Sovereignty? The Politics of a Shrinking and Fragmenting World*. Brookfield, VT: Edward Elgar. [1, 8]

CARVER, T. (1995) "Ideology: Career of a Concept." In T. Ball and R. Dagger, eds., *Ideals and Ideologies*, 1–11. 2nd edition. New York: HarperCollins. [7]

CATON, Hiram. (1988) *The Politics of Progress: The Origins and Development of the Commercial Republic, 1600–1835*. Gainesville: University of Florida Press. [1]

CHASE-DUNN, Christopher. (1981) "Interstate System and Capitalist World-Economy: One Logic or Two?" *International Studies Quarterly* 25(1) March:19–42. [1, 7]

CHAUDHURI, K. N. (1965) *The English East India Company: The Study of an Early Joint Stock Company, 1600–1640*. London: Cass. [1, 6]

———. (1978) *The Trading World of Asia and the English East India Company, 1660–1760*. New York: Cambridge University Press. [1, 6]

CHRISTIANSON, Paul. (1978) *Reformers and Babylon: English Apocalyptic Visions from the Reformation to the Eve of the Civil War*. Toronto: University of Toronto Press. [1, 4]

CIPOLLA, Carlo M. (1980) *Before the Industrial Revolution: European Society and Economy, 1000–1700*. 2nd edition. New York: W. W. Norton. [6]

CLARK, L. M. G. (1979) "Women and Locke: Who Owns the Apples in the Garden of Eden?" In L. M. G. Clark and L. Lange, eds., *The Sexism of Social and Political Theory*, 16–40. Toronto: University of Toronto Press. [2]

CLAY, C.G.A. (1984a) *Economic Expansion and Social Change: England, 1500–1700*. Vol. 1: *People, Land and Towns*. New York: Cambridge University Press. [1]

———. (1984b) *Economic Expansion and Social Change: England, 1500–1700*. Vol. 2: *Industry, Trade and Government*. New York: Cambridge University Press. [1, 5, 6]

CLOUGH, Shepard B. (1959) *The Economic Development of Western Civilization.* New York: McGraw-Hill. [6]

COATES, Willson H. (1970) "An Analysis of Major Conflicts in Seventeenth Century England." In W. A. Aiken and B. D. Henning, eds., *Conflict in Stuart England: Essays in Honour of Wallace Notestein,* 15–40. Archon Books. [1]

COKE, Sir Edward. (1628/1986) *The First Part of the Institutes of the Laws of England: A Commentary upon Littleton.* Buffalo, NY: W. S. Hein. [5]

———. (1644a/1986) *The Second Part of the Institutes of the Laws of England, Containing the Exposition of Many Ancient and Other Statutes.* Buffalo, NY: W. S. Hein. [5]

———. (1644b/1986) *The Third Part of the Institutes of the Laws of England, Concerning High Treason and Other Pleas of the Crown and Criminal Cases.* Buffalo, NY: W. S. Hein. [5]

———. (1644c/1986) *The Fourth Part of the Institutes of the Laws of England, Concerning the Jurisdiction of Courts.* Buffalo, NY: W. S. Hein. [5]

CONNELL, R. W. (1987) *Gender and Power: Society, the Person and Sexual Politics.* Stanford, CA: Stanford University Press. [2]

CONNOR, Steven. (1989) *Postmodernist Culture: An Introduction to Theories of the Contemporary.* New York: Basil Blackwell. [8]

COWLES, Virginia. (1960) *The Great Swindle: The Story of the South Sea Bubble.* New York: Harper and Brothers. [1]

COX, Robert W. (1981) "Social Forces, States and World Orders: Beyond International Relations Theory." *Millennium* 10(2) Summer:126–155. [1]

DALY, James. (1979) *Sir Robert Filmer and English Political Thought.* Toronto: University of Toronto Press. [2]

D'AMATO, Anthony. (1984) *Jurisprudence: A Descriptive and Normative Analysis of Law.* Boston: Martinus Nijhoff Publishers. [4]

DARNTON, Robert. (1984) *The Great Cat Massacre and Other Episodes in French Cultural History.* New York: Basic Books. [1, 4]

DAVIES, K. G. (1957) *The Royal African Company.* New York: Longmans, Green. [1]

DAVIS, Ralph. (1962) *The Rise of the English Shipping Industry in the Seventeenth and Eighteenth Centuries.* New York: Macmillan. [1, 6]

de GRAZIA, Sebastian. (1989) *Machiavelli in Hell.* Princeton, NJ: Princeton University Press. [5]

de JOUVENAL, Bertrand. (1957) *Sovereignty: An Inquiry into the Political Good.* Translated by J. F. Huntington. Chicago: University of Chicago Press. [1, 7]

DEMSETZ, Harold. (1967) "Toward a Theory of Property Rights." *American Economic Review* 57(2): 347–359. [1]

de VRIES, Jan. (1976) *The Economy of Europe in an Age of Crisis, 1600–1750.* New York: Cambridge University Press. [1, 6]

DOBB, Maurice. (1946) *Studies in the Development of Capitalism.* London: Routledge and Kegan Paul. [1]

DOTY, Roxanne. (1996) *Imperial Encounters: The Politics of Representation in North-South Relations.* Minneapolis: University of Minnesota Press. [1, 8]

DWORKIN, Ronald. (1977) *Taking Rights Seriously.* Cambridge, MA: Harvard University Press. [4]

DUNN, John. (1969) *The Political Thought of John Locke.* New York: Cambridge University Press. [2, 3]

EDGERTON, Robert B. (1985) *Rules, Exceptions, and Social Order.* Berkeley: University of California Press. [4]

EKELUND, Robert B., Jr., and Robert D. TOLLISON. (1981) *Mercantilism as a Rent-Seeking Society.* College Station: Texas A & M University Press. [6]

ENGELS, Frederick. (1884/1972) *The Origin of the Family, Private Property and the State.* Edited, with an introduction, by Eleanor Burke Leacock. New York: International Publishers. [2]

EPSTEIN, M. (1908/1968) *The Early History of the Levant Company.* New York: Augustus M. Kelley Publishers. [1]

ERGANG, Robert. (1954). *Europe: From the Renaissance to Waterloo.* Revised edition. Boston: D. C. Heath. [6]

FARR, James. (1989) "Understanding Conceptual Change Politically." In T. Ball, J. Farr, and R. L. Hanson, eds., *Political Innovation and Conceptual Change,* 24–49. New York: Cambridge University Press. [1]

FAY, Brian. (1987) *Critical Social Science.* Ithaca, NY: Cornell University Press. [8]

FEHRENBACH, T. R. (1968) *Lone Star: A History of Texas and the Texans.* New York: American Legacy Press. [6]

FERGUSON, Arthur B. (1979) *Clio Unbound: Perception of the Social and Historical Past in Renaissance England.* Durham, NC: Duke University Press. [1, 4]

FIELD, Barry C. (1989) "The Evolution of Property Rights." *Kyklos* 42(3):319–345. [1]

FILMER, Robert. (1680/1949) *Patriarcha and Other Political Works of Sir Robert Filmer.* Edited, with an introduction, by Peter Laslett. New York: Oxford University Press. [2, 3]

FISHER, Irving. (1911/1931) *The Purchasing Power of Money: Its Determination and Relation to Credit Interest and Crises.* Assisted by Harry G. Brown. New and revised edition. New York: Macmillan. [6]

FOWLER, Michael Ross, and Julie Marie BUNCK. (1995) *Law, Power, and the Sovereign State: The Evolution and Application of the Concept of Sovereignty.* University Park: Pennsylvania State University Press. [1]

FRANKLIN, Julian. (1978) *John Locke and the Theory of Sovereignty.* New York: Cambridge University Press. [1, 3]

———. (1992) "Introduction." In J. Bodin, ed., *On Sovereignty,* ix–xxvi. Edited and translated by J. H. Franklin. New York: Cambridge University Press. [5]

FREEDEMAN, Charles E. (1979) *Joint-Stock Enterprise in France, 1807–1867: From Privileged Company to Modern Corporation.* Chapel Hill: University of North Carolina Press. [6]

FURBER, Holden. (1976) *Rival Empires of Trade in the Orient, 1600–1800.* Minneapolis: University of Minnesota Press. [1, 6]

GAUS, Gerald F. (1980) "Property and Justice: A Select Bibliography." In J. R. Pennock and J. W. Chapman, eds., *Property,* 385–406. New York: New York University Press. [1, 2]

GEERTZ, Clifford. (1973) *The Interpretation of Cultures.* New York: Basic Books. [4, 7]

GIDDENS, Anthony. (1979) *Central Problems in Social Theory.* Berkeley: University of California Press. [2]

———. (1984) *The Constitution of Society.* Berkeley: University of California Press. [1, 4]

———. (1990) *The Consequences of Modernity.* Stanford, CA: Stanford University Press. [7]

GILL, Stephen, and David LAW. (1988) *The Global Political Economy.* Baltimore, MD: Johns Hopkins University Press. [7]

GILPIN, Robert. (1981) *War and Change in World Politics.* New York: Cambridge University Press. [1]

———. (1987) *The Political Economy of International Relations.* Princeton, NJ: Princeton University Press. [1, 7, 8]

GOLDING, William. (1959) *Lord of the Flies.* New York: Capricorn Books. [2]

GOLDSTEIN, Joshua. (1997) "Taking Off the Gender Blinders in IPE." In K. Burch and R. Denemark, eds., *Constituting International Political Economy,* 189–194. Boulder, CO: Lynne Rienner Publishers. [1]

GOLDSTEIN, Judith, and Robert O. KEOHANE, eds. (1993) *Ideas and Foreign Policy: Beliefs, Institutions, and Political Change.* Ithaca, NY: Cornell University Press. [8]

GOTTLIEB, Gidon. (1974) "The Nature of International Law." In C. Black and R. Falk, eds., *The Future of the International Legal Order,* 331–383. Princeton, NJ: Princeton University Press. [1]

GRAY, John. (1986) *Liberalism.* Minneapolis: University of Minnesota Press. [2, 7, 8]

GREENLEAF, W. H. (1964) *Order, Empiricism, and Politics: Two Traditions of English Political Thought, 1500–1700.* New York: Oxford University Press. [3]

GRIMSHAW, Jean. (1986) *Philosophy and Feminist Thinking.* Minneapolis: University of Minnesota Press. [2]

GROTIUS, Hugo. (1609/1916) *Mare liberum (The Freedom of the Seas).* New York: Oxford University Press. [6]

———. (1625/1949) *The Law of War and Peace (De jure belli ac pacis).* Translated by Louise R. Loomis. With an introduction by P. E. Corbett. Roslyn, NY: Walter J. Black. [1, 6]

———. (1625/1957) *"Prolegomena" to the Law of War and Peace.* Translated by Francis W. Kelsey. With an introduction by Edward Dumbauld. New York: Liberal Arts Press. [1, 6]

HABERMAS, Jürgen. (1973) *Theory and Practice.* Translated by John Viertel. Boston: Beacon Press. [7]

———. (1984) *The Theory of Communicative Action.* Vol. 1: *Reason and the Rationalization of Society.* Translated by T. McCarthy. Boston: Beacon Press. [4]

———. (1987). *The Philosophical Discourse of Modernity: Twelve Lectures.* Translated by Frederick Lawrence. Cambridge, MA: MIT Press. [7, 8]

HADDEN, Tom. (1979) Review of *Law and the Rise of Capitalism,* by M. E. Tigar and M. R. Levy. *International Journal of the Sociology of Law* 7(1):109–111. [1, 6]

HAMILTON, Malcolm B. (1987) "The Elements of the Concept of Ideology." *Political Studies* 1:18–38. [7]

HAMILTON, Roberta. (1978) *The Liberation of Women: A Study of Patriarchy and Capitalism.* Boston: Allen and Unwin. [2]

HANNAY, David. (1926) *The Great Chartered Companies.* London: Williams and Norgate. [1, 6]

HANNUM, Hurst. (1990) *Autonomy, Sovereignty, and Self-Determination: The Accommodation of Conflicting Rights.* Philadelphia: University of Pennsylvania Press. [1, 8]

HARDING, Alan. (1966) *A Social History of English Law.* Baltimore, MD: Penguin Books. [1, 4, 5]

HARRINGTON, James. (1656/1977) *The Commonwealth of Oceana.* In J.G.A. Pocock, ed., *The Political Works of James Harrington,* 155–358. New York: Cambridge University Press. [3]

HART, H.L.A. (1955) "Are There Any Natural Rights?" *Philosophical Review* 64:175–191. [4]

———. (1961) *The Concept of Law*. Oxford: Oxford University Press. [1, 4]

HARTSOCK, Nancy. (1983) *Money, Sex, and Power: Toward a Feminist Historical Materialism*. Boston: Northeastern University Press. [2]

HARVEY, David. (1990) *The Condition of Postmodernity: An Enquiry into the Origins of Cultural Change*. Cambridge, MA: Basil Blackwell. [7]

HECKSCHER, Eli. (1934) *Mercantilism*. 2 vols. London: Allen and Unwin. [6]

HILL, Christopher. (1965) *Intellectual Origins of the English Revolution*. Oxford: Clarendon Press. [4]

———. (1975) *The World Turned Upside Down*. New York: Pelican. [4]

HILTON, Rodney, ed. (1976) *The Transition from Feudalism to Capitalism*. London: New Left Books. [1]

HINSLEY, F. H. (1986) *Sovereignty*. 2nd edition. New York: Cambridge University Press. [1, 7]

HINTZE, Otto. (1975) "Economics and Politics in the Age of Modern Capitalism." In F. Gilbert, ed., *The Historical Essays of Otto Hintze*. Oxford: Oxford University Press. [1]

HIRSCHMAN, Albert O. (1977) *The Passions and the Interests: Political Arguments for Capitalism Before Its Triumph*. Princeton, NJ: Princeton University Press. [2]

HOBBES, Thomas. (1640/1994) *The Elements of Law, Natural and Politic:* Part I, *Human Nature;* Part II, *De corpore politico*. Edited with an introduction by J.C.A. Gaskin. New York: Oxford University Press. [5]

———. (1642/1983) *De Cive: The English Version*. Edited by Howard Warrender. New York: Oxford University Press. [2, 3]

———. (1651/1958) *Leviathan*. With an introduction by Herbert W. Schneider, vii–xvi. Indianapolis, IN: Bobbs-Merrill. [3, 5]

HOHFELD, W. N. (1964) *Fundamental Legal Conceptions as Applied in Judicial Reasoning*. New Haven, CT: Yale University Press. [3]

HOLDSWORTH, William Searle. (1922–1966) *A History of English Law*. Edited by A. L. Goodhart and H. G. Hanbury. With an introductory essay and additions by S. B. Chrimes. 16 vols. London: Methuen. [1, 6]

HOLTON, Robert J. (1981) "Marxist Theories of Social Change and the Transition from Feudalism to Capitalism." *Theory and Society* 10(6):833–867. [1]

HORNE, Thomas A. (1990) *Property Rights and Poverty: Political Argument in Britain, 1605–1834*. Chapel Hill: University of North Carolina Press. [1, 2]

HOWAT, G.M.D. (1974) *Stuart and Cromwellian Foreign Policy*. New York: St. Martin's Press. [1, 5, 6, 7]

HUNT, E. K. (1986) *Property and Prophets: The Evolution of Economic Institutions and Ideologies*. 5th edition. New York: Harper and Row. [1, 2, 6]

HUTTON, Ronald. (1989) *Charles II: King of England, Scotland, and Ireland*. New York: Oxford University Press. [1, 6, 7]

HYMA, Albert. (1928) *A Short History of Europe, 1500–1815*. New York: F. S. Crofts. [6]

INAYATULLAH, Naeem, and David BLANEY. (1995) "Realizing Sovereignty." *Review of International Studies* 21(1):3–20. [1]

ISRAEL, Jonathan I. (1989) *Dutch Primacy in World Trade, 1585–1740*. New York: Oxford University Press. [1, 6]

———. (1990) *Empires and Entrepots: The Dutch, the Spanish Monarchy, and the Jews, 1585–1713*. Roncevert, WV: Hambledon Press. [1, 6]

JACKSON, Robert H. (1990) *Quasi-States: Sovereignty, International Relations, and the Third World.* New York: Cambridge University Press. [Preface, 1, 5, 8]

JAMES, Alan. (1986) *Sovereign Statehood: The Basis of International Society.* Boston: Allen and Unwin. [1, 7]

JONES, J. R. (1987) *Charles II: Royal Politician.* New York: Unwin Hyman. [1]

KENNAN, George. (1951) *American Diplomacy, 1900–1950.* Chicago: University of Chicago Press. [2]

KENNEDY, David. (1986) "Primitive International Legal Scholarship." *Harvard International Law Journal* 27:1–98. [1, 4]

———. (1987) *International Legal Structures.* Baden-Baden, Germany: Nomos Verlagsgesellschaft. [1, 4]

KENYON, J. P. (1978) *Stuart England.* New York: Penguin Books. [1, 4, 5, 6, 7]

KEOHANE, Robert O. (1980) "The Theory of Hegemonic Stability and Changes in International Economic Regimes, 1967–1977." In O. R. Holsti, R. M. Siverson, and A. L. George, eds., *Change in the International System,* 131–162. Boulder, CO: Westview Press. [6]

———. (1984) *After Hegemony: Cooperation and Discord in the World Political Economy.* Princeton, NJ: Princeton University Press. [6]

———. (1986) "Theory of World Politics: Structural Realism and Beyond." In R. Keohane, ed., *Neorealism and Its Critics,* 158–203. New York: Columbia University Press. [7]

———. (1989) "Neoliberal Institutionalism: A Perspective on World Politics." In *International Institutions and State Power: Essays in International Relations Theory.* Boulder, CO: Westview Press. [6]

KEYNES, John Maynard. (1953a) *A Treatise on Money.* Vol. 1: *The Pure Theory of Money.* London: Macmillan. [6]

———. (1953b) *A Treatise on Money.* Vol. 2: *The Applied Theory of Money.* London: Macmillan. [6]

KINDLEBERGER, Charles P. (1973) *The World in Depression, 1929–1939.* Berkeley: University of California Press. [6]

KITCH, M. J., ed. (1967) *Capitalism and the Reformation.* New York: Barnes and Noble. [1]

KOSKENNIEMI, Martti. (1989) *From Apology to Utopia: The Structure of International Legal Argument.* Helsinki: Finnish Lawyers' Publishing Company. [4]

KRASNER, Stephen. (1988) "Sovereignty: An Institutional Perspective." *Comparative Political Studies* 21(1) April:66–94. [1]

———, ed. (1983) *International Regimes.* Ithaca, NY: Cornell University Press. [6]

KRATOCHWIL, Friedrich V. (1989) *Rules, Norms, and Decisions: On the Conditions of Practical and Legal Reasoning in International Relations and Domestic Affairs.* New York: Cambridge University Press. [1]

———. (1995) "Sovereignty as *Dominium:* Is There a Right of Humanitarian Intervention?" In G. M. Lyons and M. Mastanduno, eds., *Beyond Westphalia? State Sovereignty and International Intervention,* 21–42. Baltimore, MD: Johns Hopkins University Press. [3, 7]

KRIEDTE, Peter. (1983) *Peasants, Landlords and Merchant Capitalists: Europe and the World Economy, 1500–1800.* Translated by V. R. Berghahn. New York: Cambridge University Press. [1]

KRIEDTE, Peter, Hans MEDICK, and Jürgen SCHLUMBOHM. (1981) *Industrialization Before Industrialization: Rural Industry in the Genesis of Capitalism.* Translated by Beate Schempp. With contributions from Herbert Kisch and Franklin F. Mendels. New York: Cambridge University Press. [1, 4]

KUEHLS, Thom. (1996) *Beyond Sovereign Politics: The Space of Ecopolitics.* Minneapolis: University of Minnesota Press. [1]

KUHN, Thomas S. (1970) *The Structure of Scientific Revolutions.* 2nd edition, enlarged. Chicago: University of Chicago Press. [1]

LAKOFF, G., and M. JOHNSON. (1980) *Metaphors We Live By.* Chicago: University of Chicago Press. [4]

LASLETT, Peter. (1965) "Introduction." In *Two Treatises of Government,* by John Locke, 15–168. New York: Mentor/New American Library. [3]

LAWSON, F. H., and Bernard RUDDEN. (1982) *The Law of Property.* 2nd edition. New York: Clarendon Press. [1]

LEAPER, Campbell. (1991) "Influence and Involvement in Children's Discourse: Age, Gender, and Partner Effects." *Child Development* 62:797–811. [1]

LEVI, Margaret. (1987) *Of Rule and Revenue.* Berkeley: University of California Press. [3, 7]

LEWY, Claude. (1975) "The Code and Property." In B. Schwartz, ed., *The Code Napoleon and the Common-Law World,* 162–176. Westport, CT: Greenwood Press. [6]

LITTLE, David. (1969/1984) *Religion, Order, and Law: A Study in Pre-Revolutionary England.* Foreword by R. N. Bellah. Chicago: University of Chicago Press. [1, 4, 7]

LOCKE, John. (1690/1965) *Two Treatises of Government.* Revised edition. With an introduction and notes by Peter Laslett. New York: Mentor/New American Library. [2, 3, 4, 5]

LOVEJOY, Arthur O. (1936) *The Great Chain of Being: A Study of the History of an Idea.* Cambridge, MA: Harvard University Press. [2]

LOWI, Theodore J. (1979) *The End of Liberalism: The Second Republic of the United States.* 2nd edition. New York: W. W. Norton. [4]

LUKES, Steven. (1977) *Essays in Social Theory.* New York: Columbia University Press. [2]

LYONS, Gene M., and Michael MASTANDUNO, eds. (1995) *Beyond Westphalia? State Sovereignty and International Intervention.* Baltimore, MD: Johns Hopkins University Press. [1,8]

MACHIAVELLI, Niccolo. (1513/1975) *The Prince.* Translated and with an introduction by George Bull. New York: Penguin Books. [5]

MACPHERSON, C. B. (1962) *The Political Theory of Possessive Individualism.* New York: Oxford University Press. [1, 2, 3, 4, 7]

———. (1966) *The Real World of Democracy.* New York: Oxford University Press. [3]

———. (1975) *Democratic Theory.* New York: Clarendon Press. [4]

———, ed. (1978) *Property.* Toronto: University of Toronto Press. [4]

MANN, Michael. (1988) *States, War and Capitalism.* New York: Basil Blackwell. [8]

MANNE, Henry G. (1975) *The Economics of Legal Relationships: Readings in the Theory of Property Rights.* St. Paul, MN: West Publishing Company. [1]

MANSFIELD, Harvey C., Jr. (1983) "On the Impersonality of the Modern State: A Comment on Machiavelli's Use of *Stato.*" *American Political Science Review* 77(4) December:849–857. [5]

MARX, Karl. (1844/1964) *Economic and Philosophic Manuscripts of 1844.* Edited, with an introduction, by Dirk J. Struik. Translated by Martin Milligan. New York: International Publishers. [2, 7]

———. (1857–1858/1973) *Grundrisse.* Translated, with a foreword, by Martin Nicolaus. New York: Vintage Books. [1, 2]

―――. (1859/1970) *A Contribution to the Critique of Political Economy*. Edited, with an introduction, by Maurice Dobb. New York: International Publishers. [2]

―――. (1867/1977) *Capital*. Vol. 1. With an introduction by Ernest Mandel. Translated by Ben Fowkes. New York: Vintage Books. [1, 2]

MARX, Karl, and Frederick ENGELS. (1845–1846/1970) *The German Ideology*. Edited, with an introduction, by C. J. Arthur. New York: International Publishers. [2]

McLELLAN, David. (1986) *Ideology*. Minneapolis: University of Minnesota Press. [7]

McNEILL, William H. (1982) *The Pursuit of Power: Technology, Armed Force, and Society Since AD 1000*. Chicago: University of Chicago Press. [7]

MENDLE, Michael. (1985) *Dangerous Positions: Mixed Government, the Estates of the Realm and the Answer to the XIX Propositions*. University: University of Alabama Press. [4]

MERRIAM, C. E., Jr. (1900) *History of the Theory of Sovereignty Since Rousseau*. New York: Columbia University Press. [1, 7]

MIDDLE ENGLISH DICTIONARY. (1954–1988) 128 planned letter-parts (currently available only through part S.14). Ann Arbor, MI: University of Michigan Press. [2]

MILLER, John. (1991) *Charles II*. London: Weidenfeld and Nicolson. [1]

MORGENTHAU, Hans J. (1956) *Politics Among Nations: The Struggle for Power and Peace*. 2nd edition, revised and enlarged. New York: Alfred Knopf. [1]

MUNZER, Stephen R. (1990) *A Theory of Property*. New York: Cambridge University Press. [1]

NARDIN, Terry. (1983) *Law, Morality, and the Relations of States*. Princeton, NJ: Princeton University Press. [4]

NEF, John U. (1934) "The Progress of Technology and the Growth of Large Scale Industry in Great Britain, 1540–1640." *Economic History Review* 5(1):9–18. [6]

NENNER, Howard A. (1977) *By Colour of Law: Legal Culture and Constitutional Politics in England, 1660–1689*. Chicago: University of Chicago Press. [1, 3, 4, 5, 6, 7]

NETHERTON, Nan, Donald SWEIG, Janice ARTEMEL, Patricia HICKIN, and Patrick REED. (1978) *Fairfax County, Virginia: A History*. Fairfax, VA: Fairfax County Board of Supervisors. [6]

NEUFELD, Mark. (1995) *The Restructuring of International Relations Theory*. New York: Cambridge University Press. [8]

NEUMANN, Iver B., and Ole WAEVER, eds. (1997) *The Future of International Relations: Masters in the Making*. New York: Routledge. [1]

NEW YORK TIMES. (1997) June 12, p. A25; June 13, p. A6. [Preface]

NICHOLAS, Barry. (1962) *An Introduction to Roman Law*. New York: Clarendon Press. [2, 4]

NORTH, Douglass C. (1981) *Structure and Change in Economic History*. New York: W. W. Norton. [6]

NORTH, Douglass C., and Robert Paul THOMAS. (1973) *The Rise of the West: A New Economic History*. New York: Cambridge University Press. [1, 2, 3, 4, 6, 7]

NOZICK, Robert. (1974) *Anarchy, State, and Utopia*. New York: Basic Books. [4]

OLSON, Mancur. (1965) *The Logic of Collective Action*. Cambridge, MA: Harvard University Press. [6]

ONUF, Nicholas G. (1985) "Do Rules Say What They Do? From Ordinary Language to International Law." *Harvard International Law Journal* 26(2) Spring:385–410. [1]

———. (1989) *World of Our Making: Rules and Rule in International Relations.* Columbia: University of South Carolina Press. [1, 4, 5, 7, 8]

———. (1991) "Sovereignty: Outline of a Conceptual History." *Alternatives* 16:425–446. [1, 7]

———. (1994) "The Constitution of International Society." *European Journal of International Law* 5(1):1–19. [1, 8]

———. (1997a) "A Constructivist Manifesto." In K. Burch and R. Denemark, eds., *Constituting International Political Economy.* Boulder, CO: Lynne Rienner Publishers. [1]

———. (1997b) "Hegemony's Hegemony." In K. Burch and R. Denemark, eds., *Constituting International Political Economy.* Boulder, CO: Lynne Rienner Publishers. [1]

———. (1997c) *The Republican Legacy in International Thought.* New York: Cambridge University Press. [1, 2, 3]

ONUF, Nicholas G., and Frank F. KLINK. (1989) "Anarchy, Authority, and Rule." *International Studies Quarterly* 33(2) June:149–173. [1]

ONUF, Peter, and Nicholas ONUF. (1993) *Federal Union, Modern World: The Law of Nations in an Age of Revolutions, 1776–1814.* Madison, WI: Madison House. [5]

ONUMA, Yasuaki, ed. (1993) *A Normative Approach to War: Peace, War, and Justice in Hugo Grotius.* Oxford: Clarendon Press. [1]

OXFORD ENGLISH DICTIONARY. (1989) 20 vols. New York: Oxford University Press. [2, 4, 5, 6, 7]

PARRY, Geraint. (1978) *John Locke.* Boston: Allen and Unwin. [3]

PARRY, J. H. (1966) *The Establishment of the European Hegemony, 1415–1715: Trade and Exploration in the Age of the Renaissance.* 3rd edition, revised. New York: Harper Torchbooks. [1,6]

———. (1981) *The Age of Reconnaissance: Discovery, Exploration and Settlement, 1450 to 1650.* Revised edition. Berkeley: University of California Press. [1]

PAUL, Ellen F., F. D. MILLER, and J. PAUL, eds. (1994) *Property Rights.* New York: Cambridge University Press. [1]

PAWLISCH, Hans S. (1985) *Sir John Davies and the Conquest of Ireland: A Study in Legal Imperialism.* New York: Cambridge University Press. [1, 4]

PENNINGTON, Kenneth. (1993) *The Prince and the Law, 1200–1600: Sovereignty and Rights in the Western Legal Tradition.* Berkeley: University of California Press. [3, 5, 7, 8]

PHILPOTT, Daniel. (1995) "Sovereignty: An Introduction and Brief History." *Journal of International Affairs* 48(2) Winter:353–368. [1, 7]

PITKIN, Hanna F. (1972) *Wittgenstein and Justice: On the Significance of Ludwig Wittgenstein for Social and Political Thought.* Berkeley: University of California Press. [4]

POCOCK, J.G.A. (1957) *The Ancient Constitution and the Feudal Law: A Study of English Historical Thought in the Seventeenth Century.* New York: Cambridge University Press. [1, 4, 5, 7]

———. (1975) *The Machiavellian Moment: Florentine Political Thought and the Atlantic Republican Tradition.* Princeton, NJ: Princeton University Press. [1, 2, 3, 4, 5, 7]

———. (1977) "Historical Introduction." In J.G.A. Pocock, ed., *The Political Works of James Harrington,* 1–152. New York: Cambridge University Press. [3, 4, 7]

————. (1985) *Virtue, Commerce, and History.* New York: Cambridge University Press. [2, 3, 4, 6, 7]

————. (1987) *The Ancient Constitution and the Feudal Law: A Study of English Historical Thought in the Seventeenth Century: A reissue with a retrospect.* New York: Cambridge University Press. [4]

————, ed. (1977) *The Political Works of James Harrington.* New York: Cambridge University Press. [3]

————, ed. (1980) *Three British Revolutions: 1641, 1688, 1776.* Princeton, NJ: Princeton University Press. [3, 4, 7]

POCOCK, J.G.A, and Richard ASHCRAFT. (1980) *John Locke.* Berkeley: University of California Press. [3]

POGGI, Gianfranco. (1978) *The Development of the Modern State: A Sociological Introduction.* Stanford, CA: Stanford University Press. [1]

POLANYI, Karl. (1944) *The Great Transformation.* New York: Rinehart. [1, 7]

POSTAN, M. M. (1972) *The Medieval Economy and Society: An Economic History of Britain in the Middle Ages.* New York: Penguin Books. [1]

POULANTZAS, Nicos. (1978) *Political Power and Social Classes.* Translated by T. O'Hagan et al. London: Verso. [2]

PRAKASH, Om. (1985) *The Dutch East India Company and the Economy of Bengal, 1630–1720.* Princeton, NJ: Princeton University Press. [1, 6]

PUFENDORF, Samuel. (1672/1964) *De jure naturae et gentium libri octo.* Translated by C. H. and W. A. Oldfather. New York: Oceana Publications. [1]

————. (1673/1991) *On the Duty of Man and Citizen According to Natural Law.* Translated by M. Silverthorne. Edited by James Tully. New York: Cambridge University Press. [1]

RAHE, Paul. (1992) *Republics Ancient and Modern: Classical Republicanism and the American Revolution.* Chapel Hill: University of North Carolina Press. [2]

RAPACZYNSKI, Andrzej. (1987) *Nature and Politics: Liberalism in the Philosophies of Hobbes, Locke, and Rousseau.* Ithaca, NY: Cornell University Press. [1, 7]

RAWLS, John. (1971) *A Theory of Justice.* Cambridge, MA: Harvard University Press. [4]

RAZ, Joseph. (1990) *Practical Reason and Norms.* Princeton, NJ: Princeton University Press. [4]

REEVE, Andrew. (1986) *Property.* Atlantic Highlands, NJ: Humanities Press International. [1, 2, 4, 7]

RENNER, Karl. (1949/1976) *The Institutions of Private Law and Their Social Functions.* Edited, with an introduction and notes, by O. Kahn-Freund. Translated by A. Schwarzschild. London: Routledge and Kegan Paul. [1]

ROBBINS, Sanford. (1997) "PTTP [Professional Theatre Training Program] Presents William Shakespeare's *Henry VI.*" A theatre program from a performance at the University of Delaware. [4]

ROBERTS, James. (1997) "The Rational Constitution of Agents and Structures." In K. Burch and R. Denemark, eds., *Constituting International Political Economy,* 155–168. Boulder, CO: Lynne Rienner Publishers. [1]

ROGOW, Arnold A. (1986) *Thomas Hobbes: Radical in the Service of Reaction.* New York: W. W. Norton. [3]

RUGGIE, John G. (1983) "Continuity and Transformation in the World Polity: Toward a Neorealist Synthesis." *World Politics* 35(2) January:261–285. [1, 7, 8]

RYAN, Alan. (1984) *Property and Political Theory.* New York: Basil Blackwell. [1, 2, 4]

————. (1987) *Property*. Minneapolis: University of Minnesota Press. [1, 2, 3]

SCHEINGOLD, Stuart A. (1974) *The Politics of Rights: Lawyers, Public Policy, and Political Change*. New Haven, CT: Yale University Press. [4]

SCHUMPETER, Joseph A. (1954) *History of Economic Analysis*. Edited by E. B. Schumpeter. New York: Oxford University Press. [6]

SCOTT, William Robert. (1912/1968a) *The Constitution and Finance of English, Scottish and Irish Joint-Stock Companies to 1720*. Vol. 1: *The General Development of the Joint-Stock System to 1720*. Gloucester, MA: Peter Smith. [1, 6]

————. (1912/1968b) *The Constitution and Finance of English, Scottish and Irish Joint-Stock Companies to 1720*. Vol. 2: *Companies for Foreign Trade, Colonization, Fishing and Mining*. Gloucester, MA: Peter Smith. [1, 6]

————. (1912/1968c) *The Constitution and Finance of English, Scottish and Irish Joint-Stock Companies to 1720*. Vol. 3: *Water Supply, Postal, Street-Lighting, Manufacturing, Banking, Finance and Insurance Companies; Also Statements Relating to the Crown Finances*. Gloucester, MA: Peter Smith. [1, 6]

SEARLE, John A. (1969) *Speech Acts: An Essay in the Philosophy of Language*. New York: Cambridge University Press. [1, 4]

SEIDMAN, Steven. (1983) *Liberalism and the Origins of European Social Theory*. Berkeley: University of California Press. [1, 8]

SHAPIRO, Ian. (1987) *The Evolution of Rights in Liberal Theory*. New York: Cambridge University Press. [1, 7]

————. (1990) *Political Criticism*. Berkeley: University of California Press. [2]

SIMMONS, A. John. (1992) *The Lockean Theory of Rights*. Princeton, NJ: Princeton University Press. [3]

SKINNER, Quentin. (1989) "Language and Political Change." In T. Ball et al., eds., *Political Innovation and Conceptual Change*, 6–23. New York: Cambridge University Press. [1]

SMITH, Adam. (1776/1937) *The Wealth of Nations*. Edited, with an introduction, by E. Cannan. New York: Modern Library. [2]

SOWARDS, J. Kelley. (1969) *Western Civilization to 1660*. New York: St. Martin's Press. [4]

SPRUYT, Hendrik. (1994) *The Sovereign State and Its Competitors: An Analysis of Systems Change*. Princeton, NJ: Princeton University Press. [1]

SREENIVASAN, Gopal. (1995) *The Limits of Lockean Rights in Property*. New York: Oxford University Press. [2, 3]

STEENSGAARD, Niels. (1982) "Dutch East India Company as an Institutional Innovation." In M. Amyard, ed., *Dutch Capitalism and World Capitalism*. New York: Cambridge University Press. [1, 6]

————. (1990) "The Growth and Composition of the Long-Distance Trade of England and the Dutch Republic Before 1750." In J. D. Tracy, ed., *The Rise of Merchant Empires: Long Distance Trade in the Early Modern World, 1350–1750*. New York: Cambridge University Press. [1, 6]

STRAYER, J. R. (1970) *On the Medieval Origins of the Modern State*. Princeton, NJ: Princeton University Press. [3]

STRUIK, Dirk. (1964) "Introduction." In D. Struik, ed., *Economic and Philosophic Manuscripts of 1844*, by Karl Marx, 9–60. New York: International Publishers. [2]

SUVOROVA, Maria, and Boris ROMANOV. (1986) *What Is Property?* Moscow: Progress Publishers. [2]

SWEEZY, Paul. (1950) "The Transition from Feudalism to Capitalism." *Science and Society* 14(2) Spring:134–156. [1]

THESAURUS OF OLD ENGLISH. (1995) 2 vols. Compiled by Jane Roberts and Christian Kay, with Lynne Grundy. London: King's College, Center for Late Antique and Medieval Studies. [2]

THOMPSON, John B. (1984) *Studies in the Theory of Ideology.* Berkeley: University of California Press. [1, 7]

THOMSON, Janice. (1994) *Mercenaries, Pirates, and Sovereigns: State-Building and Extra-Territorial Violence in Early Modern Europe.* Princeton, NJ: Princeton University Press. [6, 8]

TIGAR, Michael E., and Madeleine R. LEVY. (1977) *Law and the Rise of Capitalism.* With a foreword by T. I. Emerson. New York: Monthly Review Press. [1, 4, 6]

TILLY, Charles, ed. (1975) *The Formation of National States in Western Europe.* Princeton, NJ: Princeton University Press. [1, 4, 5, 8]

TOOZE, Roger. (1984) "Perspectives and Theory: A Consumers' Guide." In S. Strange, ed., *Paths to International Political Economy,* 1–22. Boston: Allen and Unwin. [7]

TOULMIN, Stephen. (1990) *Cosmopolis: The Hidden Agenda of Modernity.* New York: Free Press. [1, 3, 5, 7, 8]

TREVOR-ROPER, Hugh. (1953) "The Gentry, 1540–1640." *Economic History Review,* Supplement 1. [3]

———. (1965) "The General Crisis of the Seventeenth Century." In T. Aston, ed., *Crisis in Europe: 1560–1660,* 59–95. London: Routledge and Kegan Paul. [1, 3]

TUCK, Richard. (1979) *Natural Rights Theories: Their Origin and Development.* New York: Cambridge University Press. [1, 3, 4, 6, 7]

———. (1989) *Hobbes.* New York: Oxford University Press. [3, 5]

TULLY, James. (1980) *A Discourse on Property: John Locke and His Adversaries.* New York: Cambridge University Press. [3, 4]

UNGER, Roberto M. (1986) *The Critical Legal Studies Movement.* Cambridge, MA: Harvard University Press. [4]

VAUGHN, Karen. (1980) *John Locke, Economist and Social Scientist.* Chicago: University of Chicago Press. [3]

WALDRON, Jeremy. (1988) *The Right to Private Property.* New York: Clarendon Press. [1, 2, 7, 8]

WALKER, R.B.J. (1993) *Inside/Outside: International Relations as Political Theory.* New York: Cambridge University Press. [1, 3, 6, 7, 8]

WALKER, R.B.J., and Saul H. MENDLOVITZ, eds. (1990) *Contending Sovereignties: Redefining Political Community.* Boulder, CO: Lynne Rienner Publishers. [1]

WALLERSTEIN, Immanuel. (1974a) *The Modern World-System I: Capitalist Agriculture and the Origins of the European World-Economy in the Sixteenth Century.* New York: Academic Press. [1, 8]

———. (1974b) "The Rise and Future Demise of the World Capitalist System: Concepts for Comparative Analysis." *Comparative Studies in Society and History* 16(4) September:387–415. [1]

———. (1980) *The Modern World-System II: Mercantilism and the Consolidation of the European World-Economy, 1600–1750.* New York: Academic Press. [3, 6, 8]

———. (1984) *The Politics of the World-Economy: The States, the Movements and the Civilizations.* New York: Cambridge University Press. [1]

————. (1989) *The Modern World-System III: The Second Era of Great Expansion of the Capitalist World-Economy, 1730–1840s*. New York: Academic Press. [8]

WALTZ, Kenneth N. (1979) *Theory of International Politics*. Reading, MA: Addison-Wesley. [1]

WALZER, Michael. (1984) "Liberalism and the Art of Separation." *Political Theory* 12(3) August:315–330. [2, 4, 5]

WASHINGTON POST (1996) "Buchanan's Swan Song Has Chorus on Comeback." August 12, pp. A15–A16. [Preface]

WEBER, Cynthia. (1995) *Simulating Sovereignty: Intervention, the State, and Symbolic Exchange*. New York: Cambridge University Press. [1, 4, 6, 7, 8]

WEBER, Max. (1958) *The Protestant Ethic and the Spirit of Capitalism*. New York: Free Press. [1, 2, 8]

————. (1978) *Economy and Society: An Outline of Interpretive Sociology*. Edited by G. Roth and C. Wittich. Translated by E. Fischoff et al. Berkeley: University of California Press. [1]

————. (1981) *General Economic History*. Translated by Frank H. Knight. New Brunswick, NJ: Transaction Books. [1]

WENDT, Alexander E. (1987) "The Agent-Structure Problem in International Relations Theory." *International Organization* 41(3) Summer:335–370. [1, 4]

————. (1992) "Anarchy Is What States Make of It." *International Organization* 46(2) Spring:391–425. [1]

————. (1995) "Constructing International Politics." *International Security* 20(1) Summer:71–81. [1]

WENDT, Alexander E., and Daniel FRIEDHEIM. (1995) "Hierarchy Under Anarchy: Informal Empire and the East German State." *International Organization* 49(4) Autumn:689–721. [1]

WESTFALL, Richard S. (1973) *Science and Religion in Seventeenth Century England*. Ann Arbor: University of Michigan Press. [3, 4]

WESTON, Corrine Comstock, and Janelle Renfrow GREENBERG. (1981) *Subjects and Sovereigns: The Grand Controversy over Legal Sovereignty in Stuart England*. New York: Cambridge University Press. [4, 5]

WHITE, Stephen D. (1979) *Sir Edward Coke and "The Grievances of the Commonwealth," 1621–1628*. Chapel Hill: University of North Carolina Press. [5]

WILLAN, T. S. (1968) *The Early History of the Russia Company, 1553–1603*. New York: Augustus M. Kelley Publishers. [1]

WILSON, Charles. (1977) "The British Isles." In C. Wilson and G. Parker, eds., *An Introduction to the Sources of European Economic History 1500–1800*, 115–154. Ithaca, NY: Cornell University Press. [1, 6, 7]

WITTGENSTEIN, Ludwig. (1968) *Philosophical Investigations*. 3rd edition. Translated by G.E.M. Anscombe. New York: Macmillan. [1, 4]

WOLIN, Sheldon. (1960) *Politics and Vision*. Boston: Beacon Press. [2]

WOOD, Alfred C. (1935/1964) *A History of the Levant Company*. London: Frank Cass and Company. [1]

WOOD, Neal. (1986) *John Locke and Agrarian Capitalism*. Berkeley: University of California Press. [3]

ZUCKERT, Michael. (1994) *Natural Rights and the New Republicanism*. Princeton, NJ: Princeton University Press. [2]

Index

Absolute sovereignty: a fiction, 145–146, 157, 160
Absolutism, 80, 82, 97, 107, 114, 115, 149
Administration, 93, 96, 97, 98–99; bureaucratic, 89, 90, 92, 94, 132, 150–151; finances and, 108–111, 114–118; institutional-legal order and, 100, 103, 109, 147, 148; by joint-stock companies, 113, 120
Africa Company, 121, 122, 123, 124, 131
Agent-structure problem, 2, 86n1, 158; constitutive principles as solution, 10
Agents (actors), agency, 2, 18n10, 70; means of action, 11, 23, 39, 141
Alienable, alienation, 30, 35, 36, 64, 74, 77, 85, 86n3, 87n6, 97, 150; rights and, 77, 158
Alva, duke of, 116
Anarchy, 6
Ancient constitution, 16n4, 92, 116, 153; foundation in common law, 80–83
Anderson, Perry, 17n5, 97
Answer to the Nineteen Propositions (English legal document), 56
Apology of the House of Commons to the King (1607), 73
Aquinas, Thomas, 57
Arbitrage, 128, 134n7, 134n8
Arblaster, Anthony, 16n2, 142, 152n3
Ardant, Gabriel, 17n5
Aristotle, 27, 28
Army, 90, 101
Ashcraft, Richard, 42, 43, 65n2
Ashley, Richard, 140, 152n3
Aston, T., 16n2

Austin, J. L. (philosopher), 85n1
Austin, John (legal theorist), 25, 157
Austria, 101
Authority, vii, 28, 29, 30, 39, 41, 56, 64, 79–83, 85, 89–97, 100, 103, 108, 114, 125, 129, 134n8, 143, 144, 145, 147, 149, 157; collapse of, 45, 49, 55, 146; as command, 94, 95, 98; constituting authority distinct from instituting sovereignty, 84, 91; claims to, 145, 146; depersonalized or impersonal, 90, 92, 96, 97, 100, 103, 139; domestic policy prerequisites and, 99–101; foreign policy prerequisites and, 100–105; foundations, 45, 61, 83; institutional-legal order and, 79–85, 91, 92, 98–105, 145; law and, 43, 69, 73–74, 80, 82, 84, 98, 134n7, 147; as making rules rather than exercising power, 100, 147; monarchs or royalty and, 56, 80, 81–82, 84, 93, 102, 105n3, 114, 116, 129; personal, 89, 91, 93, 97, 99, 102; property and, 48, 57–61, 62, 84, 90, 118–121, 140, 145–146, 152n1; sovereign, 94, 96, 99, 100, 109, 122, 132; sovereignty and, 140, 143, 144, 145–146, 147–148, 153; tension with liberty, 45, 55. *See also* Commonwealth, Cromwellian interregnum, Governance, Government, Hierarchy, Institutional-legal order, Paradox of liberty and authority, Polity, Reconstitution of authority, Royal prerogative, Sovereignty, State
Autocracy, 80–83
Autonomy, 8, 31

179

About the Book

This original work uses the concepts of *property* and *property rights* to explore the emergence of the modern international system.

Burch argues that social understandings of property and property rights contribute a crucial character to claims about the modern state, sovereignty, international law, state conflict, global political economy, and the world system as a whole. By investigating a concept, rather than a specific social condition, activity, or actor, he explores the socially shared understandings and meanings that inform individuals' outlooks and behaviors. It is these changing meanings and consequent behaviors, he demonstrates, that actually "make" the international system.

Kurt Burch is associate professor of political science at the University of Delaware.

Other Books in the Series